Fashion Marketing

The Charte ... N ... / Bu ... o..a-Heinemann Marketing Series is the ..o.. comprehensive, ..aely used and important collection of books in marketing and sales currently available worldwide.

As the CIM's official publisher, Butterworth-Heinemann develops, produces and publishes the complete series in association with the CIM. We aim to provide definitive marketing books for students and practitioners that promote excellence in marketing education and practice.

The series titles are written by CIM senior examiners and leading marketing educators for professionals, students and those studying the CIM's Certificate, Advanced Certificate and Postgraduate Diploma courses. Now firmly established, these titles provide practical study support to CIM and other marketing students and to practitioners at all levels.

The Chartered
Institute of Marketing

Formed in 1911, the Chartered Institute of Marketing is now the largest professional marketing management body in the world with over 60 000 members located worldwide. Its primary objectives are focused on the development of awareness and understanding of marketing throughout UK industry and commerce and in the raising of standards of professionalism in the education, training and practice of this key business discipline.

Books in the series

Creating Powerful Brands (second edition), Leslie de Chernatony and Malcolm McDonald

Cybermarketing (second edition), Pauline Bickerton, Matthew Bickerton and Upkar Pardesi

Cyberstrategy, Pauline Bickerton, Matthew Bickerton and Kate Simpson-Holley

Excellence in Advertising (second edition), Leslie Butterfield

Fashion Marketing, Margaret Bruce and Tony Hines

From Brand Vision to Brand Evaluation, Leslie de Chernatony

Innovation in Marketing, Peter Doyle and Susan Bridgewater

International Marketing (third edition), Stanley J. Paliwoda and Michael J. Thomas

Integrated Marketing Communications, Tony Yeshin

Key Customers, Malcolm McDonald, Beth Rogers, Diana Woodburn

Marketing Logistics, Martin Christopher

Marketing Plans (fourth edition), Malcolm McDonald

Marketing Planning for Services, Malcolm McDonald and Adrian Payne

Marketing Professional Services, Michael Roe

Marketing Research for Managers (second edition), Sunny Crouch and Matthew Housden

Marketing Strategy (second edition), Paul Fifield

Relationship Marketing for Competitive Advantage, Adrian Payne, Martin Christopher, Moira Clark and Helen Peck

Relationship Marketing: Strategy and Implementation, Helen Peck, Adrian Payne, Martin Christopher and Moira Clark

Strategic Marketing Management (second edition), Richard M. S. Wilson and Colin Gilligan

Strategic Marketing: Planning and Control (second edition), Graeme Drummond and John Ensor

Tales from the Market Place, Nigel Piercy

The CIM Handbook of Export Marketing, Chris Noonan

The CIM Handbook of Strategic Marketing, Colin Egan and Michael J. Thomas

The Customer Service Planner, Martin Christopher

The Fundamentals of Corporate Communications, Richard Dolphin

The Marketing Book (fourth edition), Michael J. Baker

The Marketing Manual, Michael J. Baker

Total Relationship Marketing, Evert Gummesson

Forthcoming

Direct Marketing, Brian Thomas and Matthew Housden

Effective Promotional Practice for eBusiness, Cathy Ace

eMarketing Excellence, Paul Smith and Dave Chaffey

Marketing Briefs, Sally Dibb and Lyndon Simkin

Market-Led Strategic Change (third edition), Nigel Piercy

Political Marketing, Phil Harris and Dominic Wring

Relationship Marketing (second edition), Martin Christopher, Adrian Payne and David Ballantyne

Successful Marketing Communications, Cathy Ace

Fashion Marketing: Contemporary Issues

Edited by

Tony Hines

and

Margaret Bruce

BUTTERWORTH
HEINEMANN

OXFORD AUCKLAND BOSTON JOHANNESBURG MELBOURNE NEW DELHI

Butterworth-Heinemann
Linacre House, Jordan Hill, Oxford OX2 8DP
225 Wildwood Avenue, Woburn, MA 01801-2041
A division of Reed Educational and Professional Publishing Ltd

ℝ   A member of the Reed Elsevier plc group

First published 2001

British Library Cataloguing in Publication Data
A catalogue record for this book is available from the British Library

Library of Congress Cataloging in Publication Data
A catalogue record for this book is available from the Library of Congress

For information on all Butterworth-Heinemann publications visit
our website at www.bh.com

ISBN 0 7506 5243 8

Composition by Genesis Typesetting, Rochester, Kent
Printed and bound in Great Britain by MPG Books Ltd, Bodmin, Cornwall

Contents

Foreword

The consumer is king. There are so many different styles and types of goods that today's customers can spend their money on, the battle for their wallets has become intense. They are feted and flattered, pushed and pulled. From mobile phones and other electronic gizmos to overseas holidays and weekend breaks; the choice is limitless and the barrage of marketing messages endless. And so, with every purchase made, the spend on clothing is hit.

At the same time, clothing is no longer the essential spend that it was – even against just a few years ago. Our wardrobes are full. The need to buy clothes is less pronounced.

All of this has had a significant impact both on the methods we use to sell clothes and how we bring them to market. In essence, the fashion market has polarized. At one end companies are pushing an aspirational sell whilst at the other there is intense price competition. This, in turn, under the weight of margin pressure and a lack of desire on the part of the consumer, has brought about a depression in the middle market.

The process of polarization has been speeded up by the development of the global marketplace. Consumers are travelling more and surfing the net frequently which means that their knowledge is growing. They are becoming increasingly aware of the international must-have brands. Yet, at the same time, they are seeing the disparity in prices between one local market and another. Each new piece of information strengthens the consumer's hand and pushes suppliers to continually adapt and change.

All of these trends and issues are covered by the chapters in this book. Not everybody will agree with some of the theories and suggested strategies but I hope those who read the book will be, at least, stimulated. Where does the clothing industry go from here? What and where are the opportunities? And, moreover, what might the solutions be?

I warmly welcome this book as a significant contribution to the debate about the issues facing our industry in the twenty-first century. There are still great opportunities for manufacturers, designers and retailers, however much we all may have to change along the way.

John Wilson OBE
Chief Executive
British Fashion Council

List of Contributors

Nick Atkinson B.Sc. is currently part of the merchandising team at River Island. Previously Nick worked with the merchandising team at Selfridges & Co., the Trafford Centre, Manchester. He graduated from UMIST in July 2000, and holds a B.Sc. (Hons) degree in Marketing and Managing Textiles.

Emma Banister B.A. M.Sc., Lecturer in Consumer Behaviour in the Department of Textiles in UMIST. Her first degree was in Politics and History at Newcastle University, and she completed an M.Sc. in Marketing at the School of Management in 1997. Her postgraduate dissertation was on the structure and transfer of meaning in the music industry, and specifically explored the consumption of imagery by adolescent consumers. After almost a year working as a research analyst within the private sector, Emma joined the Manchester School of Management at UMIST as a researcher on an ADRC/RIF funded project in August 1998, examining negative congruence and incongruence in consumer behaviour. On the basis of this she began her current doctoral research, which concerns symbolic consumption and the rejection of products – specifically the notion that the 'undesired end state' functions as an incentive to avoid products with negative images. The research draws on social psychology and sociology in its examination of possible selves and product user stereotypes. The study uses a variety of methods (including projective techniques) to generate both qualitative and quantitative data. Emma was appointed by the Textiles Department at UMIST in August 2000, and her main teaching responsibilities focus upon consumer behaviour.

Margaret Bruce B.Sc. M.Sc. Ph.D., Professor of Marketing and Design Management, and Head of Department, Textiles, UMIST, focuses on the impact of e-commerce for the textiles and retail supply chain, reviews retail strategies for the Internet and is exploring consumer behaviour of Internet shoppers. She has carried out a number of international research programmes in design and innovation, and produced over 200 papers, seven books and interactive training material in marketing, design management and innovation. She is a Fulbright Scholar and a Honorary Professor at Xi'an Institute of Science and Technology, China. Professor Bruce is the editor of the *International Journal of New Product Development, Innovation and Management*.

Steve Burt B.A. Ph.D., is Professor of Retail Marketing at the Institute for Retail Studies in the Department of Marketing, University of Stirling, and is president of the European Association for Education and Research in Commercial Distribution. He has conducted research into retailing, with a particular interest in comparative and international retailing, since graduating from the University of Oxford in 1981. Sponsors of research projects include public and private sector organizations such as the Distributive Trades EDC, the European Community, Marks & Spencer, ICL, Safeway, Scottish & Newcastle Breweries, Esslette Meto and the European Travel Research Foundation. His academic publications have covered various aspects of retail strategy, European retailing and internationalization and have appeared in journals such as the *British Journal of Management, European Journal of Marketing*, and the *International Review of Retail Distribution and Consumer Research*.

Alice W. C. Chu M.A. M.H.K.I.T.A., is currently Assistant Professor at the Institute of Textiles and Clothing, The Hong Kong Polytechnic University. Prior to joining ITC as Assistant Professor in 1996, she worked in Warner Brothers Studio Store as Deputy General Manager. Her commercial experience includes export trading, merchandising, product development, marketing and fashion retailing. Over her career in retail business, she has held different senior managerial positions in a number of retail organizations including G2000 Ltd and Goldlion. She teaches fashion retail management and is currently working within a research team examining the role of the necktie business in Hong Kong. She has carried out research on consumer behaviour, store environment and e-tailing.

Tony Hines B.A. Econ. (Hons.) Ph.D. P.G.C.E. M.C.I.M. M.Inst.Mgt. F.R.S.A., of the Department of Retailing & Marketing, the Business School, Manchester Metropolitan University has research interests in marketing-focused supply chain strategies, globalization, e-business relationships and structures and small firms. Previously he was Principal Lecturer in Fashion Marketing at London College of Fashion where he was founding Director of the Management Research Group and Academic Leader for the Marketing Group. He has been an invited plenary speaker at a number of World Textile Conferences most recently in India, Greece, Turkey and the United States where he presented papers on supply chain strategies and e-business relationships. In November 2000 he was an invited plenary speaker at the International Forum for Fashion Training Institutes held in London, a platform shared with the UK Government Minister for the Creative Industries. He was joint author of a report on a Department of Trade and Industry (DTI) Mission to the USA to examine e-commerce developments in the textile and apparel supply chain (July 2000). He has also undertaken market research for the Consumer Association and has been an invited expert on consumer issues, marketing and retailing for the BBC on radio and television. Tony is one of only three international academics invited to be a member of the Strategic Planning Committee for the Milano

Project in South Korea. He is editor of the *Textile Institute Journal of Economics, Management and Marketing* and on the distinguished editorial board of the *Fashion Marketing Journal*. He holds external examiner positions at Oxford Brookes University Business School for their South African programmes, the University of Ulster, Glasgow Caledonian University (M.Sc. Marketing), Bournemouth University (M.A. Services Marketing) and he is a Senior Examiner for the Chartered Institute of Marketing.

Margaret K. Hogg M.A. M.A.B.A. Ph.D., is Senior Lecturer in consumer behaviour at Manchester School of Management, UMIST. She read Politics and Modern History at Edinburgh University, followed by postgraduate studies in history at the Vrije Universiteit, Amsterdam and then by an M.A. in Business Analysis at Lancaster University. She spent 6 years working in Marketing with K Shoes, Kendal. Prior to joining UMIST in September 1995, she completed a Ph.D. at Manchester Business School in Consumer Behaviour and Retailing. Her research interests include consumer behaviour, retailing and marketing history. Her work has appeared in refereed journals, including the *Journal of Marketing Management*, the *European Journal of Marketing* and the *International Journal of Advertising*. She has presented papers at a number of international conferences, including US meetings of the Association for Consumer Research and the Society for Consumer Psychology.

Cynthia L. Istook Ph.D., is currently an Associate Professor, Department of Textile and Apparel Technology and Management at North Carolina State University. Dr Istook received her Bachelor's degree in Fashion Merchandising, Clothing, and Textiles from Texas Christian University in 1976. She worked for Sanger Harris (a Federated Department store) for almost 3 years in the management training programme as an assistant buyer and department group manager. Dr Istook obtained a Master's degree in 1989 and a Ph.D. degree in 1992 from Texas Woman's University. Her master's thesis research concerned the durability of Texcellana 80% Cotton–20% Wool fabric. Research for her dissertation was centred on Computer-Aided-Design (CAD) in the apparel industry. She has taught at Baylor University in Waco, Texas, the University of North Texas in Denton, Texas, and Texas Woman's University.

Tim Jackson Dip.M. M.A., is a Senior Lecturer in Marketing at the London College of Fashion responsible for developing and leading a Post Graduate Certificate in Fashion Buying and Merchandising, and a member of the Management Research Group. Having worked both in retail management and in buying and merchandising for a number of fashion retailers, including Dash, Jaeger and Burton, he has co-written the first UK textbook on fashion buying and merchandising with David Shaw, published by Macmillan in January 2001. Tim is qualified in marketing, having gained an M.A. in Marketing and the CIM Diploma; he has undertaken considerable research into the fashion industry while based at the London College of Fashion. In addition to lecturing at the LCF, he has lectured at the University of Westminster and Surrey University.

M. C. Lam B.A., graduated from ITC in 1998. After graduation she worked in Next (Asia) Ltd as Assistant Merchandiser. She now works for the Hong Kong Government's Health and Environment Hygiene Department.

Beatrice Le Pechoux B.Sc. M.B.A. M.Sc. Ph.D. After having graduated from the Textile Technology Management Ph.D. program at the College of Textiles of North Carolina State University in May 2000, Beatrice initially conducted a post-doc research project related to the design process models developed during her dissertation work in collaboration with the Computer Science department of the College of Engineering, NCSU. Since 1 January 2001, she has been working as a Visiting Assistant Professor in the Textile and Apparel Technology and Management department of the College of Textiles, NCSU. As from 1 August 2001, she will be a Global Marketing Manager for Cotton Incorporated based in Cary, North Carolina. This position will focus mainly on Europe and Turkey. Beatrice has published several articles in refereed journals regarding the link between marketing, design and creative processes, standard sizing issues, and knowledge management.

Trevor J. Little B.Sc. Ph.D., is currently Professor and Head of Department of Textile and Apparel Technology and Management at North Carolina State University. Professor Little received his Bachelor's degree in Textile Industries from the University of Leeds in 1971. He then went on to obtain a Ph.D. degree in 1974 from the University of Leeds. Professor Little's research interests include apparel manufacturing and management, production and assembly systems, design for manufacturability, automated manufacturing systems, handling systems, manufacturing simulation, human factors, technology development, and information technology.

Christopher M. Moore M.A.(Hons) M.B.A. Ph.D., is Scotmid Professor of Retailing at Glasgow Caledonian University and is the Course Director for the M.Sc. in Fashion Marketing. He has published widely in the area of fashion marketing and the focus for his doctoral research was the international expansion of fashion retailers into the UK. He has consulted to a wide variety of fashion companies, ranging from Issey Miyake to Marks & Spencer. He is also a regular guest columnist on consumer issues for Emap media.

Ruth Murphy B.A.(Hons) PgD. M.B.A., is a Senior Lecturer in Retail Marketing in the Business School at the University of North London where she teaches retail marketing, retail strategy and strategic management at undergraduate and postgraduate level. Her research interests centre on the operationalization of Internet strategies of fashion retail companies. To this end, she has published a number of articles in the *Journal of Fashion Marketing and Management* and the *International Journal of Retail and Distribution Management*, together with presenting papers at both national and international conferences.

Andrew J. Newman Ph.D., is a lecturer in retailing at the Department of Textiles, UMIST, where he teaches retailing, market research and consumer behaviour. His research interests lie in the impact of the physical setting or built environment on customer behaviour, retail store design and the application of e-commerce techniques in retailing. His most recent collaborative research activity involves government funded work on customer in-store tracking, and the use of this knowledge in the design of retail layouts and format designs. He has presented academic papers that deal with consumer behaviour and the impact of the built environment at numerous retailing and marketing conferences. He has established links with a number of UK universities for collaboration in areas of sourcing, managing the distribution and logistics function, and Internet-based approaches to supply chain issues. Before returning to higher education in 1993, he worked for the commercial airline British Airways in areas of marketing and customer service. During this period he travelled extensively throughout the world.

Martin Raymond M.A., is editor of *Viewpoint* magazine, a twice yearly trends, brands, intelligence and lifestyle predictions journal. He lectures in journalism and fashion lifestyle at the London College of Fashion, and is a regular contributor to *The Independent on Sunday* and BBC Radio 4's *Front Row* arts programme. He is also co-author of *100 Years of Change; Design and Style in the Twentieth Century* and creative director of The Future Laboratory, a consultancy and trends mapping group that specializes in analyzing current and future consumer behaviour patterns.

Pammi Sinha B.Sc.(Hons) B.A.(Hons) M.A. Ph.D., trained as a fashion designer at the University of Central England, from where she received the B.A. (Hons) and M.A. in fashion and textiles. She continued her studies for a Ph.D. at Salford University, which examined the fashion design process across market levels in the UK womenswear sector. She has had a varied career, working in design studios and retail, as well as completing enterprise and industrial manufacturing courses; she finally settled down when she taught fashion marketing and foundation studies in fashion and textiles at the University of Salford, and gained her Ph.D. from there in 2000. She is currently senior fashion tutor at UMIST.

Bill Webb M.A.Cantab, Executive Director of the Institute of Retail & Distribution Management and Senior Lecturer at The London Institute. Bill Webb has an Exhibition and Masters degree in Economics from The University of Cambridge. He lectures in Retail Management at The London College of Fashion (London Institute). A member of the Management Research Group, his research interests include branding, e-commerce, and retail internationalization. He has recently been engaged on a project sponsored by IBM, examining the impact of 'mass customization' and e-commerce on the clothing sector. He has published a number of papers relating to retail marketing in academic journals and at conferences, most recently the Academy of Marketing Science congress in Columbus, Ohio, USA. Bill has held senior marketing positions with three major companies and served as a Director of Management Horizons Europe, the leading retail consulting firm, for eight years. He how runs his own successful consulting practice (IRDM). He is a panel judge for the UK 'Retailer of the Year' awards and is a regular speaker at commercial conferences, and on TV and radio. He regularly contributes to practitioner publications such as *Retail Interiors*.

Acknowledgements

We would like to thank and dedicate this book to our partners Janice Hines and Stephen Glennon, for all their support and encouragement. This book is also dedicated to Joyce and Ivan Bruce.

We would also like to thank Delia Alfonso at Butterworth-Heinemann for her enthusiasm and commitment to this project.

Finally, many thanks to the contributors.

Introduction

Fashion is a global business. It is an exciting, dynamic and creative business. Fashion is about self-expression, emotion and identity. Fashion reflects *and* pushes cultural and social boundaries. The mix of aesthetic, technology and business makes fashion a special and fascinating industry. Fashion is big business and employs a host of people with different talents and skills to bring fashion apparel to the consumer. Designers, merchandisers, buyers, marketers, technologists, logistics managers, strategists, etc. are all involved with getting the best product to the marketplace in the fastest time, and at the most competitive price. This is not easy – fashion changes constantly. The traditional seasons of Spring, Summer, Autumn and Winter are still apparent, but in-season changes are frequent. Colour, form, texture, label, etc. can be extremely short-lived. This makes forecasting, planning and marketing risky and complex.

The growth of the 'new economy' affects the structure of the fashion business. New dotcom companies offer fashion apparel via the Internet. But, are these operating as wholesalers or retailers? What 'added value' do they offer consumers? How do they deliver customer fulfilment and cope with distribution issues? Nonetheless, they pose a potential threat to the 'bricks and mortar' retailers, in terms of being a new channel to market and, in many cases, offering cheaper prices for branded goods. The emergence of 'clicks and mortar' retailers – traditional retailers offering Internet sites – has stimulated Internet shopping. Boundaries between retailers, manufacturers and dotcom companies are becoming blurred. Alongside this reorganization of the industry, consumers are less loyal. Consumers do 'shop around' for the best deal, based on price, quality, convenience or brand awareness, but how they shop on the Internet for fashion is not predictable. It is in 'business to business' transactions where the new economy seems to be gaining a foothold. Ordering and shipping dyestuffs from Japan to factories in India, tracking the movement of goods as they are being transported from China to the UK and other similar business activities are where e-commerce is beneficial. New partnerships and strategic alliances are being formed with e-commerce.

The 'old' paradigms of management thinking in the fashion industry are being challenged. Quick response, flexible approaches and the constant drive to offer innovative products to consumers have to be managed effectively. How can new design talent be spotted and given the opportunity to flourish?

Fashion futures are influenced by new materials and advanced technologies. These will present new challenges and create new aesthetics and sensibilities. Seamless garments offer a comfortable fit; partly finished garments may be bought and then 'finished' by a local micro-manufacturer based at a local supermarket; dyeing a garment may be available at the 'touch of a button' and be another programme offered on a domestic washing machine, etc. How can the needs of the 'green consumer' be met?

This book covers the main themes that affect marketing in the fashion world. The first two chapters by Tony Hines outline the dynamics of the global fashion industry and the machinations of the supply chain. The shift of apparel manufacture to the Far East is shown and the importance of global brands is stressed. A new approach to supply chain management – the iceberg theory – is advanced and the implications of e-commerce for supply chain management are mapped out. Christopher Moore embellishes the theme of globalization in Chapter 3. He focuses on the problems fashion retailers face with expanding internationally. Chapters 4–6 consider marketing issues faced by fashion retailers. William Webb identifies three issues that fashion retailers have to address: culture, strategy and operations. Andrew Newman and Nick Atkinson present an in-depth case study of the UK retailer of luxury goods, Selfridges. They focus on how store image was paramount in the re-branding of Selfridges. Building on the theme of store image and atmospherics, Alice Chu and M. C. Lam discuss the situation in Hong Kong for fashion retailers. Chapters 7–9 examine the key issues of brand development, design and creativity in fashion. Tim Jackson describes the process of trend forecasting in the fashion industry. Innovation management in fashion is discussed in the chapter by Beatrice Le Pechoux, Trevor Little and Cynthia Istook. They develop a Product Development Framework, which incorporates Consumer Needs and links this with the requirement of retailers to have a stream of successful products. Following on from this, Pammi Sinha describes the role of designers in the fashion industry. She considers design management from the perspective of a high street retailer, an independent design label and a large manufacturer. The next two chapters focus on the consumer. Negative self-identity is the theme of the chapter by Emma Banister and Margaret Hogg. They note that the user images and stereotypes that accompany negative selves may explain why consumers reject fashion items and avoid shopping in certain retail environments. Moving onto the world of Internet retail, Ruth Murphy and Margaret Bruce show how consumer value can be developed to create effective Internet sites. Capturing the zeitgeist is the final chapter of the book. Martin Raymond reveals different fashion marketing futures that are appropriate for the global world of fashion.

1

Globalization: an introduction to fashion markets and fashion marketing

Tony Hines

Introduction

This introductory chapter is structured to provide an overview of the impact of globalization upon fashion markets and fashion marketing. In this context, it is essential to understanding the competitive landscape for this important international industry before examining some of the key themes and contemporary issues that consume time and effort of policy makers, managers, consultants and researchers. The chapter begins by examining meanings of fashion markets and fashion marketing before examining in detail the changing business environment. Globalization is then explored through two key industries that underpin fashion markets – textiles and clothing. Structures and conditions that have caused the phenomenon of globalization are examined before moving on to identify consequences for textiles and clothing, and subsequently fashion markets and fashion marketing.

Fashion markets and fashion marketing

The textile, apparel and footwear industries are what many consider to be elements of a fashion industry. Textiles in the shape of home furnishings, fabrics, curtains, various upholstery, wall and floor coverings are what many consider fashionable items, as indeed are clothing and footwear. However, the term fashion can cover a much greater range of goods and a glance at any contemporary style magazine would lead one to conclude that many of the issues raised in relation to fashion markets and fashion marketing as applied to these sectors that we commonly think of as making up the fashion industries could equally apply to food, music, automobiles, perfumery and beauty products. Indeed, modern lifestyles and consumerism rely heavily on and are influenced by these wider fashion trends. Nevertheless, much of the focus for this book in terms of product and markets will remain with textiles and apparel.

The changing business environment

Global capital markets are predicted to grow in value by 10 times in the next 10 years increasing from $20 trillion in 2000 to $200 trillion by 2010 (Means and Schneider, 2000). The last 20 years of the twentieth century witnessed a growth from $2 trillion in 1980 to $20 trillion by 2000. The start of the first decade in the twenty-first century is witnessing an unleashing speed of change in worldwide economic and business conditions. The e-revolution is transforming the ways in which business to business (B2B) markets are interacting. The e-business revolution is upon us all. It is not just or simply the technological impacts that are leading to long-term market change, but a series of changes that have developed during the last decades of the twentieth century. These factors influencing conditions are: globalization; organizational restructuring; information and communication technologies; a growing recognition that differentiation strategies and not simply cost-based strategies are required to survive and thrive in the twenty-first century; and finally, the rise in consumerism with more fickle buying behaviour. The more *'savvy'* consumers in the start of the new century are migrating to e-business, digital shopping, telephone commerce, e-retail and e-finance. They also have more choice, are likely to be less loyal, are not prepared to accept second best, and have become more sophisticated in their tastes and their approach to buying goods and services. In many developed economies, consumers have become time poor and cash rich, creating marketing opportunities for doing business differently and presenting traditional retailers with new and different challenges.

Competitive markets are being shaped by global companies who want to achieve market dominance through developing their powerful brands in order to transcend local domestic markets. These organizations need to satisfy their customers by understanding better their needs. They are developing powerful information systems that provide their owner(s) with vast databases that they can mine to identify market trends and utilize for targeted promotional activity.

New product innovation and creativity to leverage both the brand and the vast arrays of information that these global brand owners have at their disposal requires them to think in new ways about their business and the competition they face. Owning assets is no longer as important a consideration as owning customers. This belief is evidenced by recent trends to restructure organizations and to outsource many of the functional and traditional activities previously regarded as essential to the well-being of the organization. Efficient and effective supply chains are required to manage customer demand and brand operations. Customer relationship management is supported through e-commerce. Back-office support activities are more focused on satisfying customers and fulfilment of the marketing promise is critical to the organization's future. Organizations are focused on value creation rather than merely short-term profitability. Creating value streams is important as markets, marketing processes, supplier networks and operations throughout the globe become integrated through e-linkages in a complex chain moving parts, products and information around the network in order to meet customer demand. Different strategies are required to pursue this goal as time and distance shrink (Cairncross, 1998). Internet strategies present opportunities to integrate complex supply chains from concept design to store, and on to the final consumer. Markets and market opportunity may be both local and global. Organizations will be managing networks to leverage brand values and this can be achieved using global communication systems from anywhere in the world.

Globalization and economic growth

Historically, the textiles and clothing industries have played a prominent role in the process of economic development. In the eighteenth century, the textiles and clothing industries led the Industrial Revolution in Europe, and more recently were crucial to the success of export-led growth in the dynamic newly industrializing economies of East Asia (OECD, 1995, p. 11). Globally, the textiles and clothing industries are large employers of labour, with 13 million directly employed in textiles and a further 10 million in clothing manufacture. However, as Dicken (1998, p. 284) remarks, these figures are likely to grossly underestimate the actual numbers of people involved who are not recorded in any official statistics or estimates. In 1998, the figures for employment in the clothing industry alone were estimated at 10.7 million, a substantial increase on previous estimates (OETH, 2000, p. 10). The increase is attributed to more accurate statistics from the People's Republic of China. Between 1995 and 1999, EU employment in clothing fell by 9.1%. Globally, 14.2% of all employment is accounted for by textiles and clothing manufacture. In the EU, 7.5% is the comparable figure. World production in textiles was valued at US$485 billion and clothing at US$335 billion in 1998. Table 1.1 provides details for world exports and imports for both clothing and textiles. It is worth noting that the export and import of textiles are dominated by Western Europe and Asia. Asia is also the largest exporter of clothes and Western Europe the largest importer.

Table 1.1 Percentages of world exports and imports of textiles and clothing 1998

	Exports		Imports	
	Textiles	Clothing	Textiles	Clothing
W Europe	44.0	33.7	40.3	45.2
Asia	40.2	42.9	25.1	13.0
N America	7.4	5.8	11.7	28.5
Latin America	2.8	7.1	5.8	5.4
Other	5.6	10.5	16.1	7.9

Source: OETH (2000).

Table 1.2 Percentages of world employment in 1998

	Textiles	Clothing
Europe	16.6	22.3
Asia	72.5	60.4
Oceania	0.4	0.0
Africa	2.9	5.3
America	7.6	12.0

Source: OETH (2000).

Table 1.2 shows the patterns for world employment in both the textile and clothing industries with Asia by far the largest employer.

According to Dicken (1998, p. 283), the textiles and clothing industries were the first manufacturing industries to take on a global dimension and are the most widely dispersed industries across the developed and developing world.

> Indeed, global shifts in the textiles and clothing industries exemplify many of the intractable issues facing today's world economy, particularly the trade tensions between developed and developing economies. These changes continue to cause intense political friction.
>
> Dicken (1998, p. 283)

Globalization defined

Ghoshal and Bartlett (1998, p. 18) refer to companies that are multinational, international and global in the context of developing key strategic capabilities. *Multinational* companies build a strong local presence through sensitivity and responsiveness to national differences. *International* companies exploit parent company knowledge and capabilities through worldwide diffusion and adaptation, whereas *global* companies build cost advantages through centralized global-scale operations. The turbulent economic environments of the 1970s and 1980s had led to a rash of reports, studies and recommendations to managers offering prescriptions to run their businesses more effectively in the new 'global' environment. As Ghoshal and Bartlett (1988, p. 21) comment, globalization became a term in search of a definition. The term was interpreted in a variety of ways and given new meanings. A *Newsweek* article[1] offered advice to managers to reorganize and streamline their businesses by offering standard global products and managing operations through a centrally coordinated home office, a method, it was stated, that the Japanese had used for years. However, many managers and academics remained unconvinced by this formula of standardization, rationalization and centralization. It was true that for some Japanese companies the formula had worked, but it was equally true that for others it had not. Ghoshal and Bartlett (1998, p. 22) give a number of examples where the formula had failed in Japan for companies such as NEC and Kao, whereas some European and US companies not working to any prescribed formulas had been successful (Unilever, Ericsson and Procter & Gamble). The quest for global formulas was replaced by a search for fit. The dominant strategic requirement of the business and the development of strategic capabilities to match the requirement were seen as important. Nevertheless, the forces of global change act very differently on different industries, and any analysis of global strategy and organization must begin with an understanding of where the industry is placed.

Lévy (1995, p. 353) provides an economic definition for the phenomenon of globalization as follows:

> To economists globalization is seen as the increasing internationalization of the production, distribution and marketing of goods and services.

Govindarajan and Gupta (1998, p. 3) provide a number of different ways to define globalization, but at the level of the specific country they refer to:

> The extent of the interlinkages between a country's economy and the rest of the world.

They state that the key indicators defining globalization of an industry are:

- the extent of cross-border trade within the industry as a ratio of total worldwide production;
- the extent of cross-border investment as a ratio of total capital invested in the industry; and
- the proportion of industry revenue accounted for by companies that compete in all major regions.

---

[1] *Newsweek*, 14 April 1986, 'Rebuilding Corporate Empires: A New Global Formula'.

In this respect, the textiles and clothing industries would score highly against all the criteria given. This will become clearer as the chapter unfolds. Dicken (1998, p. 5) views globalization as a complex of inter-related processes rather than an end-state, and in taking such a process-oriented approach he makes an important distinction between the processes of internationalization and globalization:

> Internationalization processes involve the simple extension of eco-
> nomic activities across national boundaries. It is, essentially, a
> quantitative process which leads to a more extensive geographical
> pattern of economic activity . . . Globalization processes are qual-
> itatively different from internationalization processes. They involve not
> merely the geographical extension of economic activity across national
> boundaries but also – and more importantly – the functional integration
> of such internationally dispersed activities.

The textile and clothing industries are both international and global in nature. It is clear that by any current definition of globalization these industries qualify.

Market definition

Standard Industrial Classification (SIC) codes are used by the Department of Trade and Industry (DTI) within the UK to define the scope of an industry. This is done according to product characteristics. The SIC codes were redefined in 1992, making some statistical comparisons to earlier periods more problematic, since some codes were merged and aggregated differently. SIC(92) 18 encompasses the various sectors making up the UK Apparel Industry.[2] Companies that comprise the industry tend to specialize in a sector: Menswear, Ladieswear, Childrenswear, Knitwear, Lingerie, Street Fashion, Designerwear or Accessories (scarves, ties, hats and gloves). SIC codes such as those used by the UK government are important and provide a mechanism for gathering statistics and supplying information about an industrial grouping. Definitions about the types of organization comprising the group are important if accurate statistical data are to be available. Similarly, in other countries there are similar mechanisms for gathering statistics relating to these industries. Trade bodies also gather statistics about the industry and they too use government data. For example, the British Clothing Industry Association (BCIA), The National Textile Center (US), American Apparel Manufacturers Association and Korean Federation of Textile Industries, to name but a few organizations. Statistical data are useful for making comparisons between different competing countries comprising an industry, although one has to be careful in drawing comparisons 'like with like'. It has already been stated that there may be difficulty in

[2] *Source*: Department of Trade and Industry, 'The UK Clothing, Footwear and Textile Industry – An Overview'. London: DTI, 1998.

comparing data from different time periods when classification codes change. However, it is also the case that it is difficult drawing comparisons across different countries or regions of the world when the definitions of firms comprising the industrial groupings differ. Furthermore, it may also be difficult when statistical data collection methods differ and estimates become less accurate. Nevertheless, the next section will attempt to draw comparisons with these points in mind.

Structure and size of textiles and clothing manufacturing industries

In 1996, there were over 1 million people employed in clothing manufacture across the EU. By 1999, this had fallen to an estimated 923 500 and this trend is continuing into 2000. It is estimated that there were around 57 000 enterprises in the EU clothing sector in 1996, falling to 52 500 by December 1999. More than 80% of enterprises had fewer than 20 employees in both 1996 and 1999. These small enterprises account for some 30% of employment and 25% of the turnover. In 1999, there was a trade deficit in clothing amounting to 27.9 billion Euro, with imports to the European Union (EU15) standing at 40.5 billion Euro and exports at 12.7 billion Euro. The total turnover amounted to 68.9 billion Euro (OETH, 2000). This trade deficit for the EU15 and the rest of the world has declined significantly in recent years. In 1996, the trade deficit for the UK stood at £2.5 billion. This had risen to £4 billion in 1999. The turnover in the industry in the UK at retail prices was £26.5 billion[3] and the value of UK manufacturing in the sector at factor prices stood at around £8 billion (EMAP, 1997). In the legitimate[4] sector of the UK economy there were some 210 000 employees in the clothing sector during 1996 (ONS, 1997). The UK lost 6.8% of its clothing employment between 1998 and 1999 alone (OETH, 2000). Estimates vary, but in 2000 fewer than 150 000 employees were thought to remain in UK clothing manufacturing jobs and those losing their jobs were casualties of intensifying global competition in the sector.

From a global perspective, the largest concentration of clothing employment is in China with 1.6 million, followed by the US with 770 000, the Russian Federation (630 000) and then Japan (450 000) (Dicken, 1998, p. 289). Other major concentrations of clothing workers include Indonesia, Thailand, Philippines, South Korea and Hong Kong, while in Western Europe clothing manufacturing remains important to the UK, Germany, France and Italy, despite the decline in employment. Table 1.3 gives details of the numbers officially employed in textiles and clothing in the EU. Table 1.4 shows an analysis of EU15 clothing employment by member states in 1996.

---

[3] This figure includes footwear as well as clothing.
[4] In this context, it is important to recognize that there is a 'black economy' in the manufacture of clothes whereby numbers employed are not registered in any official statistics.

Table 1.3 EU15 textile and clothing employment

	1995	1996	Change 1996 on 1995 (%)	1999	Change 1999 on 1996 (%)
Textiles	1 278 000	1 230 300	3.73	1 159 300	5.77
Clothing	1 068 000	1 017 700	4.71	923 500	9.26
Textiles and clothing	2 346 000	2 248 000	4.18	2 082 800	7.35

Source: OETH (1997, 2000).

Table 1.4 Employment in the EU clothing sector, 1996

Country	% of EU employment	Number employed
Austria	1.2	12 212.40
Belgium	1.6	16 283.20
Denmark	0.7	7 123.90
Finland	0.8	8 141.60
France	12.5	127 212.50
Germany	11.7	119 070.90
Greece	2.6	26 460.20
Ireland	0.8	8 141.60
Italy	21.3	216 770.10
Netherlands	0.8	8 141.60
Portugal	13.6	138 407.20
Spain	11.5	117 035.50
Sweden	0.3	3 053.10
UK	20.6	209 646.20
	100.0	1 017 700.00

Source: table adapted from OETH (1997) and OETH (2000).

Textiles and clothing taken together accounted for 4.2% of the value added for manufacturing industries as a whole and 7.6% of manufacturing employment within the EU (OETH, 1997). Textile production fell by 4.9% and clothing output by 3.7%. Employment in these sectors also fell in 1996 by 4.2% in comparison with a fall of only 2.8% in 1995. The rate of decline in the sector has been higher than for all manufacturing employment, according to OETH (1997) data. Imports grew by 3.4% in volume terms and by 4.9% in value, whilst exports rose by 2.5% in volume and 8.5% in value between 1995 and 1996. Outward Processing Trade (OPT) represented 20% of all EU15 clothing imports and rose by 7% in 1996. Competitiveness in the sector was helped by falling exchange rates for the major member states, apart from Italy, during 1996 and also through productivity gains measured in value added terms mentioned previously. Productivity in the clothing sector alone rose by 1.4% in 1996, compared to a rise of 6.1% in 1995. Important improvements in productivity since 1995 were attributed to subcontracting and the application of information technologies within the sector (Hines, 1997). It is recognized that Information and Communication Technologies (ICT) have enabled major purchasing groups to buy further from their home base and still maintain a reasonable degree of control over the supply chain.

It is estimated that 70% of the UK workforce are women and that 25% of total employment is accounted for by the knitwear sector. However, during 2000 this sector has also become a casualty of intensifying competitive forces, and the continuing migration of major UK retailers searching to lower their own costs and maintain high street margins in the face of fickle consumer demand has led to factory closures and more job losses. It is further estimated that the bulk of clothing production is carried out by small and medium-sized firms with fewer than 200 employees accounting for 50% of the total industry output. This compares to around 33% of output being produced by SMEs for the manufacturing sector as a whole in the UK (EMAP, 1997, p. 192). The UK has the second largest number of people employed in the EU after Italy (Table 1.4). Furthermore, there are geographical pockets of employment within specific regions of the UK in Scotland, the East Midlands, East London, the North East and the North West.

Growing liberalization with the demise of the Multi-Fibre Arrangement (MFA) by the end of 2004 and the World Trade Organization (WTO) Agreement on Textiles and Clothing (ATC) will mean lower tariffs for textile and clothing products, thereby reducing trade barriers for the developing world to export goods to the EU. Commercial policy has been an important protection mechanism for the countries of the EU. Countries outside the WTO often have bilateral agreements with the EU. For example, in 1996 the EU developed a preferential relationship with Turkey eliminating trade barriers between the EU and Turkey. Therefore, in terms of trade policy, Turkey has in substance become a member of the EU, if not in form. The same can be said for the Central Eastern European Countries (CEEC) from January 1998. Two areas of major concern and yet to be resolved for the EU are the re-integration of China and policy towards the Russian Federation.

GATT Textile and Clothing Agreement[5]

This agreement was formerly referred to as the Multi-Fibre Arrangement (MFA). It was established under the General Agreement on Tariffs and Trade (GATT) in 1974 as a means of countering unfair trading practices. The aim was to restrict imports from low labour cost countries by negotiating bilateral quotas. It is an umbrella agreement signed by most developed countries and about 30 developing countries. In the EU, the agreement takes the form of a series of bilateral agreements with a number of textile supplier countries. The

[5] Renamed in 1994 at the Uruguay Round.

agreements limit the export of textile and clothing products from the supplier country into the EU by a system of quantitative restrictions, i.e. quotas. It is a specific derogation from the free trading principles of the WTO. The MFA has two stated objectives:

1 To give the textile and clothing industries in the developed world time to restructure and diversify.
2 To guarantee a share of the developed market to developing countries.

It was only ever envisaged as a temporary measure. The WTO Textile and Clothing Agreement, which took effect from 1 January 1995, prescribes the way in which the MFA will be phased out, thereby returning the textile and clothing sector to free trading principles of the WTO.

Phasing out the Multi-Fibre Arrangement

There are four specific steps to the phasing out of the MFA which began on 1 January 1995 with 16% of the EU 1990 volume of textile and clothing imports integrated into the WTO system. The products concerned covered yarns, fabrics, made up textiles and clothing products that had not been under quota. In 1998, step 2 required a further 17.8% to be integrated with the WTO system. The same four product groups were covered with 24 categories under MFA quota and 19 of those categories represent one or more important quotas. This is significant for EU production, since about one-third of the 1990 volume of EU textiles and clothing imports will no longer be subject to quota and the licensing requirements. Since 1995, EU tariffs on textiles and clothing have reduced annually by around 10% and this will continue through to 31 December 2004. The EU market is one of the most open in the world, and exporters to the EU such as Turkey and the CEEC countries have taken advantage. In contrast, it has been difficult for EU producers to export to some countries, notably the US, because of their rules of origin. Intensifying global competition will no doubt witness further declines in EU production, employment and investment. One consequence of this will be a worsening balance of trade deficit for the EU in this sector as imports increase and exports decline.

EU industrial policy in the sector is concerned with technological development, training, diversification and conversion, information and communication. Emphasis has been placed upon development and more effective use of existing industrial networks, know how and technology transfer.[6]

It is important to recognize that quotas and the removal of those quotas will not necessarily remove all the barriers to trade. There are still environmental restrictions. For example, products containing Azo dye stuffs are banned in Germany and the Netherlands. Children's nightwear is subject to far more

[6] The Competitiveness of Subcontracting in the Textile and Clothing Industry in the EU, DG III, European Commission, Brussels, 1996.

rigorous legislation in other European countries, for example flammability restrictions. Other barriers come in the form of non-standard anthropometrics (sizing of garments) or in labelling legislation. Quotas may disappear but trade barriers still exist.

Government policies in a global context

Government intervention throughout the globe has focused upon two specific aims:

1 Restructure and rationalization of textiles and clothing industries within the country concerned.
2 Stimulating the industry through offshore assembly provision and preferential trading agreements.

It is worth briefly examining the impact of each policy aim upon the global industry.

Textile industry reforms since 1945

Developed countries, most noticeably in Europe, where the industries may be regarded as mature, have had various subsidies and investment assistance programmes. As Dicken (1998, p. 299) reports, the UK faced severe competition from low labour cost countries in the 1950s and the government introduced the Cotton Industry Act with the aim of removing half of the textile industry's capacity for cotton, the aim being to re-equip and modernize what remained. Firms were encouraged to engage in voluntary euthanasia in return for compensation for scrapped plants and grants for re-equipment. Similar schemes of national assistance were offered as inducements by other European governments in an effort to restructure their industries. Despite the UK government broadly achieving its target through these policy instruments in the 1950s, the problem of over-capacity has not disappeared and subsequent decades have seen continued rationalization.

The problem of restructuring is not, as one might expect, unique to the developed countries of Europe. At the end of the 1960s, Japan actively encouraged a reduction in capacity and plant modernization with the aim of repositioning the industry in markets with higher value products. Newer textile producers in Taiwan and South Korea have also had similar interventions by government.

For example, Korea's textile industry in 1998 accounted for 13.5% of the country's exports, 18.5% of the total number of companies, 15.2% of total employment and 8.3% of total production. Korea accounted for 4.7% of the global market for textiles, trailing only China, Italy, Germany and the US in terms of market share. Korea trades with more than 180 countries. The industry in Korea has invested heavily in automation to reduce costs and improve productivity. Automation in textile factories has increased from 45% to 70% between 1995 and 2000. It is expected to reach 85% by 2005. Key changes encouraged by government have been environmental protection, energy conservation and the introduction of information technology systems, e.g. local area networks (LANs), management software and computer integrated manufacture (CIM), with a move towards agile production systems producing smaller quantities and multiple product production.[7]

Offshore assembly and preferential trading agreements

These types of government intervention can have a significant impact upon the global distribution, development and location of the industry. They form part of a country's customs and excise regulations, and have been used extensively as protection measures by the US and Germany.[8]

The US government established the '807' Programme in the 1960s. Item 807 of the tariff schedule operated by US Customs and Excise encouraged garment manufacturers to undertake apparel assembly in lower cost Caribbean and South American countries. The duty payable on the garment was then limited to the value-added component since leaving the US and being re-imported as a finished item. In effect, duty was paid only on the labour cost element. The developing country keen for the additional business allowed cut cloth to be imported for assembly free of any duty. As a result of such a favourable bilateral agreement, the total cost of manufacturing garments was lower than it would have been if manufactured in the US.

The US established the Caribbean Basin Initiative (CBI) in February 1986 that allowed access to US markets, under specific conditions, for garments produced within the Caribbean (Steele, 1988). Item 807.0010 of the US Customs and Excise Schedule, more commonly referred to as 807a, was added to the existing 807 Programme. The main difference between the two programmes was critical for the US textile industry. Whereas 807 allowed the use of fabric imported from anywhere in the world so long as it was cut in the US before being exported to the low cost labour country, 807a demanded that only US produced fabric could be used within the scheme. This addition removed an earlier major objection from textile suppliers that had continually been levelled at the original 807 scheme. The major developing countries benefiting from the 807a Programme have been the Dominican Republic and Mexico, who between

---

[7] A recent visit to Korea (June 2000) as a member of the Strategic Planning Committee for Taegu's Textile Industry Development Strategy – Milano Project confirmed the people's, organization's and government's long-term commitment to this industry. Statistics for the Korean Textile and Clothing Industry were taken from Textile Korea 2000 supplied by the Korea Federation of Textile Industries and supplemented by KITECH statistics.

[8] It is West Germany that is being referred to for the period before re-integration and Germany since re-integration. Statistics and other data would need to be gathered separately for anyone wanting to pursue this avenue of investigation.

them have accounted for approaching 50% of all throughput. It is significant that labour costs in the Dominican Republic were $0.82 (1992) including social charges and $1.17 in Mexico (1992). These figures would represent 10% or less of the US hourly rate.

The more recent North American Free Trade Area (NAFTA) agreement established between the US, Canada and Mexico is for a 12-year period from 1992. This agreement effectively replaces the 807a Programme for Mexico. Three hundred and sixty million people are covered by the terms of the agreement, making NAFTA the largest trading bloc in the world. As far as clothing and textiles are concerned, any outsourced production to Mexico would need to use fabric developed in US mills in the same way as the 807a schedule. There are some further important additional restrictions, e.g. that fabric must be made from yarn produced in North America. Quota limits have been eliminated between the parties to the agreement, as has the requirement that fabric is cut in the US. The NAFTA agreement extends a competitive advantage to Mexico as near neighbours of the US. It is significant that Mexico is the largest exporter of clothing into the US market.

Demand for textile and clothing products

Examining the EU clothing industry, it can be seen that demand comes from two sources: domestic demand from within the EU and external demand from outside the EU. Domestic demand can be measured in a number of ways, one of which is a strange term called *apparent consumption*[9] (see Table 1.5). Domestic production within the EU represented 75.73% of apparent consumption in 1990 and by 1999 this had fallen to 53.82%, whilst imports accounted for a growing proportion, increasing from 24.27% in 1990 to 46.18% in 1999. Hence import penetration increased. Domestic demand has been in decline since 1990; as a consequence, producers have focused their attention on export markets in the face of growing competition for the domestic market from outside the EU. However, exports increased by a smaller percentage, from 9.86% of apparent consumption in 1990 to 14.86% in 1999.

It is interesting to note that the relative increase in apparent consumption between 1990 and 1999 is largely due to a significant increase in imports, particularly between 1990 and 1998. Apparent consumption increased by 10.9% between 1990 and 1999 in value terms at current prices of producers.[10] Production declined steadily between 1990 and 1998, and then more rapidly between 1998 and 1999. One explanation for this might be the impact of the removal of MFA restrictions discussed earlier in the chapter.

A narrower measure uses final demand, the largest part of which is consumption by EU households and a smaller part accounted for by

[9] Apparent consumption is calculated by the following formula: production + imports – exports.
[10] This percentage includes knitwear.

Table 1.5 EU apparent consumption, ECU billion (current prices)

	1990	1998	1999
Production	67.7	64.5	59.9
Imports	19.2	38.0	40.5
Exports	7.8	13.1	12.7
Apparent consumption	79.1	89.3	87.7

Source: OETH (2000).

Table 1.6 Final demand for textiles and clothing in the EU

Sector	Percentage demand
Manufacturing	10.9
Services	9.3
Household textiles	11.1
Household clothing	68.7

Source: OETH 1997

consumption in other sectors of the economy. Table 1.6 shows the structure of final demand for textiles and clothing within the EU. The demand for textiles is significantly dependent upon the clothing industry.

The structure of clothing retailing in the EU – routes to market

Table 1.7 shows the changes that have occurred in clothing retailing channels throughout the EU between 1988 and 1999. Throughout the EU there has been an increasing trend towards retail concentration, as detailed in Table 1.7. Independent stores have fallen from 48% in 1988 to 32.5% in 1999, meaning that 67.5% (59% in 1996) of the market for clothes is now served by specialized chains, department and variety stores, supermarkets and hypermarkets, mail order and other. However, the level of concentration is still nowhere near UK proportions. Retail concentration is a phenomenon that UK analysts are familiar with. The top seven clothing retailers in the UK account for 45% of the market and they dominate the market for clothes. Independent stores account for only about 15% of the market. Marks & Spencer is the largest UK retailer, accounting for nearly 16% of the market and for 25% of all UK manufacturing (Hines, 1997). Italy is still the least concentrated retail market, but even in Italy the trend is towards concentration. Nevertheless, independent family owned stores represent more than 50% of all clothing sales, whereas elsewhere

Table 1.7 Structure of EU retailing

	Channels of distribution (%)			Change 1999 on 1996 (%)
	1988	1996	1999	
Independent stores	48	41	32.5	−20.73
Specialized chains	18	22	25.0	13.64
Department and variety stores	12	12	15.2	26.67
Supermarkets and hypermarkets	5	7	8.0	14.29
Mail order	7	9	7.7	−14.44
Other	10	9	11.6	28.89

Source: adapted from OETH (1997, 2000) data.

throughout major economies their share is less than 30%. In Germany, speciality chains dominate with 35% compared to France, where speciality chains and independent stores each account for just over 20% of the total market share. General chain stores dominate the Japanese market with 40%, whereas speciality chains dominate in Hong Kong with 40% of the market. Compare this to Korea, where hypermarkets and street markets dominate with close to 30% for each category. Street markets are also an important distribution channel in Taiwan. As retail buying concentration increases, it is important for the large retailing groups to have both flexibility and certainty in terms of satisfying consumer demand. Their supply chains become extended geographically and focused in terms of developing 'safe suppliers' who are able to respond quickly.

European retailing has witnessed a wave of takeovers. In France, Carrefour has taken over Promodes to create the world's second biggest retailer, with a combined turnover of US$54 billion, a figure that is almost double that of the UK clothing industry. Carrefour also acquired Gruppo, the Italian supermarket chain. As a result of these takeovers, Carrefour has become a market leader in Belgium, Spain, Portugal, Greece, Italy, Brazil, Argentina and Chile, and has a significant presence in the People's Republic of China, Taiwan and Indonesia. In the UK, Wal-Mart (US) has taken over ASDA and is the world's largest retailer. The world's 25 largest retailers already have 15% of the total world market and are forecast to control around 40% of world markets by 2009 (OETH, 2000, p. 85).

In the US, clothing retailing is structured differently to the EU discount stores, off-price retailers and factory outlets being more significant distribution routes to market. Table 1.8 illustrates the US clothing retail distribution by market share.

The US clothing market was worth US$183.9 billion (201.2 billion Euro) in 1999 compared to an estimated expenditure within the EU of 227.8 billion Euro in 1999. In the US market, the shift towards a more casual lifestyle is offered as

Table 1.8 US clothing retailing distribution channels by percentage value

	1990	1999	Change 1999 on 1990 (%)
Speciality stores	11.7	22.0	88.03
Discount stores	18.1	20.1	11.05
Department stores	23.7	18.7	−21.10
Major chains	16.7	15.9	−4.79
Off-price retailers	6.3	6.2	−1.59
Factory outlets	3.3	3.6	9.09
Others	20.2	13.5	−33.17
	100.0	100.0	

Source: OETH (2000).

an explanation for the growth of speciality and discount stores. Casual clothing comprises knit tops, work shirts, sweaters, jeans and casual trousers, whereas tailored clothing would consist of suits, sports coats, dresses, dress trousers and formal shirts. From 1995 to 1999, the sales of casual clothing rose by around 50%, while tailored clothes grew more slowly at around 9%. The US market is forecast to grow to US$225.9 billion by 2003, with more than 30% of the market accounted for by designerwear. Major losers have been department stores and major chains selling more traditional lines. Lifestyle changes account for the switch in expenditure by consumers. For example, dress-down Fridays which have extended to dress-down everyday in many organizations have eroded formal-wear.

Consumer expenditure on clothing

Analysis of UK expenditure by category

UK consumer spending on clothing in 2000 was almost three times what it was in 1974, but most of the increase is represented by price inflation rather than increases in volume. According to MTI (1996),[11] expenditure on consumer clothing and footwear is expected to increase in monetary terms at 1996 prices from £26.97 billion in 1996 to £36 billion by the year 2006. However, this represents a fall in expenditure as a percentage of total expenditure from 5.8% of disposable income to 5% by 2006. Disposable income and the propensity to spend is an important consideration when trying to predict how markets will perform in future. Table 1.9 illustrates the changes that occurred in consumer expenditure by product sector between 1992 and 1996 in the UK.

---

[11] Market Track International, London.

Table 1.9 Consumer expenditure in £millions on clothing by product sector 1992–1996*

Product sector	1992	1993	1994	1995	1996
All clothing	18 384	19 544	20 506	21 404	22 367
Womenswear	7 170	7 622	8 010	8 442	8 864
Menswear	4 669	4 964	5 229	5 330	5 490
Childrenswear	2 692	2 856	2 996	3 143	3 300
Lingerie	1 264	1 303	1 435	1 575	1 722
Sportswear	1 220	1 350	1 450	1 550	1 633
Jeans	1 155	1 133	1 142	1 175	1 260
Men's underwear	550	568	606	625	640
Hosiery	440	440	400	405	415
Total	19 160	20 236	21 268	22 245	23 324

Source: Industry estimates and ONS data

* ONS All clothing figure is lower than the total from MTI industry data because certain categories of sportswear are not included in the ONS data.

Consumer expenditure on clothing in the EU

EU household consumption of clothing was estimated at 228 billion Euro in 1999, an increase of 2.7% over 1998. Consumer spending per head on clothing was 606 Euro.

The balance of trade

The balance of trade is an important measure for most economies and provides an indication of how the economy in a particular country is performing in terms of its competitiveness by examining exports and imports. Table 1.10 gives an

Table 1.10 Exports, imports and trade balance in UK clothing

Year	Value of UK exports in apparel (£ billion)	Index of exports 1990 = 100	Value of UK imports in apparel (£ billion)	Index of imports 1990 = 100	Value of trade balance in apparel (£ billion)	Index of trade balance 1990 = 100
1990	1.70	100.0	3.90	100.0	−2.20	100.0
1991	1.92	113.0	4.13	105.7	−2.21	100.2
1992	2.08	122.6	4.48	114.7	−2.39	108.6
1993	2.41	141.6	4.80	123.0	−2.39	108.6
1994	2.68	157.9	4.86	124.6	−2.18	98.8
1995	2.94	173.3	5.29	135.4	−2.34	106.1
1999	2.20	129.4	6.20	159.0	−4.00	129.4

Source: Adapted from base data from Office of National Statistics, Keynote (1996) and OETH (2000).

indication of the value of exports, imports and the trade balance for the UK from 1990 to 1999. From the data in the table, it is clearly evident that exports and imports are rising during the period in monetary terms. Calculating an index of output with 1990 = 100, it becomes clearer that although exports have been rising rapidly, resulting in a 73.3% increase to 1995, this has only managed to contain the balance of trade. The balance of trade position had worsened by 1999 as exports slipped back considerably and imports continued to rise. More product was by now being sourced from abroad and of those manufacturers that remained, more were using outward processing trade (OPT) to reduce cost.

The trade balance is an important macroeconomic measure for government given that a major economic policy objective is to maintain balance of payments equilibrium. The declining trade balance demonstrated in Table 1.10 highlights the decline in the UK's competitive position in this industry. Imports have risen markedly while exports have declined between 1995 and 1999.

Labour costs

Labour costs are an important element of cost for the manufacture of most items of clothing. Estimates vary, but it is not unusual for this cost element to be between 30% and 50% of the total garment cost in the UK.[12] The industry is still very labour intensive and it is acknowledged that many parts of clothing manufacturing operations cannot be mechanized. Fabric is flexible, unlike steel, where robotics can be used to improve manufacturing throughput in industries such as motor vehicles. Furthermore, many sewing operations require skilled handling. It is because of this that the industry has focused attention upon reducing labour content within garment manufacture. Production processes are measured in standard minute values (SMVs) and controlling SMVs has been a focus for management attention. This explains paradoxically why more complicated garments tend to be constructed in developing countries, where labour costs are lower. Overhead and material costs tend to be less easy to control. Most overheads are fixed costs and material costs are often determined by the retailer's choice of fabric. It is often not left to the manufacturer to select materials for input to the manufacturing process, as in other industries. The input costs apart from labour are therefore often not controllable or determinable by the manufacturer. Focus therefore moves to the only cost left within their control – labour. Table 1.11 gives comparative cost data in the EU for clothing.

Portugal is the lowest labour cost country in the EU and Denmark is the most expensive. The UK is below the average hourly cost for labour by $1.48 ($2.48 in 1990). The People's Republic of China at $0.43 ($0.25), India at $0.39 ($0.29), Pakistan at $0.24 ($0.29), Vietnam at $0.22 ($0.29) and Indonesia at $0.16 ($0.33) are the lowest labour cost countries in the world, while European

---

[12] Figures are taken from my own estimates of costs at many UK clothing manufacturing firms over several years.

Table 1.11 Labour cost comparisons in the EU for clothing (US$)

Country	1990	1999	Change 1999 on 1990 (%)
Austria	9.96	14.32	43.78
Belgium	12.92	16.49	27.63
Denmark	15.93	18.71	17.45
Finland	14.16	13.96	−1.41
France	12.52	13.03	4.07
Germany	7.23	18.04	149.52
Greece	4.33	6.55	51.27
Ireland	7.50	8.72	16.27
Italy	12.50	13.60	8.80
Netherlands	14.71	14.71	0.00
Portugal	2.30	3.70	60.87
Spain	7.08	3.79	−46.47
Sweden	17.78	16.30	−8.32
UK	8.02	10.86	35.41
Average	**10.50**	**12.34**	**17.59**

Source: Werner International data (Summer 1990) and OETH (2000).

neighbours in Poland at $2.77 ($1.42), Hungary at $2.12 ($1.68), the Czech Republic at $1.85 ($1.55) and Romania at $1.04($1.08) are also very low cost producers, competing effectively with Turkey at $1.84 ($1.52), Morocco at $1.36 ($1.22) and Egypt at $0.58 ($0.51).[13]

UK government support for the industry

Capital investment in the industry was reported to be £2.5 billion between 1990 and 1995 (EMAP, 1997), the main thrust for investment being focused on modernization and productivity improvements rather than expansion. Since the formation of the British Apparel and Textile Confederation (BATC) in 1992, the Department of Trade and Industry has been keen to form better links between government and industry.

> The DTI is currently working with industry through trade associations on a variety of projects to encourage companies to become more competitive. The areas targeted include technology, management of

---

[13] Source data extracted from Werner International Labour Cost Report (Spring 1996) and OETH (2000) based on Werner International data for Spring 1998. According to Werner International, the quality of data for the clothing industry is not as accurate as for the textile industry.

the supply chain, development of skills, and encouraging greater use of design. The aim is to enable British companies to compete in world markets, not just the UK.

(DTI, 1998)

Competitiveness is a major concern for government, with the increasing threat to UK suppliers coming from lower labour cost producers in the developing world. The demise of the GATT quotas formerly applied through the MFA means that the UK market will be open along with other EU markets and all developed markets throughout the world. The global market for clothing and textile products will be a free market after 31 December 2004, but it may not be a fair market, with labour costs being the major element of cost for many clothing products. Countries employing low cost labour (women and children) in low cost countries have an advantage that some regard as unfair. Ethical considerations may play a greater part in an organization's strategy and marketing communications to fashion conscious consumers in future.

In the UK, the DTI advocate competitive strategies based on design, speed of response, niche markets and use of high technology. It is acknowledged that UK suppliers will not be able to compete on price.

The overall challenge to this industry is to seek out and exploit these markets and business methods which will allow them to compete in fiercely competitive global markets.

(DTI, 1998)

The main interest of government policy has focused upon the following measures to provide support for the UK clothing industry:

- Promoting exports by organizing inward missions, sponsoring visits to trade fairs and providing advice and information to the firms in the industry.
- Support and sponsorship of the Apparel and Textile Challenge, which has been set up to encourage UK manufacturers and retailers to work together, forging stronger partnerships with the aim of improving supply chain performance.
- In 1996, a project was established with the aim of attracting youngsters aged 16 and above to the industry. Educational resource packs were produced with help from the Department of Employment and Education, the DTI, Marks & Spencer, the BATC and CAPITB National Training Organization (NTO) for Clothing in the UK, previously the Industry Training Board.

A national strategy for the UK textile and clothing industry was published in June 2000. This report (DTI, 2000) provides a clear summary of the challenges facing the clothing industry in the UK. It also illustrates the competitive landscape in the global marketplace and the challenges and opportunities that most EU and Western developed economies face from other parts of the globe. In this document, it is reported that these industries contribute about £7 billion to the UK economy annually. It was the largest manufacturing sector with a turnover of £17.7 billion at production cost in 1998 and exported £5.5 billion in 1999, employing 277 000 in January 2000 with concentrations of employment in the East Midlands, Yorkshire, Scottish Borders and Northern Ireland. It also has a significant impact upon the local economies throughout the North East of England, East London, the West Midlands and the North West.

Key factors impacting upon the UK industry's competitiveness were identified as:

- Low labour cost competition securing a greater share of world markets.
- State aid in a number of overseas countries distorting competition.
- Sourcing patterns in the UK high street are changing consumer spending patterns.
- Weakness of European currencies has had a significant impact upon UK exporters.
- Macroeconomic factors include recent devaluations of Asian currencies and the progressive phasing out of the MFA.

Strengths were identified as being:

- Manufacturer/retailer co-operation to establish stronger supply chain links.
- More efficient use of design talent.
- Better exploitation of technical expertise and resources available in UK universities and colleges.
- Effective promotion of the industry's reputation for quality and excellence in specific product areas.

Weaknesses identified included:

- Enhancing innovation by collaboration.
- Improving and formalizing training and career development.
- Strengthening marketing skills.
- Improving the industry's image to attract recruits.

Recommendations to government policy included:

- Ensuring a level playing field with competitors.
- Easier access to the right kinds of public support.
- The need for universities and colleges to offer appropriate training opportunities.

Conclusions

The more difficult challenges face those firms located in the developed countries of Western Europe and the United States as they grapple with worldwide free trade and the demise of protective tariffs and quotas with the end of the MFA in January 2005. The main impact upon the most Western developed economies will be severe in terms of higher imports, lower exports, reduced production, employment and investment. The UK industry is and will continue to suffer from this specific policy change as a consequence of opening up developed markets throughout Europe to competitors from low labour cost countries in the Far East, Eastern Europe and, more importantly perhaps, Mediterranean Rim countries of North Africa and Turkey.

A further challenge facing most Western economies, including the UK and US clothing manufacturers, is how to compete with suppliers from low labour cost countries not simply in their home market, but overseas. In the UK, government initiatives under the auspices of the DTI are supporting supply chain improvements. The focus of these improvements is currently upon productivity by driving unnecessary cost out of the pipeline. Whilst the focus of this initiative is not unimportant, it is probably insufficient to improve the overall competitive position of UK suppliers, and perhaps more attention needs to focus on how to add value for key customers. In other words, perhaps the centre of attention needs to move from an input focus to focus upon examining outputs. A marketing perspective rather than a product oriented or production driven approach is required if these industries are to compete and survive the intense global competitive pressures. As the DTI has already recognized, it is not possible for UK suppliers to compete solely on price. In terms of comparative advantage, lower labour cost countries can compete on price and will win orders from UK suppliers every time. UK suppliers must therefore focus on Porter's (1980) differentiation strategies to distinguish their offering to customers.

It is important that the remaining clothing manufacturing firms are able to maintain the support of major UK retailers. In particular, Marks & Spencer have a critical role to play in continuing to source a high percentage of their clothing products from UK suppliers. It has been estimated and reported earlier in this chapter that they alone are still responsible for a significant proportion of the UK industry's output. No other single retailer is so influential. However, during 2000, Marks & Spencer openly shifted its policy of sourcing from around 70% UK to 30% overseas towards a 50–50 policy in the short term and to its ultimate currently stated goal of 30% UK and 70% offshore. Many long-standing suppliers to Marks & Spencer have suffered by losing contracts, in particular, William Baird and the contract clothing division of Coats Viyella. Estimated job losses in the UK as an immediate consequence of this announcement were in the region of 20 000 clothing workers, mainly women.

In the US since the early 1980s, competitive strategies have focused upon the application of quick response (QR). QR approaches aim at reducing the holding costs of inventory and increasing throughput (i.e. increasing efficiency). QR is useful to retailers by enabling rapid replenishment of 'hot-styles'. QR reduces the traditional requirement of stock holding to satisfy consumer demand by focusing resources to achieve just-in-time supply (JIT).

Local replenishment of supplies can often be achieved in a 4- to 6-week supply cycle, whereas offshore supplies often take longer. Longer supply lead times increase the risk of lost sales by not having the right stock in store at the right time. The counterbalance to this equation is will it be at the right cost price (i.e. bought in price) to achieve the required margin? Sourcing, purchasing and supply decisions are complex algorithms. Unfortunately, historically many such decisions have been divorced from marketing decisions, having undesirable consequences for 'bottom line' profit. More enlightened organizations have or are beginning to realize that these supply chain decision-making processes must be integrated if they are to satisfy consumer demand efficiently. Sourcing, purchasing and supply chain decisions have to be informed by marketing information.

The trend in retailing is towards further concentration, both in the UK and across Europe. This provides retailers with increasing buying power. Smaller and medium-sized firms will need to become more professional in terms of developing their management and organization capabilities in order to co-operate with larger manufacturers and retailers. Their future is inextricably linked to both larger manufacturing firms and with large retailing groups, if not directly then simply by the disciplines that these larger organizations are imposing upon their own suppliers trickling down to smaller retailers and their suppliers.

The UK industry has been slow to adopt OPT and as a result the resistance has meant higher costs and lower profits for many manufacturing firms in the industry. It is understandable that they might have had a natural reluctance to enter the scheme and that pressure may have been applied from trade union groups fearing job losses for their members. Nevertheless, there is a reasonable argument that rather than hastening job losses the adoption of OPT could indeed buy valuable time for the industry to reposition itself in the world markets before the removal of all trade barriers and a return to free trade wreak havoc. It is important that firms seek to gain equal advantage with their competitors by exploiting any government or European schemes at their disposal, however limited they may be. There has been a recent trend of some larger manufacturing firms seeking ways of lowering their cost by setting up facilities in places like Morocco. On the face of it, this trend does not bode well for the future of the UK industry or for national income, the balance of trade, employment and tax revenues that are associated with the loss of UK capacity.

It might be argued that this is an industry where government policy, far from helping the industry, has hindered its development and impeded its capability through well-meaning interventions that have merely encouraged long-term dependency. It may also be argued that support for the textile and clothing industries from UK government has not matched the rhetoric. Very small sums of public money have been made available in comparison with overseas competitors of similar size, such as South Korea, where these industries are seen as central to their economic well-being and public investment is much greater.

Globalization as a phenomenon is itself a consequence of competitive pressures that have led textile and clothing producers towards an endless search for ways to lower production costs, firstly through efficiency measures often internal to a single organization or network of organizations locked in a continuous supply chain. Secondly, the search for lower cost sources of supply shifts production and organizations controlling production to offshore locations throughout the globe, where conditions are more favourable than in the home market where the products will be sold and consumed. Often, these global shifts have a devastating impact upon domestic markets, where production jobs are lost, investment declines and the trade balance worsens. Investment declines not simply as a consequence of production erosion, but also in relative terms for those organizations that remain locked into industrial decline, because investors and governments are unwilling to take the financial and political risks that investment in the future requires. This reduction in investment is a consequence of perceived increasing uncertainties.

For retailers, the future requirement that they become large is predominant in the 'psyche' of major retail groups. Being large when markets are saturated in domestic economies requires retailers to develop beyond their own geographical boundaries. For the very large retailing groups it is a matter of who can get to the future first. Who can dominate market share. These large retail groups have enormous purchasing power and are able to extract economies of scale from their operations and economies of scope from their existing and developing supply chains. Globalization is not only identified through economic shifts, but also through cultural and social change that has been hastened by rapid communication and transportation infrastructures. Consumer behaviour has changed as markets have converged. Consumer behaviour patterns are also shifted not simply by consumers themselves, but by the professional purchasing and procurement officers of retailing groups who exert enormous influence over consumer choice. For example, designers, range selectors, sourcing decisions and decisions about what merchandise to stock or replace will paradoxically limit consumer choice. Adopting an integrated marketing approach is a necessary condition to achieving consumer satisfaction. Supply chain structures, strategies and processes are interdependent upon and a corollary of consumer demand patterns identified through market intelligence and marketing information. Supply chains are in effect the corollary of demand chains.

The phenomenon of globalization, conditions that give rise to it, and shape the structure, strategies and consequences are probably more transparently evident in the textile and clothing industries than in many other sectors. Markets from Manchester to Manchuria and suppliers from Singapore to Sacramento are subject to the phenomenon of global forces and global shifts. This is what makes fashion markets and fashion marketing an exciting area to study.

References

Cairncross, F. (1998). *The Death of Distance*. London: Orion Business Books.
Dicken, P. (1998). *Global Shift*. London: Paul Chapman.

DTI (1998). *The Clothing, Footwear and Textile Industry – An Overview*. London: DTI.

DTI (2000). *A National Strategy for UK Textile and Clothing Industry*. Textile and Clothing Strategy Group. London: DTI.

EMAP (1997). *The UK Fashion Report*. London: EMAP.

Ghoshal, S. and Bartlett, C. A. (1998). *Managing Across Borders – The Transnational Solution*. London: Random House Business Books.

Govindarajan, V. and Gupta, A. (1998). Setting a course for the new global landscape. *Financial Times*, 30 January, Section 1, 3–5.

Hines, T. (1997). Core competence and global retailing in fashion. *The Journal of Fashion Marketing*, **2** (1).

Keynote (1996). *The UK Clothing Industry Report*. London: Keynote.

Lévy, B. (1995). Globalization and regionalisation: toward the shaping of a tripolar world economy? *The International Executive*, July/August, **37** (4), 349–71.

Means, G. and Schneider, D. (2000). *Meta-Capitalism – The E-Business Revolution and the Design of 21st Century Companies and Markets*. New York: John Wiley.

MTI (1996). Market Track International data. In *The UK Fashion Report*. London: EMAP.

OECD (1995). *Beyond The MFA: Third World Competition and Restructuring Europe*. Paris: OECD.

OETH (1997). *Eurostat – European Textile and Clothing Industry Statistics*. Brussels: OETH.

OETH (2000). *Key Trends in 2000*. L'Observatoire European Du Textile Et De L'habillment. Paris: OETH.

ONS (1997). *Overseas Trade Statistics*. London: HMSO (replaces National Stats Office, 31st Edn).

Porter, M. E. (1980). *Competitive Strategy – Techniques for Analyzing Industries and Competitors*. New York: Free Press.

Steele, P. (1988). *The Caribbean Clothing Industry: The US and Fareast Connection, Special Report No. 1147*. London: Economist Intelligence Unit.

Werner International (1990). *Labour Costs in the Textile and Clothing Sector, Summer*. Werner.

Werner International (1996). *Labour Costs in the Textile and Clothing Sector, Spring*. Werner.

2

From analogue to digital supply chains: implications for fashion marketing

Tony Hines

Introduction

Supply chain management is seen as a critical factor in managing contemporary fashion businesses. It is worth noting the following quote from the UK Fashion Report:

> Focus on the supply chain has sharpened since the beginning of the decade. Market responsiveness and meeting the demands of the ultimate consumer are given as reasons. The supply base has contracted and there has been a greater shift to overseas sourcing. This has led to changes in culture and philosophy whereby retailers and suppliers work with rather than against each other. The key influencing factor is Information Technology and the speed of information exchange.
>
> (EMAP, 1997, p. 417)

However, what does the term convey to different managers? Is it considered an operational, tactical or strategic weapon in competing for customers? Is the terminology itself problematic when we consider issues in relation to managing demand? These are just a few of the important questions that need to be addressed by academics and practising managers in mapping out the terrain of supply chain management. This chapter will address these and other critical issues to provide the reader with an informed view of supply chain management and its impact upon customers, marketing decision-making and organizational strategies.

The chapter begins by reviewing some of the key ideas located within the supply chain literature, and demonstrates the eclectic nature of the field and its location within several management disciplines. A description of traditional supply chains is given within the context of the apparel and textile industry, together with an analysis of current practices drawn from a number of organizations located within Europe, the US and the Far East. Implications are drawn for marketing and strategic managers of organizations located within this global industry. There are also a number of key issues that policy makers need to address when considering conditions under which this industry operates. These conditions are discussed before concluding that supply chains in the fashion industries deserve and require much more attention by academic researchers, practitioners and policy makers, especially in a digital global economy.

Supply chains

Traditional supply chains view flows of goods from upstream raw material suppliers through manufacturing processes and on to the customers. In the apparel and textile supply chains, one might expect to start the chain with raw materials from animals (wool), agricultural crops (cotton) or synthetically produced fibres (polyester), that are then woven into fabric, dyed and passed on to apparel manufacturers. The apparel manufacturer will cut the cloth, make it up and trim to a specific design template before finishing (packing, labelling, pricing) and delivering to a retail customer, who sells the item on until it reaches its final destination – the consumer (Hines, 1994a). The ways in which these chains are described give us some clues as to the literature bases that contribute to the debate. Figure 2.1 provides a summary map of these literatures. The ways in which the traditional supply chain language addresses the topic gives an impression of being supplier push. It is a push-through distribution system. The literature is drawn from different discipline areas relating to purchasing, supply, distribution (logistics), operations management

Figure 2.1 A traditional analogue supply chain literature base.

and in recent times marketing. In contrast, the modern supply chain concept begins and ends with the customer. Contemporary views draw on a wider literature base, as depicted in Figure 2.2. The chain is viewed from a marketing perspective and as being demand driven by customers. This is a pull-through concept as opposed to a supplier push. It may seem like splitting hairs, but this distinction is extremely important to the discussions that follow. This is because it places the control within a chain not with any single supplier, but with the customer. This has implications for the ways in which these supply chains need to be managed. Traditional perspectives focus upon operations, tactical initiatives and emphasize cost reduction as a major goal. Contemporary views of supply chain management view it as being strategic in nature (i.e. having longer term implications), with competitive advantages to be gained in terms of differentiation and not simply cost alone.

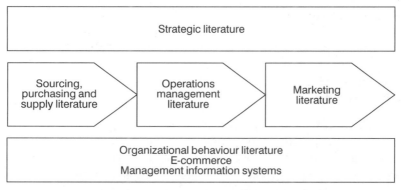

Figure 2.2 A contemporary digital supply chain literature base.

Modern supply chains are described differently by various commentators using terminologies that shape contemporary views on the topic. The adjectives applied include: flexible, responsive, agile, lean, value adding networks and value streams. Supply chains are more than the term suggests. They are value creation mechanisms for customers. They are not simply 'supply' focused, nor are they necessarily 'chains'. Supply chains are dynamic, efficient, effective response networks delivering customer requirements flexibly and on time. These high performance networks consist of customers, suppliers and information travelling through organizational 'arterial systems'. These arterial systems cut across functional, organizational and geographical boundaries. What distinguishes the traditional supply chain approach from a contemporary view is the capability for customers to self-design products/services at a price they find acceptable. Information enables production decisions to be taken much later in the cycle. The storage of expensive items that no one wants to buy is not necessary in a 'digital supply chain'.

Definitions of the term 'supply chain management'

Drucker (1956) once referred to this aspect of management as being the *dark continent* taking a narrower view focusing upon distribution. Nevertheless, until recently this has been the case for supply chain management. Saunders (1997, p. 28) comments that concepts and theories are borrowed from other management disciplines. The term *'supply chain management'* entered the literature in the early 1980s. Originally, Oliver and Webber (1982) were referring to the integration of internal business functions and the flow of materials and information coming into and going out of the business. This particular definition equates closely to the traditional materials management perspective (Houlihan, 1984; Stevens, 1989; Jones and Riley, 1985). The definition draws on pre-existing concepts in the materials management literature (Ammer, 1968, 1989; Lee and Dobler, 1965; Baily and Farmer, 1982, Chapters 11 and 12). It is also closely related to the value chain concept (Porter, 1985; Kogut, 1985; Johnstone and Lawrence, 1988). The term *supply chain management* has also been used to refer to supplier–buyer relationships (Hayes and Wheelwright, 1984). A further meaning has been applied in reference to managing relationships with a number of businesses in the chain, including the immediate supplier's supplier and the immediate customer's customer and so on (Buzzell and Ortmeyer, 1996, pp. 85–96; DTI, 1995). Fearne (1998, p. 4), in an editorial in *The Supply Chain Management Journal*, reports a debate about definition conducted on the logistics-research-network@mailbase.ac.uk and comments that:

> Supply Chain Management is now well established as a key source of competitive advantage, yet there remains some confusion (or at least disagreement) over what aspects of business activity are covered by the term. Logistics is primarily concerned with products and processes of procurement, manufacturing and distribution, whereas supply chain management is a business philosophy – a way of doing business with customers and suppliers.

This view supports that taken by Buzzell and Ortmeyer (1996, p. 85) and adopts a strategic rather than simply an operational view of supply chains. It is an extension from purchasing operations to include relationships ('a way of doing business'), and is clearly inclusive in its focus upon the customer. Christopher (1992, p. 12) defines the supply chain as:

> . . . the network of organisations that are involved, through upstream and downstream linkages, in the different processes and activities that produce value in the form of products and services in the hands of the ultimate consumer. Thus, for example, a shirt manufacturer is a part of a supply chain that extends upstream through the weavers of fabrics to the manufacture of fibres, and downstream through distributors and retailers to the final consumer.

It is interesting to note the use of an apparel and textile example to illustrate the concept. There is also a recognition that the chain is perhaps better described as a network, since at each link in the chain there may be a number of different organizations involved.

A useful categorization of each of the different approaches is given by Harland (1995, p. 63), who refers to four main uses of the term *supply chain management*, which are:

1 The internal supply chain integrating business functions involved in a flow of materials and information from the point of entry to a business to the point of exit.
2 The management of a dyadic or two-party relationship with immediate suppliers.
3 The management of a chain of businesses including a supplier, the supplier's supplier, a customer and a customer's customer and so on.
4 The management of a network of interconnected businesses involved in the ultimate provision of products and services required by the end customer. (N.B. The word constellation and a constellation diagram have been used by some to depict this relationship.)

Managerial competence

A recent report suggested that two management skills in particular marked out winners in today's fashion retail marketplace: managing product cost and speed to market (Merrill-Lynch, 2000). It suggested that speed and flexibility are required to satisfy customers who expect increasingly good value and more fashion content. To these management competencies can be added a third that is probably more important, and that is the skill to anticipate, identify and satisfy customers profitably; in other words – marketing. These management competencies are focused around the supply chain. There are a number of critical issues management need to address when it comes to applying the marketing concepts towards fashion. These issues can be explained simply as follows: fragmented markets leading to targeting and segmentation difficulties. Increasingly more demanding consumers make it difficult to spot a sustainable winning formula, individualism is breaking down traditional fashion trend prediction influences, fashion cycles are shorter leading to a more volatile marketplace and fashion icons are less predictable. Capturing the zeitgeist is a search for the 'holy grail'. Shifting demographics in the UK and Western Europe mean that an increasing proportion of consumer spending is attributed to the affluent over 45-year-old age group. This trend is here to stay, with 50% of the population expected to be over 50 by 2020 (Hines, 1997). Older consumers may have become more fashion conscious in recent times, but they are less likely to purchase as frequently as younger consumers. A recent report in *The Economist* stated that one major difficulty facing Marks & Spencer in the UK was the fact that mothers approaching middle age did not want to dress like their parents. This had historically been the case, but nowadays they preferred to dress like their children (*The Economist*, 2000, p. 32).

Harrison and Storey (1996, p. 63) classify several operational supply chain concepts as New Wave Manufacturing (NWM). They group together Lean Production (LP), Just-in-Time (JIT), World Class Manufacturing (WCM) and Total Quality Management (TQM), and coin the phrase NWM to describe these techniques. According to Harrison and Storey (1996, p. 64), NWM strategies have often been expressed as a set of absolutes, such as the 'five zeros' (zero paper, zero inventory, zero downtime, zero delays and zero defects). The authors make an important contribution to the literature relating to supply chains by identifying two sets of literature (operations management and organizational behaviour) that are addressing the same phenomenon but from different perspectives, and they conclude 'that these different approaches end up talking past each other'. By this statement they mean that operations management literature focuses upon processes and tends to ignore or pay scant attention to social and organizational dimensions reported in the organizational behaviour literature.

There is no doubt that the digital supply chains now being created by world class businesses, be they in fashion or other industries, are transforming the ways in which business can be conducted. The focus is global not local, whether at the consumer end of the chain or upstream in making sourcing decisions. At the heart of this shifting business paradigm are information and communication technologies (ICTs). These technologies are having profound influences shaping consumer behaviour from Singapore to Bangalore to Beijing, to San Francisco, to New York, to Milan, to London, to Paris, to Tokyo, Seoul and Madrid. There are global trends emerging that characterize great similarities between different countries and their consumers. The dichotomy is that there are also great disparities in historical culture, economic wealth, standards of living and political freedom. However, hitherto unheard of similarities emerge as ICT breaks down the barriers between different nation states. It is not only consumer attitudes that are being shaped by these new technologies, but the technologies themselves bring new opportunities for those with the ability and capability to do business differently. Differences can be observed in the ways in which fashion retailers and fashion brands source supply and manage their global digital supply chain to create value for their customers and for themselves.

Managing product cost

Managing product cost begins with product design and product sourcing decisions made by organizations. Most fashion retail organizations in Western Europe, the US and Japan would estimate that between 20% and 40% of stock keeping units (SKUs) are those that they would regard as fashion items and highly time sensitive. Conversely, 60–80% are better explained as commodity clothing items that need replenishing, and these SKUs are more price sensitive than time sensitive. These estimates will vary depending upon the exact nature of the fashion business and the conditions under which it finds itself operating. Nevertheless, it is with the sourcing of fashion items that lifetime product and organizational costs are determined. One estimate in the automobile industry stated that up to 60% of life cycle cost was determined at the product design stage. Therefore, where SKUs are deemed to be more price than time sensitive a different approach to sourcing decisions is required. In price-sensitive markets cost control is emphasized. Sourcing decisions and purchases made by high street 'commodity clothing' stores often make choices based upon lowest bought-in prices with the aim of acquiring margin flexibility. For example, Arcadia Group in the UK estimate between 80% and 90% of SKUs are supplied by overseas manufacturers. The major benefit of having a high percentage of overseas supply is deemed to be cost saving against local supply. This is because labour is the highest cost element within apparel manufacture, somewhere between 30% and 60% of the total cost depending on the product. Lower labour costs can be found offshore for most of the developed world in lesser-developed countries (LDCs). In some places like Vietnam, labour costs can be as low as 20–30 cents per hour compared to $10 per hour in the UK. Labour cost may be low but skill levels are often comparable to higher priced production areas. Arcadia are by no means unique in adopting this strategy. NEXT plc sources a very high proportion of its fabric from outside the UK, although its customer base is in the UK. The company has a mixed sourcing strategy, procuring goods from home-based and overseas suppliers. One reason often put forward for the declining profitability of Marks & Spencer in the UK is that they have purchased a higher percentage of product from UK-based suppliers. The company is in a transition period, having switched its policy to procure a higher percentage of goods from outside the UK. Until 1999, the company stated that it obtained around 70% of its clothing products locally. In March 2000, the company stated that it was shifting the balance of overseas supply more in line with its competitors. This would result in 70–80% of clothing being supplied from outside the UK within 2 years. Termination of long-standing contracts with UK suppliers has forced many to lay off their work forces and in some cases factory closure and firm closure has followed. The unique position of Marks & Spencer within the UK clothing industry has meant that the impact of the switch in policy has sent a chill wind throughout the clothing manufacturing sector. In the latter half of the 1990s, about one quarter of all output from the UK clothing manufacturing sector found its way on to Marks & Spencer's shelves. The purchasing power of the company was equivalent to a significant proportion of the trade deficit in clothing items. Pundits have often argued for Marks & Spencer to adopt the policies it has now implemented, with little regard for the knock-on effect within the industry or the impact it will have upon the trade balance. Some commentators argue that Marks & Spencer have done too little, too late (*The Economist*, 2000). Nevertheless, they appear to ignore one further fundamental significant issue which is that unfortunately the company has failed to satisfy its customers in recent times. No matter by how much they are able to lower cost, if their customers are not attracted by the products on offer then lowering unit cost is irrelevant. Managing product cost is of course important, but it has to be balanced against the prices the fashion retailer is able to charge and, more importantly, what the customer is willing to pay. It has already been noted that fashion markets are time sensitive and therefore it is argued that having the right product in the right place at the right time at the right price with the right promotion is more important to a retailer's margin. Simply achieving the lowest cost price from a supplier becomes less important than ensuring the product is of acceptable quality and available. On-time deliveries and order completeness become a higher priority. If SKUs are not available at the times that customers want to buy the item, you may not simply lose a sale but the customer too. Managing customer demand through effective supply chain management is critical to success.

Sourcing decisions

There is a paucity of literature relating to sourcing decisions within the clothing industry given its significance to managing supply chains. One notable exception is the work of Lui and McGoldrick (1996), where they: attempted to define international sourcing and draw distinctions between the activities of retailers and manufacturers; discussed the growth of international sourcing and identified data deficiencies; reviewed the literature on this topic; developed frameworks to explain sourcing in this context, presenting evidence from case study interviews, and identified implications for policy makers, suppliers and retailers. These authors draw a distinction between importing and sourcing by attributing the latter with pro-active behaviour. Sourcing in the cases examined in this research took the form of retail organizations searching for new suppliers who would either (a) make goods to retailer specifications or (b) supply goods the retail organization required. Retailers also used existing suppliers to design and develop new products. Although this was an investigation of the UK industry, it inevitably had international dimensions caused by competitiveness. Sourcing is a context where global influences are strongly evident, as explained earlier. There are a number of different theoretical propositions that may explain sourcing in terms of international trade, foreign direct investment (FDI), offshore production, product life cycles and strategy (Swamidass, 1993). Kotabe and Omura (1989) made use of a value chain approach to sourcing. However, none of these theoretical models sufficiently explains the complex nature of modern sourcing by organizations in the UK clothing industry. Lui and McGoldrick (1996, p. 13) suggest that any new theory must introduce the dimension of product attributes. They conclude that it is a combination of low factor cost and product attributes that determines sourcing decisions. Nevertheless, the most prevalent reason given by retail buyers in the UK is cost price. My own research in this area reveals that even in circumstances where they mention other reasons they are of secondary importance. This is especially the case in price-sensitive markets. These market conditions usually imply that the apparel has a low design content. In essence they are non-fashion.

The iceberg theory of costs and opportunity

The focus on offshore sourcing as a way to lower costs may be ignoring some key data relevant to the decision-making process. This myopia would seem to be overlooking an 'iceberg' of costs, many of which have been identified within my own research (Hines, 1998). The iceberg beneath the waterline contains a number of hidden costs that are often ignored (the view from the bridge). These hidden costs could be substantial. Furthermore, these costs are often disguised or never traced back to the SKUs. Examples of some of the hidden costs are given in the model. Costs include: procurement, management time consumed in acquisition and monitoring progress or in re-work. More importantly, something that is hardly ever measured is lost sales due to late delivery or incomplete delivery (wrong size ratios, style mix, colour mix).

Procurement costs

Evidence from a number of retail fashion buyers who spend a significant amount of their time travelling abroad to search for new products suggests that the cost is not unimportant. Buyers often spend two or more months travelling to source merchandise during any given year. The cost includes airfares, hotel bills, telephone calls and subsistence payments, not to mention the human cost of broken relationships, loneliness and fatigue measures that reflect in staff turnover measures. Furthermore, if one considers the time spent against orders placed, there will be times when the cost of procurement is extremely expensive and significantly more than the final invoiced bought-in price, which may be the only cost that is measured. Thus, procurement costs may never be traced back to products. Such costs are more likely to reside in an overhead category. What is worse, such costs may be allocated or apportioned arbitrarily to products that did not incur the costs, if at all.

Management time

Management time is consumed communicating with suppliers before acquisition, during acquisition and post acquisition. The number of managers involved and the amount of time spent can be significant. One major retailer in the UK has a team of managers that co-ordinate activities with offshore suppliers in Morocco. The management team frequently visits the plants to monitor and plan production, to resolve operational difficulties and to help improve efficiencies. The time spent is not always traced back to the products that are consuming this resource.

Opportunity cost of lost sales

By far the greatest cost and perhaps the most significant part of the iceberg could be the opportunity cost of lost sales. If merchandise is not available within a store at the time the consumer wants to buy it the sale is lost. Consumer behaviour theory might suggest substitution. However, substitution of one product for another may not happen within the same retail store. Substitution may unwittingly help competitors to achieve a sale. This part of the iceberg is where an overseas supplier is at greater disadvantage. A UK supplier is closer to market and a short delay in production will not necessarily result in late delivery or incomplete delivery, whereas a delay in production from an overseas source would more probably result in missing a shipping date. This may require drastic action to airfreight goods, which adds significantly to cost and a cost that has not been built into the retailer's price point. Typically, it takes 8–12 weeks to source from a Far Eastern source, whereas it will be 4–6 weeks from the UK, and perhaps just 1 week more from Morocco, Portugal, Egypt and Eastern Europe. For many non-fashion items, these lead times are less significant than would be the case for 'time-sensitive' fashion items.

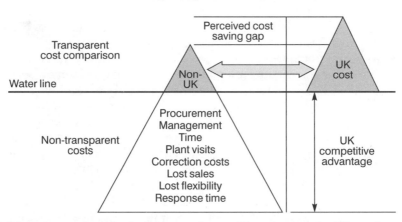

The iceberg theory of cost comparison

Figure 2.3 Iceberg costs and potential areas of competitive advantage for UK suppliers. *Source:* Hines (1998).

Figure 2.3 illustrates the iceberg costs, together with potential areas whereby UK suppliers could build competitive advantage. Assuming that the iceberg costs for a UK supplier are less significant than for an overseas supplier would suppose that UK suppliers could build on strengths that an overseas source would find it difficult to achieve.

Sources of competitive advantage for UK suppliers

The iceberg theory creates a number of possibilities that would enable UK, Western European and US suppliers to achieve competitive advantage vis-à-vis an overseas supplier, even an overseas supplier located within near reach of Europe or the US. However, it is not simply the iceberg but the size of the iceberg that will determine the relative advantage. In some cases an iceberg may exist but it may not be sufficiently deep to allow the UK supplier to exploit it. The stronger the relationship between a supplier and a UK retailer the less likelihood of a large iceberg lurking. On the other hand, the weaker the relationship between a UK retailer and a supplier the more likelihood of a larger iceberg that may be exploited by an alternative supplier who is able to differentiate itself using variables listed in the model.

Time to market

Quick response (QR) was a phrase coined in 1985 by Alan Hunter, a professor at North Carolina State University, as a method of improving response time in the textile pipeline (Fernie, 1994). Hunter's original conceptualization was concerned with improving the response times of textile suppliers in the face of severe price competition from developing countries. The term has since evolved over time to represent a method of improving response time from the selection of a garment by a retailer to its replenishment by a manufacturer. It has therefore expanded in meaning to reflect the responsiveness of the whole clothing supply chain. Ko and Kincade (1997), 12 years on, define quick response as being a business strategy to optimize the flow of information and merchandise between channel members to maximize customer service. In order to accomplish QR, retailers must employ a variety of technologies. EPOS, barcodes and EDI are all classified as enabling quick response technologies (QRTs). Web-based EDI has opened up the technology to a wider market. This has been achieved by lowering the cost to users using Internet browsers and removing the requirement for dedicated systems networks. From a retail point of view, the ultimate aim is to provide their customers (the consumers) with what they want to buy, when they want to buy it, and at a price that attracts and persuades them to make the purchase. Retailers and contemporary retailing literature refers to Efficient Consumer Response (ECR), whereas manufacturers refer to quick response. A critical aspect of this buying decision is for retailers to make sure they have sufficient stock to meet the demand. If stock is not available immediately within a clothing store, it is likely that the customer will substitute a product that is available immediately either from the same retailer or from a competitor. The substitute product may be a lower price offering, even if bought from the same retailer. Either way the retailer risks losing business.

Many of today's supply chain practices are an attempt to replicate the external resource management model pioneered by Toyota. This is often referred to as 'lean thinking'. According to Cox (1999, p. 167), the predominant orthodoxy of supply chain management thinking is devoted to 'discovering tools and techniques that provide increased operational effectiveness and efficiency throughout the delivery channels that must be created internally and externally to support and supply existing corporate product and service offerings to customers'. Cox goes on to attribute this thinking to studies of the Japanese automobile industry in the 1970s and 1980s by Womack et al. (1990). Contrast this view with the earlier view expressed by Fearne (1998), which emphasizes the importance of the customer and building relationships – 'a philosophy of doing business'. These two approaches highlight the differences between product push and market-led strategies. Historically, apparel retailing has adopted product push strategies and some organizations still do. Large retailing giants have adopted a monolithic planning approach to filling their stores with product volumes at the lowest cost. They have ignored customers at their peril, and many have paid a high price in terms of lost customers and reducing profitability, and in a few cases market withdrawal. Witness C&A in the UK and Marks & Spencer in the UK and in some overseas locations. Contrast these retailers with 'the new kids on the block' Zara, New Look and George at ASDA. These companies have been more responsive to customer needs, and they have developed sourcing and supply chain strategies focused on their customers. These organizations claim to have products from design to in store within 3 or 4 weeks.

Recent practices observed in US and Western European retailing organizations that have been adopted from practices in the automobile supply chains have focused upon time compression and include:

1 Reducing the numbers of suppliers in order to increase supplier dependency and to provide the retailer with increased dedication and flexibility.
2 Eliminating agents except where they are deemed to add value by bringing in suppliers who have special capabilities. Superior technology, innovation and design are examples.
3 Increasing application of Internet technologies to source or develop products faster, to obtain better prices through auction site bidding or to search for specialist suppliers without the need to have agents.
4 Shifting responsibility to the supplier through vendor-managed inventory systems (VMI), pre-retailing services (ticketing, labelling, steaming, pressing, packaging for store ready display) and devolving responsibility for quality – hence lowering costs for stock holding and other services.

Supply chain strategies and organizational learning

Pine et al. (1995, p. 103) refer to 'learning relationships' in the supply chain – an ongoing connection that becomes smarter as they interact with each other, collaborating to meet the consumer's needs over time. The customer teaches the supplying company more and more about their preferences and needs. The more the supplier learns the more difficult it is for competitors to entice the customer away. Because a learning relationship has developed, even if a competitor could develop the same capabilities the investment in time and energy to teach a competitor is not worthwhile. According to Hines et al. (2000), early myopia of mass production efficiency focused attention internally. This mechanistic approach to managing organizations had earlier been observed by Burns and Stalker (1961) and by Merli (1991), who identified this type of management structure as a barrier to innovation. These organizations were in effect operating 'closed systems' that were little affected by the environment in which they were operating. Organizations were able to ignore the environment at the time that mass production was at its height in the 1920s and 1930s because of the conditions identified by Merli (1991) as low levels of uncertainty and low levels of domestic competition prevailing. Stevens (1989) identified the following arrangements in terms of a staged model of development of supply chain competencies:

- *The baseline organization* – focused upon short-term distribution efficiency and is preoccupied with cost management.
- *Functional integration* – short-term budget focused. Management attention is applied to customer service and order processing.
- *Internal integration* – medium-term focus and measurement against annual goals. Management attention is focused upon productivity improvements, and sourcing and planning are the most important aspects of managing the supply chain.
- *External integration* – long-term attention integrating strategies and policies. Flow management techniques and cross-functional teams enable a platform to be developed to provide world class manufacturing to be achieved.

Merli (1991) also provided a parallel four-stage model, but this model was chronologically staged:

1 The early myopia of mass production efficiency (1920s–1950s).
2 Competition and internationalism (1960s).
3 The involvement stage (1970s) – characterized by Japanese manufacturing techniques.
4 The market in stage (1980s) – the strategic integration of two organizations where information systems are integrated: trust characterizes this type of relationship.

It is only when organizations reach stages 3 and 4 in both these conceptual models that learning is able to take place between the parties. As a consequence, it is only at these stages that organizations are able to jointly develop their capabilities to achieve an improved competitive position.

Edmondson and Moingeon (1998) identify organizational learning as a source of global competitive advantage. They suggest that this learning takes two forms: learning how and learning why. Learning how involves the transfer and improvement of existing skills and routines. Programmes that reduce errors or increase yields focus on the how. Learning why leads to establishing and maintaining relationships. These authors also note that learning why is difficult to copy. This model of organizational learning mirrors closely the two approaches to supply chain management. How is focused on technical competencies (speed, consistency, productivity, quality and product excellence) and measuring performance. Learning why focuses on the importance of supply chain relationships. Technical competency improvements lead to efficiency, whereas relationship improvements enhance effectiveness.

Globalization and supply chain management

According to Christopher (1992, p. 111) companies that need to organize globally fall into three categories:

1 Commodity companies where the task is to move bulk raw materials from countries with a surplus to countries that either have markets or labour to process the materials.
2 Companies taking advantage of low cost labour, maximizing profitability in labour intensive manufacturing operations.
3 Companies that have concentrated their investment in R&D and manu-facturing, focusing each of their sites on a specific product–technology combination. Christopher refers to this grouping as being the most significant in terms of the rate of change in the global economy. It is sometimes referred to as the centre of excellence strategy. It is worth noting that apparel manufacturers have often moved offshore to take advantage of lower labour costs in production, Christopher's type 2 grouping.

Hamel and Prahalad (1994, p. 272) comment that managers now give much attention to reducing product development cycle times. Speedy product development is important to pre-empt competitors. It is pointed out that it is not just speed to market that is important, but rather from 'concept to global market'. Although being first to market is important, the real returns go to companies able to exploit their products by being first to spread the product round the globe. The primary goal is therefore to drive a new product or marketing concept around the globe as quickly as possible, the main critical success factor (CSF) being to access channels of distribution and to have developed an internal capacity to propagate new product innovation. In this context, a core capability is competence in managing global supply chains. Hence, it is relationships that are an important competence.

Christopher and Peck (1997, p. 63) identify the volatility of fashion markets that are characterized by short product life cycles, high demand volatility, uncertainty of forecasting demand and the high impulse nature of fashion purchases. They argue for greater integration within the supply chain to overcome these problems. They identify the trend to source more offshore production as problematic and as having a causal effect upon lead times that can be severe. These writers also identify the trend of larger organizations to deal with fewer suppliers. Three critical lead times are identified as: time to market – how long it takes a company to translate a market opportunity into a product or service; time to serve – the time it takes to capture a customer order and deliver the goods or service to the satisfaction of the customer; and finally, time to react – the time it takes to respond to demand volatility by turning on or off the production tap. Agility and lean supply chains are offered as solutions to the problems identified. Shared information, quick response and greater systems integration are seen as critical to the process. Although interesting, one is left wondering about the 70+% of supply within the clothing industry that could rightly be regarded as 'non-fashion', and are the solutions and the prescriptions necessarily the same? Nevertheless, these commentators do present some useful insights into the problems involved in managing supply chains in this industry and in a global context.

Supplier partnerships and alliances

Partnerships and alliances are terms often used in relation to supply chains. To gain a thorough understanding of meaning it is important to examine definitions of the terms.

Definition of terms

A great deal of the more recent literature related to the supply chain has emphasized a partnership approach (Christopher, 1996; Gattorna and Walters, 1996) and referred to the strategic nature of partnerships (Kanter, 1994). Partnerships usually involve a relationship between two or more different types of organization at different stages of the supply chain, for example a retailer and a contract clothing supplier. A partnership is distinguished from a strategic alliance, which is more usually referred to when two or more organizations at the same part of the chain agree to co-operate, for example a number of retailers combining to supply a particular market segment, to cover a specific geographical area or to create a purchasing consortium.

Importance of building supplier partnerships

Wheelright and Clark (1992) recognized that firms are able to get new products to market faster and more efficiently by establishing strategic partnerships with suppliers. Strong relationships between a lead supplier and other outside suppliers nearby play a fundamental role in flexibility according to a number of commentators who have observed the Japanese automobile industry (Fruin, 1992; Imai, 1986). Nishiguchi (1993) referred to this phenomenon as *'clustered control'*. Much attention has focused upon strategic alliances in the automotive industry (Lamming, 1993; Womack et al., 1990; Smitka, 1991). 'Co-makership' and lean supply are terms used to characterize customer-driven integrated systems of manufacture and informational relationship systems (Lamming, 1993; Womack and Jones, 1996; Hines, 1994b; Womack et al., 1990). It has been argued that two dimensions were particularly important in supplier partnerships: the timing of involvement in the product development process and the degree of competition among suppliers (Merli, 1991). The importance of these two dimensions is further supported by the work of Stevens (1989).

Strategic alliances

Table 2.1 gives a useful delineation between strategic alliances, operational partnerships and opportunistic partnerships. Many supply chain relationships could be categorized into one of these three types.

Table 2.1 Delineation between strategic alliances, operational partnerships and opportunistic partnerships

Strategic alliance	Operational partnership	Opportunistic partnership
Integrate core competencies of each partner and perform the activities that add most value to the relationship	Partnership based on one partner leveraging another partner's core competence	Based on one party performing activities that the other no longer will
Power is moved towards the consumer and the alliance with equal partners acting to serve the consumer	Power equality exists at only one place in the supply chain	Power inequality results in greater demands being placed on one party
Consumer enjoys measurable value from the alliance	Both partners benefit but not always equally	Results in one partner gaining at the other's expense
Information analysis is performed jointly and information is shared	Risk is greater for one of the partners	Risks are always greater for one party
The alliance results in a more efficient supply chain	Consumer receives only some value from the partnership	Consumer does not receive greater value as a result of the agreement
	Information is shared on a selective basis	Information is rarely shared
	Partnership has the effect of shifting costs and efficiencies within the supply chain	Cost reduction or inefficiency in the supply chain is ignored
←———— Co-operation		————→ Control

Source: The table is based on KSA's description of different relationships that exist in industry between merchant and vendor (retailer and supplier), KSA (1997)

Supply chain efficiency and cost reduction are control relationships whereas the other themes emerging would be categorized as co-operating relationships. Co-operating relationships might well lead to cost reduction and efficiency, and therefore could be seen as causal relationships. However, cost reduction or an efficiency gain in the supply chain could be the catalyst to move towards co-operation. It may be a necessary condition that could cause change to happen, but in itself may not be sufficient to determine co-operative behaviour. Nevertheless, co-operation is likely to be a necessary and sufficient condition for a firm to achieve both efficiency and cost reduction in any supply chain.

Taking the notion of integration raised by Christopher and Peck (1997) a stage further, Barney (1999) refers to a firm's capabilities affecting boundary decisions, and comments that under certain conditions a firm's capabilities and those of its potential partners can influence boundary decisions. Although the argument put forward by Barney is mainly concerned with transaction cost analyses, one is able to conceptualize how a firm's boundary could be affected by decisions relating to supply chain strategies, structures and relationships. In particular, one organization may wish to acquire capabilities that it does not yet possess through a co-operatively structured arrangement to integrate parts of the supply chain managed by two distinct organizations. Such an arrangement avoids heavy investment by one party. However, it would also need to demonstrate some benefits to the other party for such an arrangement to develop into a successful relationship.

Supplier networking

There is an extensive literature on networking. Network theory potentially provides a way of explaining business relationships in the supply chain. The reality is that the literature relating to networks is full of ambiguity both in terms of terminology and conceptually (Szarka, 1990, p. 10). Johannison (1987) identified three types of network, which are:

1 Production networks between trading organizations.
2 Personal networks based on friendship and trust.
3 Symbolic networks based on social bonds, community ties and conformity to collective values.

Mitchell (1973) recognized exchange networks, communication networks and social networks, which are closely aligned to those categories given by Johannison. Although these typologies may be useful in different contexts to examine the nature of relationships, they may in themselves be limited or constraining when examining supplier relationships that could potentially have characteristics of all three types identified.

The language used to describe supplier networks more usually refers to partnerships and alliances, whereas networking per se refers to formal and informal networks based upon exchange/production, personal/social or communication/conformity.

Conclusions

This chapter has synthesized current thinking with regard to the importance of managing supply chains from sourcing through the supply network and onto the consumer. Historically, a functional approach treated each aspect of managing a supply chain not as an integrated whole but in a fragmented way, focusing upon single parts of the chain in isolation. Today's supply chain requires effective co-ordination and an integrated approach. Integration has been made possible by thinking differently about the whole supply chain as a system that encompasses not simply physical stock movements (the analogue supply chain) but one where technologies are enabling more effective information and communication to take place (digital supply chains). These digital supply chains are thus replacing inventory with information creating transparency within the supply chain at each stage. As a consequence the supply chains become flexible and responsive systems that deliver customer needs effectively and efficiently whilst simultaneously delaying the commitment of resources that may result in obsolete or redundant stock. A number of strategic and financial consequences emerge from this change. Most importantly flexibility and responsiveness allow the focus to shift from a product orientation towards a market-focused perspective. Financial outflows can be delayed as resources are committed much later in the market cycle. Some costs may be avoided completely or may be significantly reduced, especially the iceberg costs discussed earlier in the chapter. Market responsiveness should improve as indicated and result in faster cash inflows as goods are made closer to the selling period. Holding costs will be reduced for both the supplier and the retailer when information replaces inventory. Finally, because costs can be reduced and revenue flows in faster this will improve profitability.

Table 2.2 Perspectives revisited

Focus on processes	Focus on relationships
Just-in-Time manufacture/retailing and Inventory models, e.g. Vendor managed inventory, category management, MRP1, MRP2, DRP, ERP New Wave Manufacturing (NWM) (Harrison and Storey, 1996)	Partnerships – historically referred to relations between two or more parties at different stages in the supply chain, e.g. supplier/ buyer
Continuous improvement models Japanese manufacturing improvement models – Business Process Re-engineering (BPR)	Alliances – historically alliances referred to two or more firms at the same stage in the chain (suppliers or customers) joining forces Japanese – Kieretsu – networks of suppliers
Benchmarking – against competitors, the best in the industry, the best in the world	Contingency approaches

Table 2.2 Continued

Focus on processes	Focus on relationships
Throughput and line balancing models	Improving communications
Lean manufacturing	
Total Quality Management (Demming and others)	Inter and intra firm relations
Efficient Consumer Response – a systems approach	Efficient Consumer Response and customer-driven relationships
Information flows – a systems approach	Information flows – change the nature of relationships
Electronic Data Interchange	Electronic Data Interchange – can change the nature of relationships
Quick Response – Time from design concept to realisation in New Product Developments – impact of shortening product life cycles – Improved forecasting models – Time to manufacture – Time to market	QR as augmented product/service development – transparency and intangible benefits
Economies of scale	Economies of scope
Flexible manufacturing	Flexible supply and flexible customer response
Computer Aided Design Computer Aided Manufacture Computer Integrated Manufacture	Improving communications Improving time compression Co-makership, co-design
Cost Models and Cost Improvements – Direct Product Costing – Activity Based Costing/Management – Performance measurement – Value chain analysis	Value added through service and differentiation – established through relationship marketing approaches (Zeithaml et al., 1990) Value stream (Hines et al., 2000) Value nets (Bovet and Martha, 2000)
Statistical Process Control	
Material Requirement Planning	
Manufacturing Resource Planning	
Environment Resource Planning	Enterprise resource planning
Learning how	Learning why
Control	Trust
Emphasis on quantitative research approaches – Hypothesis testing – Using statistical tools	Emphasis on qualitative research approaches – Ethnographic approaches – Grounded theory

The chapter began by examining recent developments in supply chain management. It moved on to examine definitions and interpretations given to the term. It then reviewed different foci for supply chain management in terms of sourcing, operations, learning relationships and marketing, before drawing conclusions that have implications for managers, policy makers and academics. Some of the main differences in focus between processes and relationships in the context of supply chain management are illustrated in Table 2.2. There is little doubt that there is great value in conducting further research into the different aspects of the supply chain that have been drawn to the reader's attention within this chapter. Practising managers, industry policy makers and academics would benefit from a study that examined the detailed structures, strategies and relationships to be found in the different strata of the global fashion industry. Integration and the digital supply chain bring with them further opportunities and threats at each level in the supply chain, and present new opportunities for fashion marketing.

References

Ammer, D. (1968). *Materials Management*. Holmewood, US: Irwin.

Ammer, D. (1989). Top management's view of the purchasing function, *Journal of Purchasing and Material Management*, Spring.

Baily, P. and Farmer, D. (1982). *Materials Management Handbook*. Aldershot: Gower.

Barney, J. B. (1999). How a firm's capabilities affect boundary decisions. *Sloan Management Review*, Spring.

Bovet, D. and Martha, J. (2000). *Value Nets – Breaking the Supply Chain to Unlock Hidden Profits*. New York: John Wiley.

Burns, T. and Stalker, G. M. (1961). *The Management of Innovation*. London: Tavistock Institute.

Buzzell, R. and Ortmeyer, G. (1996). Channel partnerships streamline distribution. *Sloan Management Review*, Spring, 85–96.

Christopher, M. (1992). *Logistics and Supply Chain Management – Strategies for Reducing Cost and Improving Service*. London: FT/Prentice Hall.

Christopher, M. G. (1996). *Marketing Logistics*. Oxford: Butterworth-Heinemann.

Christopher, M. and Peck, H. (1997). Managing logistics in fashion markets. *The International Journal of Logistics Management*, **8** (2).

Cox, A. (1999). Power, value and supply chain management. *Supply Management: An International Journal*, **4** (4), 167–75.

Drucker, P (1956). *The Practice of Management*. Oxford: Butterworth-Heinemann.

DTI (1995). *Logistics and Supply Chain Management*. London: DTI.

Edmondson, A. and Moingeon, B. (1998). The how and why of organisational learning. In *Mastering Global Business, Financial Times Supplement*, 14 (week 2).

EMAP (1997). *The UK Fashion Report*. London: EMAP.

Fearne, A. (1998). *Supply Chain Management Journal*, **3** (1), 4.

Fernie, J. (1994). Quick response – an international perspective. *International Journal of Physical Distribution & Logistics Management,* **24** (6), 38–46.

Fruin, W. M. (1992). *The Japanese Enterprise System.* Oxford: Clarendon Press.

Gattorna, J. L. and Walters, D. W. (1996). *Managing the Supply Chain – A Strategic Perspective.* London: Macmillan.

Hamel, G. and Prahalad, C. K. (1994). *Competing for the Future.* Boston, US: Harvard Business Press.

Harland, C. M. (1995). Supply chain management: relationships, chains and networks. *British Academy of Management Proceedings,* pp. 62–79, Sheffield.

Harrison, A. and Storey, J. (1996). New Wave Manufacturing strategies – operational, organisational and human dimensions. *International Journal of Operations and Production Management,* **16** (2), 63–76.

Hayes, R. and Wheelwright, S. C. (1984). *Restoring our Competitive Edge: Competing Through Manufacturing.* London: John Wiley.

Hines, T. (1994a). Globalisation and the seductive search for competitive advantage – myth or reality? *75th Textile Institute World Conference Proceedings,* September. Atlanta, US: The Textile Institute.

Hines, P. (1994b). *Creating World Class Suppliers: Unlocking Mutual and Competitive Advantage.* London: Pitman.

Hines, P., Lamming, R., Jones, D., Cousins, P. and Rich, N. (2000). *Value Stream Management – Strategy and Excellence in the Supply Chain.* London: FT/Prentice Hall.

Hines, T. (1997). Core competence and global retailing in fashion. *The Journal of Fashion Marketing,* **2** (1).

Hines, T. (1998). The Iceberg Theory of cost comparison – overseas v. UK sourcing dilemma, *Drapers Record/Apparel Challenge Conference.* London: Bloomberg.

Houlihan, J. (1984). Supply chain management. *Proceedings of the 19th International Technical Conference,* BPICS.

Imai, K. (1986). *Kaizen.* New York: McGraw Hill.

Johannison, B. (1987). Beyond process and structure: social exchange networks. *International Studies of Management and Organisation,* **17** (1), 3–23.

Johnstone, R. and Lawrence, P. R. (1988). Beyond vertical integration – the rise of the value-adding patnership. *Harvard Business Review,* July/August, 94–101.

Jones, T. C. and Riley, D. W. (1985). Using inventory for competitive advantage through supply chain management. *International Journal of Physical Distribution and Materials Management,* **15** (5), 16–26.

Kanter, R. M. (1994). Collaborative advantage: the art of alliances. *Harvard Business Review,* **72** (4), July/August.

Ko, E. and Kincade, D. H. (1997). The impact of quick response technologies on retail store attributes. *International Journal of Retail and Distribution Management,* **25** (2), 90–8.

Kogut, B. (1985). Designing global strategies: comparative and competitive value added chains. *Sloan Management Review,* Summer, 15–28.

Kotabe, M. and Omura, G. S. (1989). Sourcing strategies of European and Japanese multinationals: a comparison. *Journal of International Business Studies,* **20**, Spring, 113–40.

KSA (1997). *The ABCs of Strategic Alliances*, Women's Wear Daily reprint in WDinfotracs. New York: WDinfotracs.

Lamming, R. (1993). *Beyond Partnership Strategies for Innovation and Lean Supply.* Hemel Hempstead: Prentice Hall.

Lee, L. and Dobler, D. (1965). *Purchasing and Materials Management.* Maidenhead: McGraw Hill.

Lui, H. and McGoldrick, J. (1996). International retail sourcing: trend, nature and process. *Journal of International Marketing,* **4** (4), 9–33.

Merli, G. (1991). *Co-Makership.* Cambridge, MA: Productivity Press.

Merrill-Lynch (2000). *Clothing Retailers 2000 – The Source of Competitive Advantage (Europe, September).* Global Securities Research & Economics Group, RC860226301. London: Merrill-Lynch.

Mitchell, V. W. (1973). Quoted in Johannison, B. (1987). Beyond process and structure: social exchange networks. *International Studies of Management and Organisation,* **17** (1), 3–23.

Nishiguchi, T. (1993). *Strategic Industrial Sourcing: The Japanese Advantage.* Oxford: Oxford University Press.

Oliver, R. K. and Webber, M. D. (1982). *Outlook.* US: Booz, Allen & Hamilton.

Pine II, B. J., Peppers, D. and Rogers, M. (1995). Do you want to keep customers forever? *Harvard Business Review,* March/April.

Porter, M. E. (1985). *Competitive Advantage: Creating and Sustaining Superior Performance.* New York: Free Press.

Saunders, M. (1997). *Strategic Purchasing and Supply Chain Management,* 2nd Edn. London: Pitman.

Smitka, M. (1991). *Competitive Ties: Subcontracting in the Japanese Automotive Industry.* New York: Columbia University Press.

Stevens, G. C. (1989). Integrating the supply chain. *International Journal of Physical Distribution and Materials Management,* **19** (8), 3–8.

Swamidass, P. M. (1993). Import sourcing dynamics: an integrative perspective. *Journal of International Business Studies,* **24** (4), 671–91.

Szarka, J. (1990). Networking and small firms. *International Small Business Journal,* **8** (2), 10–22.

The Economist (2000). Does M&S have a future? *The Economist,* **357** (8194), 28 October–3 November, 32–5.

Wheelright, S. C. and Clark, K. B. (1992). *Revolutionising Product Development.* New York: Free Press.

Womack, J. P. and Jones, D. T. (1996). From lean production to the lean enterprise. *Harvard Business Review,* March/April, 93–103.

Womack, J. P., Jones, D. T. and Roos, D. (1990). *The Machine that Changed the World.* London: Macmillan.

Zeithaml, V. A., Parasuraman, A. and Berry, L. (1990) *Delivering Quality Service: Balancing Customers' Perceptions and Expectations.* New York: Free Press.

3

Developing a research agenda for the internationalization of fashion retailing

Christopher M. Moore and Steve Burt

Introduction

While fashion retailer activity is essentially a domestic market-based activity, now for a significant minority of fashion retailers, operating within a foreign market is essential to their reputation and makes a significant contribution to their overall turnover. Foreign market expansion is not a new phenomenon, however. For example, Liberty opened their first store in Paris in 1890, while Burberry opened their first store in the French capital in 1909. However, it is true to say that in the past two decades, the international expansion of fashion retailers has been unprecedented, and has been fuelled by a variety of facilitating factors, the most notable of which has been the emergence of fashion retailer super-brands (examples of which include The Gap, Benetton and Gucci), whose image positioning makes them appealing to customers across the globe, regardless of their cultural background and ethnic origin. Consequently, fashion retailers are now identified as amongst the most important international companies.

Hollander (1970), in his review of the internationalization of retailers in general, noted that fashion retailers were amongst the most prolific and successful when it came to foreign market expansion. Dawson (1993) identified a number of factors which he suggested serve to explain why internationalizing fashion retailers enjoy considerable success abroad. These various factors are listed in Table 3.1.

However, despite the international success of fashion retailers, there has been little reference to that success within the literature, and consequently, there has been insufficient consideration of their international strategies and activities. Therefore, the purpose of this chapter will be to explore in depth the pan-national expansion of fashion retailers.

Akehurst and Alexander (1996) proposed an agenda for future research in the area of retailer internationalization in general. The details of their agenda are provided in Table 3.2.

Table 3.1 Factors enabling the internationalization of fashion retailing

Factors

- Small format requiring limited capital and management set-up costs
- Ease of entry and exit compared to manufacturing
- Single brand format enables internationalization
- More suited to franchising than food formats
- Economies of replication

Source: Dawson (1993).

Table 3.2 Future agenda for the study of the internationalization of retailing

Six questions of retailer internationalization	Key issues to be addressed
What is the internationalization of retailing?	Development of a definition
Who are internationalizing?	Identification of the key determinants which identify categories of international retailer
Why are retailers internationalizing?	Examination of the motivations for internationalization
Where are retailers developing international operations?	Identification of the direction of international expansion
How are retailers developing international operations?	Examination of the methods of foreign market entry
When does internationalization occur?	Examination of the conditions in which internationalization occurs

Source: Akehurst and Alexander (1996).

These research questions readily apply to a consideration of the international expansion of fashion retailers, and these will be addressed here and will serve as a structure for the remainder of this chapter.

What is the internationalization of fashion retailing?

The internationalization of fashion retailing is apparent in three ways. The first to be considered, and ostensibly the most prevalent, is the sourcing of products from foreign markets. Sourcing raw materials and finished and unfinished product for abroad has been a long-established feature of the British and European clothing sectors. Buying from foreign markets is largely motivated by economic and competitive considerations, as retailers seek to take advantage of low labour costs within underdeveloped economies. A further motivation for foreign market sourcing relates to the power of country of origin as a factor which influences consumer perception of the style, reliability and quality standards of a garment. For example, the Italian fashion industry has recognized that consumers worldwide perceive products originating from Italy as superior in style and quality, and has therefore adopted the 'Made in Italy' mark as a means of further exploiting these positive perceptions.

Furthermore, as a result of the advent of the global fashion brand, many fashion retail buyers are forced, as a response to consumer demand, to stock the world's most successful brands, such as those created by Ralph Lauren, Calvin Klein, DKNY, Lacoste and Diesel. The 'pulling power' of these brands is such that the fashion buyer has little choice but to stock these brands, often at the expense of lesser known brands from their home market.

Within the context of the British fashion market, it has to be recognized that the disintegration of the country's textile manufacturing sector has also made it increasingly difficult for British fashion retailers to source products of an acceptable quality standard and at an acceptable competitive price within the UK. Furthermore, because the British textile industry has suffered from a chronic lack of investment over the past 30 years, buyers who seek to offer a differentiated product range must source from abroad because of the lack of sufficient technical expertise within the domestic market.

The second dimension of fashion retailer internationalization relates to the internationalization of 'management know-how'. This 'know-how' may be in the form of expertise in particular trading methods, marketing techniques or technological competence. With the international flow of management personnel from one company to another, improvements in management intelligence gathering and the advent of multi-market participation by fashion retailers, it is increasingly the case that ideas, techniques and policies adopted in one country are soon replicated by another retailer in another country. One has only to consider the speed by which fashion retailers copied the just-in-time design to manufacturing processes of Benetton in the 1980s and the 'brand as communicator' advertising of The Gap in the 1990s to appreciate the extent of inter-company influence within the fashion sector.

Finally, the third and easily the most obvious aspect of fashion retailer internationalization is the operation of retail shops by fashion retailers within foreign markets. A number of questions arise as a result of this direct form of participation within a foreign market by a fashion company, and these relate to such issues as the reasons for opening stores abroad, the direction of that opening, as well as the operating methods that companies adopt in order to operate stores abroad. These various questions are the focus for the remainder of this discussion.

Who are the international fashion retailers?

To definitively identify which fashion companies operate stores abroad is highly problematic for a number of reasons. The first is that no international database appears to exist which has tracked the international activities of fashion companies. Secondly, if such a database did exist, then it would be impossible to ensure its accuracy, since this is a dynamic and fast-changing market sector; retailers enter and exit from national markets at great speed, for as Dawson (1993) identified, the replication of a fashion retailer's trading format abroad is limited in terms of capital and management costs, and their single brand format lends itself to economies of replication.

However, despite the difficulties of locating exactly who are the international fashion retailers, it is possible to identify categories of fashion retailer likely to engage in foreign market expansion. This can firstly be done on the basis of country of origin.

Studies undertaken by Corporate Intelligence on Retailing (1997) found that, within a European context, the most prolific international fashion retailers, in terms of the number of European countries to be entered, and the number of stores operated within these markets, originated from France, Italy, the US, The Netherlands, Germany, Denmark and the UK. No clear explanation is provided as to why these markets should produce such internationally oriented retailers, but possible suggestions include the recognition that these countries have long been established as reputable exporters of clothing products and their fashion retailers are expert in product and brand development, distribution management and information technology.

A further categorization of international fashion retailers drawn from an analysis of the most prolific fashion retailers is provided in Table 3.3, and identifies their product focus, the number of stores and their size, their market positioning and target customer groups.

Where are fashion retailers developing international operations?

Studies which examine the direction of fashion retailers' foreign market expansion are limited, both in terms of the volume and the breadth of

Table 3.3 The four types of international fashion retailer

1 **The product specialist fashion retailers**: These are companies that focus upon a narrow and specific product range, such as Hom Underwear, La Senza, Tie Rack, Nike, Sock Shop and Jacadi and have a clearly defined target customer group either based upon demography (such as childrenswear), gender (such as La Senza and Hom Underwear) or a specific interest (such as sport and Nike and Reebok). While there are some obvious exceptions, such as Nike Town, these retailers typically operate small-scale stores either within busy customer traffic sites, such as adjacent to airports/railway stations or major mass market shopping areas, such as Oxford Street in London and Fifth Avenue in New York.

2 **The fashion designer retailers:** Fernie et al. (1997) provided a clear definition of the international fashion designer retailers which states that these have an international profile in the fashion industry as evidenced in their having a bi-annual fashion show in one of the international fashion capitals (i.e. Paris, Milan, London and New York) and have been established in the fashion design business for at least 2 years. These firms retail merchandise through outlets bearing the designer's name (or an associated name) within two or more countries and market their own label merchandise.

   Company examples of this group include Gucci, Valentino and Chanel, who normally locate within premium locations within capital and other important cities.

3 **The general merchandise retailers**: Corporate Intelligence on Retailing (1997) identified these as retailers that include a mix of fashion and non-fashion goods within their merchandise offer. Examples include department stores such as Marks & Spencer, Harrods and Sogo. These foreign stores are often located within key shopping centres and tourist locations, the merchandise offer increasingly extends beyond two trading floors (Corporate Intelligence on Retailing, 1997).

4 **The general fashion retailers**: Unlike the product specialist fashion retailers which tend to concentrate upon one or two fashion product groups, the general fashion retailers are described by Corporate Intelligence on Retailing (1997) as offering a broad range of fashion merchandise and accessories, either to a broad (e.g. The Gap) or highly defined target segment (e.g. Kookai). This group are typically low to mid-priced and locate in 'city centre' locations so as to allow maximum access for mass market customers (Corporate Intelligence on Retailing, 1997).

Source: Hollander (1970), Fernie et al. (1997, 1998), and Corporate Intelligence on Retailing (1997).

companies considered. Those studies which examined the direction of expansion of specific fashion retailers have found that the choice of market to be entered is largely determined by the market positioning of the retailer concerned. For example, Lualajainen (1992) found that the luxury goods retailer Louis Vuitton focused its international expansion upon the world's leading centres, specifically the capital cities of the most prosperous nations.

Hollander (1970) found that a focus upon capital city expansion was a common trait of the internationalizing luxury fashion retailers and he termed this expansion strategy the 'New York, London, Paris syndrome'. He explained that luxury fashion retailers adopted this strategy of opening flagship stores within the world's leading centres in order to create an allure and sophistication for their organizations. As such, the operation of a flagship store in Paris, Rome or the like communicated to consumers that the company was cosmopolitan, successful and accessible to the world's richest and most beautiful people.

While the luxury fashion retailers typically focus their expansion upon geographically disparate foreign markets, other studies have found that general fashion retailers have tended to concentrate their expansion upon the markets that are geographically and culturally proximate to their local market. Again, drawing from the work of Lualajainen (1991), the international expansion of Hennes & Mauritz of Sweden attests to the fact that those retailers which seek to serve the broad mass market typically opt to enter those markets which are culturally and geographically close, so as to minimize the associated risk and maximize their control over their operations there. It is only when this adequate coverage is achieved within adjacent foreign markets that consideration is given to entering into markets that are culturally and geographically distant from the home market.

Moving from the firm-specific level, a series of patterns relevant to the geographic expansion of fashion retailers can be identified as follows:

- European fashion retailers typically confine their foreign market entry to other European markets, as well as the North American market.
- American retailers typically enter into Canada, followed by the markets of Western Europe, specifically the UK.
- European designer retailers have extended their international participation into the Japanese and Pacific Rim markets.

In the 1990s, partly as a consequence of the highly competitive conditions within the European Union and as a result of the opportunities afforded by the demise of the USSR, fashion retailers have reorientated their international expansion to include Russia and the other markets of Eastern Europe. Furthermore, the previously underdeveloped markets of South America and the Middle East have emerged as the new centres for fashion retailers' foreign market expansion (Fernie et al., 1998).

When does fashion retailer internationalization occur?

Drawing from the international expansion of European fashion retailers provided by Corporate Intelligence on Retailing (1997), it is possible to identify distinct time periods within which the international expansion of retailers has occurred. The period 1990–1995 can be identified as the most significant in terms of number of fashion retailers entering a foreign market for the first time, followed by the period 1985–1989. In contrast, the period 1980–1984 is identified as a lean period, unlike the late 1970s, when a significant number of companies went abroad for the first time.

In many respects these fluctuations very broadly mirror the changing economic conditions of the respective periods, whereby, for example, the growth in international participation by fashion companies in the late 1980s appears to have been precipitated by the positive economic conditions of the period. However, economic conditions alone fail to account for the variations in foreign market participation levels. For example, the unprecedented growth in international expansion within the early 1990s occurred within the context of a significant international economic recession. Therefore, other explanations must be found in order to explain the timing of fashion retailers' expansion into foreign markets.

On the one hand, embarking upon an expansion strategy during a recessionary period is sensible, since the associated costs are likely to be less. However, financial reasons alone cannot account for the volume of expansion. Instead, consideration must also be given to social factors which facilitate the global expansion of a fashion retailer's brand. Dimensions such as the emergence of a more cosmopolitan, better informed fashion consumer precipitate the demand for products abroad, and the availability of pan-national advertising media, the Internet and an increased convergence in global lifestyles has enabled fashion retailers to communicate cost-effectively with consumers from a wide variety of foreign markets.

The issue of the timing of fashion retailer internationalization is also concerned with the range of preconditions which may facilitate and encourage foreign market expansion, as well as the obstacles which inhibit a retailer from achieving success abroad. The advantages of a strong brand image with associated values of cosmopolitanism, exclusivity and design excellence have been identified as a key factor contributing to the success of the international fashion design houses (Fernie et al., 1997). In a similar vein, the international success of such companies as Hennes & Mauritz of Sweden and Kookai & Morgan from France has been attributed to their ability to offer product ranges which are distinctive and perceived to be value for money, within retailer environments which are memorable and capable of easy replication across a variety of markets (Lualajainen, 1991; Moore, 1997, 1998). Furthermore, the international success enjoyed by fashion retailers has also been attributed to their ability to develop internationally appealing brands, such as in the case of Benetton and The Gap (Simpson and Thorpe, 1996), and serve customer segments inadequately catered for by indigenous retailers, or to create segments where none had previously existed (Sternquist, 1997; Johnson and Allen, 1994).

Scant attention has been given to the problems that internationalizing fashion retailers may face. Hollander (1970) argued that the major obstacles that mass market fashion retailers face within foreign markets are more likely to be cultural than technical. The importance of cultural affiliation and understanding was seen to impact upon the decision to enter, as well as avoid, certain countries on the part of retailers such as Hennes & Mauritz of Sweden (Lualajainen, 1991). Corporate Intelligence on Retailing (1997), while recognizing that internationalizing fashion retailers may face problems related to supply chain inefficiencies, the activities of local competition, and the control and management of foreign operations from a distance, stated that the main reason for failure within foreign markets was because fashion retailers often underestimate the cultural differences that exist between foreign and domestic markets. As such, these retailers invariably fail to make necessary adjustments to their offer in order to suit local market conditions.

Given the inextricable relationship between cultural context and the very notion of what is deemed fashionable, it is perhaps surprising that greater consideration has not been given to the role of culture within the process of fashion internationalization. No study would appear to have considered the critical factors that foreign fashion retailers require for success, or the obstacles that such firms potentially face, when entering the UK market.

Why do fashion retailers internationalize?

Of the research areas related to retailer internationalization, that which considers the reasons for retail firms' involvement within foreign markets has arguably attracted greatest attention (Hollander, 1970; Jackson, 1976; Waldman, 1978; Kacker, 1985; Salmon and Tordjman, 1989; Treadgold, 1990/91; Alexander, 1994, 1997; Tordjman, 1995; Crewe and Lowe, 1996). Variously described as driving forces (Treadgold, 1990/91), international inducements (Hollander, 1970) as well as strategic motivations (Alexander, 1994), all of these terms relate in some way to those factors that encourage retailers to consider international market involvement as a strategy for growth (Williams, 1992).

Alexander (1997) noted that 'push' and 'pull' factors have emerged as an important method for interpreting retailers' motives for expanding into foreign markets. Derived principally from the work of Kacker (1985), the 'push–pull' dichotomy seeks to explain why retailers are pulled towards a foreign market and/or are 'pushed' out of their home market in order to further their growth objectives. Based upon a review of the expansion activities of European retailers into the American market, Kacker (1985) claimed that these two sets of factors were the key drivers for the significant growth in European retailer acquisition of American firms from the early 1970s to the mid-1980s. Accordingly, European retailer activity was prompted by 'push' factors evident in the various home markets and by 'pull' factors in the American market.

Alexander (1997) provided a comprehensive, but not exhaustive, listing of the significant 'push' and 'pull' factors associated with retailers' international expansion. In addition, he also emphasizes the fact that these factors do not exist in isolation, but are mutually inclusive. Indeed, these factors serve to delineate the political, economic, social, cultural and retail structural conditions of the period. Table 3.4 summarizes the key 'push' and 'pull' factors, and sets these within their wider environmental context.

Other than the 'push' and 'pull' factors, the literature also acknowledges the importance of facilitating factors which support and enable retailers to successfully internationalize. Among the facilitating factors identified are those which relate to corporate philosophy and the vision of senior management to succeed abroad, the accumulation of in-company expertise, financial stability

Table 3.4 Push and pull factors behind retailer internationalization

Boundary	Push	Pull
Political	Unstable structure, restrictive regulatory environment, anti-business culture dominant, consumer credit restrictions	Stable structure, relaxed regulatory environment, pro-business culture dominant, relaxed consumer credit regulations
Economic	Poor economic conditions, low growth potential, high operating costs, mature markets, small domestic market	Good economic conditions, high growth potential, low operating costs, developing markets, property investment potential, large market, favourable exchange rates, depressed share prices
Social	Negative social environment, negative demographic trends, population stagnation	Positive social environment, positive demographic trends, population growth
Cultural	Unfamiliar cultural climate, heterogeneous cultural environment	Familiar culture reference points, attractive cultural fabric, innovative business/retail culture, company ethos, homogeneous cultural environment
Retail structure	Hostile environment, high concentration levels, format saturation, unfavourable operating environment	Niche opportunities, company owned facilities, 'me too' expansions, favourable operating environment

Source: Alexander (1997).

and capability, and expertise in communication and data technologies (Treadgold, 1991; Treadgold and Davies, 1988).

Other studies have provided classifications of the inducements which encourage retailer internationalization, and these are clearly founded upon the 'home market push' and 'foreign market pull' premise. Tordjman and Dionisio (1991) classified retailer motives in terms of constraints and opportunities, the former relating to issues such as market saturation and legislation aimed at restricting growth, and the latter to the opportunities that a foreign country can provide for the development of an international image and increased profitability. Tordjman (1995) provided a refinement of the earlier classification by identifying external motives, such as the emergence of homogeneous consumer tastes, saturation of national markets, improvements in logistics and international information exchange, and internal motives which include the exploitation of brand image and corporate know-how over a wider range of markets.

Fragmentary accounts can be found within the wider motivational studies on retailer internationalization which include reference to fashion retailers (Hollander, 1970; Treadgold, 1990/91; Dawson, 1993; Salmon and Tordjman, 1989; Alexander, 1994; Sternquist, 1997), or from the very limited literature which considers the international migration of individual fashion retailers (McHarg et al., 1992; Johnson and Allen, 1994; Lualajainen, 1991, 1992).

Identifying the 'commercial objectives' which induce international expansion by retailers, Hollander (1970) suggested that luxury fashion houses developed international chains for reasons of prestige, while department store retailers went abroad because of saturation in the domestic market. Other studies which have considered the internationalization of high fashion and luxury brand retailers have suggested that the motivation to expand into foreign markets has been premised not so much upon the need to escape from home market restrictions, but instead upon the desire to exploit the potential of distinctive brands and innovative product offerings within receptive markets (Lualajainen, 1992; Fernie et al., 1997).

The adoption of a proactive approach to internationalization is not necessarily restricted to the activities of exclusive fashion design houses. As part of a general review of the features of retailer internationalization, Treadgold (1990/91) maintained that specialist fashion retailers (focusing upon specific product types), such as Damart, Tie Rack and High & Mighty, all have entered foreign markets in order to maximize the opportunities afforded by their respective merchandise expertise and specialization. Similarly, according to trade press sources, there is evidence to suggest that other clothing firms with a highly focused product offering (such as the lingerie retailer, La Senza of Canada, and ski-wear specialist, Helly Hansen of Norway: Murphy and Bruce, 1999; Moore and Murphy, 2000) have engaged in foreign market expansion in response to foreign market demand for their products. In addition, retailers focusing upon highly specific customer segments, such as young female fashion retailers Kookai & Morgan of France, have been reported as stating that the decision to engage in foreign expansion was motivated primarily by the desire to exploit the opportunities afforded by under-developed competition in markets.

It cannot be assumed, however, that the international expansion of all clothing retailers serving clearly defined customer segments can be attributed to proactive motivations. For example, the entry into Spain by British childrenswear retailer Adams in the mid-1990s has been described as a reactive response by the company to imminent market saturation and increased competition within the domestic market (Johnson and Allen, 1994). Similarly, Lualajainen (1991) concluded that home market saturation within Scandinavia encouraged the expansion of youth fashion retailer Hennes & Mauritz of Sweden into the UK.

Research which has considered the internationalization of general merchandise retailers (McHarg et al., 1992; Whitehead, 1991) pays scant attention to the motives which have led to their cross-border expansions. Assuming that Laura Ashley can be categorized as a clothing retailer serving a broader market through varied ladies' and childrenswear collections, Treadgold (1991) argued that the firm's motivation for foreign market development was essentially proactive, determined by a brand and retail formula with a cross-market appeal. In contrast, Sternquist (1997) identified a clear relationship between the expansion of American clothing retailer The Gap into Canada, the UK, France and Germany and the saturation of the domestic market, and of opportunities within regional shopping malls in particular.

Furthermore, the literature has acknowledged that no one motivation or set of motivations for internationalization could be regarded as dominant over time, either for a specific company or sector (Alexander, 1994). Of those studies identified above, it would appear that none has considered how time and differing circumstances may serve to influence a fashion retailer's motivation and attitude towards foreign market participation.

It has been suggested that an examination of a retailer's motivation(s) for international expansion potentially provides rich insights into the nature of the company's strategic decision-making and its ability to interpret and respond to operating environments (Hollander, 1970; Alexander, 1994). By implication, the fact that only a perfunctory understanding of the reasons why fashion retailers have internationalized into the UK or elsewhere is available also means that our understanding of how these fashion retailers assess, understand and respond to their operating environments (as evidenced in their strategic decision-making) is essentially limited.

How are fashion retailers developing international operations?

The 'how' of retailer internationalization is a complex concept, and is essentially concerned with the alterations that a retailer makes with respect to their marketing mix elements in response to local market conditions. Furthermore, the 'how' of retailer internationalization also involves those entry methods that retailers adopt in order to facilitate the opening of stores abroad. Both dimensions will be considered here within the context of the international expansion of fashion retailers.

Sparks (1996) suggested that the strategies that retailers adopt for internationalization and the methods of foreign market entry that they use reflect the variations in the degree of direct involvement and control required by the retailer and the level of knowledge and transfer borrowing, in relation to management expertise and business ideas, that may exist between the entering retailer and associates within the local market. Similarly, the internationalization strategy and the market entry strategies that are adopted are linked to the place of decision-making for the retail business operating within the host country (Dawson, 1993).

Treadgold and Davies (1988) identified a range of strategic options available to a retailer seeking to operate within a foreign market and suggested that the manner in which a company entered a market and conducted operations served to reflect the availability of resources for foreign market development and the degree of operational control they sought to retain over foreign operations. Recognizing that a high degree of control implies a high cost entry strategy and that a low cost entry approach necessitates a considerable loss of control, Treadgold identified three strategic options for the development of foreign operations. The first is a high cost/high control strategy, adopted mainly by firms with limited foreign market experience, which can be achieved through organic growth or the outright acquisition or dominant shareholding of a company currently operating within the foreign market. The alternative approaches include a medium cost/medium control strategy, achieved normally by joint venture arrangements, or a low cost/low control strategy, achieved through a franchise arrangement.

The themes of resource availability, the degree of control required by the internationalizing retailer and the extent of their experience in foreign market trading, identified by Treadgold (1991), are also apparent in the review of retailer internalization strategies provided by Salmon and Tordjman (1989). Without doubt, their work has proved to be highly influential to the understanding of the strategic approaches adopted by retailers in respect of internationalization (Dawson, 1993; Sparks, 1996).

Salmon and Tordjman (1989) identified three strategic approaches to retailer internationalization, *international investment*, *global* and *multinational*, and suggest that a retailer's choice of strategy is ultimately dependent upon the trading characteristics and internal competencies of the company. The *international investment strategy* involves the transfer of capital from one country to another, with the aim of acquiring part-share or total shares in another operating company. Retailers typically adopt this approach in the early stages of their international involvement in order to diversify their business for reasons of financial and political risk, to gain rapid market share within countries where the organic development of a chain of outlets would involve high risk and high cost, as well as to obtain the trading advantages inherent to that market.

Accordingly, Salmon and Tordjman (1989) assert that the type of retailer likely to use this type of international growth strategy would typically be large, highly diversified within their own domestic market (although this was clearly less evident among internationalizing British grocery retailers: Burt, 1993; Wrigley, 1997, 1998), and are committed to exploiting the growth opportunities available within foreign countries, mainly through the part or full acquisition of existing retail chains and other businesses. Within a fashion retailing context, the acquisition by the Paris-based LVMH Group of companies including Christian Dior, Givenchy, Loewe, Christian Lacroix, Fendi, Kenzo, Guerlain and Gant underlines their adoption of an international investment strategy which seeks to spread their corporate risk across a number of different brands serving disparate customer segments. Consequently, should the LVMH conglomerate find that any one brand falls out of fashion favour, then the company has an alternative brand to promote and therefore an alternative source of income.

The internationalizing fashion retailer typically must respond to two conflicting pressures. The first is to adapt to local market conditions in order to fully respond to the needs of consumers, while the second is the desire to benefit from operational scale economies (Salmon and Tordjman, 1989). Following from Levitt's (1983) assertion of the worldwide convergence of consumer needs and wants, retailers who follow the second of Salmon and Tordjman's strategies, *the global strategy*, do so on the basis that they have access to consumer groups with shared lifestyle characteristics and purchase requirements, independent of their place of residence. A global strategy is therefore defined as a faithful replication of a trading concept abroad, and involves the standardization of the fashion marketing mix and the faithful replication of the same product range, communications methods, corporate identity, service and price levels within all stores, regardless of their geographical location.

The fashion retailers that use this strategy typically have a clearly defined corporate image and market positioning, often with a strong own-brand and possibly with a unique product range or trading format. Companies that replicate a standardized marketing strategy include general fashion chains such as The Gap, the designer companies including Gucci, Prada and Kenzo, and specialist fashion retailers like Lacoste and Nike. Product exclusivity, the influence of a founding personality (such as Laura Ashley within her company), the interplay between the product on sale and the store environments within which they are sold, all serve to shape the distinctive characteristics which are central to the success of a global strategy. In addition, Salmon and Tordjman highlighted the significance of an integrated supply chain, and suggested that the most successful global fashion retailers exert considerable influence over the design and quality standards of their products so that the reputation of their corporate brand can be managed and controlled at all times. Consistency in terms of all dimensions of the retailer's positioning is highly significant for the global retailer and can only be achieved through high levels of centralization. Consequently, successful global fashion retailers seek to retain and centralize tactical and strategic decision-making, and the standardization of their activities provides for economies of scale through the consistent replication of store format elements, marketing communications, product development and management control systems. In order to facilitate this centralization, global fashion retailers must invest in computerized management information systems in order to monitor and control the flow of stock and information.

There are also disadvantages associated with such centralization, and these are identified by Salmon and Tordjman (1989) as those related to inflexibility in responding to local market needs, which may result in the non-identification of market trends, demotivation and a lack of commitment among local management, as well as the danger of being associated with a particular specialization which may leave the company vulnerable in the face of competitor attack or changes in consumer attitudes.

A variety of studies have examined the utilization of globalization strategies by retailers in general and have questioned the extent to which this approach is viable within a retailing context. Waldman (1978) argued that environmental differences, such as those related to consumer culture, competitive conditions and economic and legal restraints, made standardization of the retailer's marketing mix across a range of markets impossible to achieve. Similarly, Martenson (1987) suggests that, while a retailer may be able to achieve a pan-national replication of their core trading values and philosophy, it is unlikely that they will, at the same time, be able to achieve the successful implementation of a standardized trading approach.

The third internationalization strategy identified by Salmon and Tordjman (1989) is *the multinational strategy*, which seeks to preserve a basic trading concept or image across a range of geographically dispersed markets, but also adapts the formula to fit local market conditions and the expectations of local customers. Salmon and Tordjman identify C&A as an example of a multi-national retailer. In all of the countries in which C&A trades, the company operates the same basic strategy of offering recognizable ranges of clothing for men, women and children, inexpensively. However, at a national level, the firm's marketing mix elements are adapted to suit local needs. As a result, each country has its own range of products, pricing and margin policy, while advertising and promotions methods are adapted to suit local market conditions.

While C&A are identified as a retailer that adapts their positioning mix to best suit national characteristics, French hypermarket chains, with representations across Europe, are identified by Salmon and Tordjman (and latterly by Dupuis and Prime, 1996) as having adapted their marketing mix elements at a regional level and increasingly at store level. This allows local managers the flexibility to select products and adjust prices in response to near trading environments. In order to respond to local conditions, multinational retailers develop decentralized management control structures, based upon a clear demarcation of responsibilities, whereby strategic decision-making resides with the parent company and is undertaken in the home country. Tactical and operational decisions are delegated to local management teams, either at national, regional or local level. This devolution of power to the host nation requires a management team that is able to identify local market trends and credibly respond to these through their marketing mix decisions. However, while this may suggest a loosening of centralized control on the part of the internationalizing retailer, Salmon and Tordjman emphasize that firms still retain control over the original business concept, using formal and informal communications channels, such as through the deployment of parent company personnel to co-ordinate and 'head-up' local operations. In such cases, the devolvement of power from the retailer's central administration can prove to be somewhat limited.

As a result of pursuing a multinational strategy, Salmon and Tordjman (1989) have identified three principal strategic consequences. The first is that the scale of investment (both in terms of time and financial resources) required in order to open each new shop, adapt the offering to suit local market conditions and recruit management capable of undertaking such initiatives is so significant that it invariably limits the speed of replicating such formats. Secondly, because of their adaptive techniques, multinational fashion retailers fail to benefit from the economies of scale associated with retailing, supply and advertising to the extent that is achieved by global fashion retailers, although those retailers that develop a large local presence within one country or region may benefit from scale economies within these markets. Thirdly, but not to their disadvantage, the multinational retailer, through the range and diversity of their market involvement and experience, may be able to integrate the know-how techniques and best practice found within foreign markets into their domestic and international business strategies.

Salmon and Tordjman predicted that the multinational retailers would gain market share within markets where the international procurement of goods is inhibited by the physical characteristics of the products, such as in relation to size or perishability. As such, the multinational retailer is expected to grow in significance within the food sector and other product categories that are less subject to abrupt changes in consumer tastes and lifestyle features. However, it is also their contention that it is the global strategy that will realize the greatest growth rate, which is partly attributed to the increased homogenization of consumer groups around the world and the homogenization of standards which will serve to facilitate the distribution of products between countries. Treadgold (1991) also predicted that the multinational approach would increase among retailers who seek to satisfy the requirements of local consumers while maintaining cost and scale economies where possible.

Dawson (1993), in a review of Salmon and Tordjman's typology, and specifically their choice of C&A as a classic example of a multinational retailer, argued that, while C&A may seek to adapt their marketing mix to suit local market conditions, any changes that are made happen in the context of a corporate brand framework that is both highly defined and uniform in its application. The elements of C&A's brand identification, store interiors and corporate colours are consistent across all countries, and while products may vary across markets in terms of their type and design, there is nevertheless a constancy in their styling and quality that is in keeping with the overall image of the C&A brand and their market positioning. Any devolvement in power is likely to be operational and possibly tactical in nature, and the flexibility that does exist is constrained by the prescriptive nature of the C&A brand identity.

Therefore, Dawson proposed that there is a case to be made which sees globalization and multinationalization not as two discrete and mutually exclusive approaches to transnational expansion, but instead as a continuum which marks the extent to which a fashion retailer's proposition is both capable and required to adapt to the needs of the foreign market. This continuum extends between the extremes of a standard global identity and a locally tailored one, and where a retailer is positioned on this scale is dependent upon the nature and importance of the retailer as a distinct brand entity, both at corporate and product level. Where the brand is regarded as central to the identity of the retailer and is clearly positioned within the mind of the actual and potential consumer, then the retailer is more likely to follow a global strategy. However, even within such a prescriptive strategy, there is the possibility that the operational and tactical elements of the retailer's positioning may be altered to suit the trading environment of the non-domestic market. As such, Dawson proposed that Salmon and Tordjman's (1989) classification must be 'loosened' and perhaps not taken as literally in order to adequately reflect the reality of international retailing.

Concluding comments

Fashion retailers are the most international of retailers, as was noted by Doherty (2000), who recognized that the international expansion of fashion retailers in Europe far outweighs the foreign market activities of retailers operating within other product sectors. However, despite the prominence of fashion companies as international retailers, the attention invested by researchers in this area has largely been perfunctory, and our appreciation of the nature and characteristics of the internationalization of fashion retailing remains largely incomplete.

The application of Akehurst and Alexander's (1996) research agenda to fashion retailer internationalization not only provides a clearer direction and focus for research activity within the area, but also highlights the many dimensions which seek to differentiate the process of internationalizing fashion retail operations.

In summary, the internationalization of fashion retailing is distinguished by its clear emphasis upon the exploitation of the brand as the fundamental driver for foreign market expansion and the fact that the possibilities for future expansion show little signs of abatement in the near future.

References

Akehurst, G. and Alexander, N. (eds) (1996). *The Internationalisation of Retailing*. London: Frank Cass.

Alexander, N. (1994). UK retailers' motives for operating in the single European market. *Proceedings, Annual Conference of the Marketing Education Group: Marketing Unity in Diversity*, Vol. 1, pp. 22–31.

Alexander, N. (1997). *International Retailing*. London: Blackwell.

Burt, S. (1993). Temporal trends in the internationalization of British retailing. *The International Review of Retail, Distribution and Consumer Research*, **3** (4), 391–410.

Corporate Intelligence on Retailing (1997). *Clothing Retailing in Europe*. London: CIG.

Crewe, L. and Lowe, M. (1996). United colours? Globalization and localization tendencies in fashion retailing. In *Retailing, Consumption and Capital. Towards the New Retail Geography* (N. Wrigley and M. Lowe, eds), pp. 271–83. London: Longman.

Dawson, J. (1993). The internationalization of retailing. In *Retail Change. Contemporary Issues* (R. D. F. Bromley and C. J. Thomas, eds), pp. 15–40. London: UCL Press.

Doherty, A. M. (2000). Factors influencing international retailers' market entry mode strategy. *Journal of Marketing Management*, **16**, 223–45.

Dupuis, M. and Prime, N. (1996). Business distance and global retailing: a model for analysis of key success/failure factors. *International Journal of Retail and Distribution Management*, **24** (11), 30–8.

Fernie, J., Moore, C., Lawrie, A. and Hallsworth, A. (1997). The internationalisation of the high fashion brand : the case of Central London. *Journal of Product and Brand Management*, **6** (3).

Fernie, J., Moore, C. and Lawrie, A. (1998). A tale of two cities: an examination of fashion designer retailing within London and New York. *Journal of Product and Brand Management*, **7** (5).

Hollander, S. C. (1970). Who are the multinational retailers? In *Multinational Retailing*, pp. 14–53. Michigan State University Press.

Jackson, G. I. (1976). British Retailer Expansion into Europe. Unpublished Ph.D. Thesis, UMIST, Manchester.

Johnson, M. and Allen, B. (1994). Taking the English 'apple' to Spain: the Adams experience. *International Journal of Retail and Distribution Management*, **22** (7), 39.

Kacker, M. P. (1985). *Transantlantic Trends in Retailing: Takeovers and Flow of Know-How*. Connecticut: Quorum Books.

Levitt, T. (1983). The globalisation of markets. *Harvard Business Review*, **16** (3).

Lualajainen, R. (1991). International expansion of an apparel retailer – Hennes and Mauritz of Sweden. *Zeitschrift fur Wirtschaftsgeographie*, **35**, Heft 1, 1–15.

Lualajainen, R. (1992). Louis Vuitton Malletier – a truly global retailer. *Annals of the Japanese Association of Economic Geographers*, **38** (2), 55–70.

Martenson, R. (1987). Is standardisation of marketing feasible in culture bound industries? *Interntional Marketing Review*, **4** (3), 7–17.

McHarg, K., Lea, E. C. and Oldroyd, M. (1992). *European Market Entry Strategies of UK Clothing Retailers*. Working Papers Series, University of Sheffield.

Moore, C. (1997). *La Mode Sans Frontiers? – The Internationalisation of Fashion Retailing*. Working Paper, Institute for Retail Studies, University of Stirling.

Moore, C. (1998). La mode sans frontiers: the internationalisation of fashion retailing. *Journal of Fashion Marketing and Management*, **1** (4), 345–56.

Moore, C. and Murphy, R. (2000). The strategic exploitation of new market opportunities by British fashion companies. *Journal of Fashion Marketing and Management*, **4** (1).

Murphy, R. and Bruce, M. (1999). The structure and organisation of UK clothing retailing. *Journal of Fashion Marketing and Management*, **3** (3).

Salmon, W. J. and Tordjman, A. (1989). The internationalisation of retailing. *International Journal of Retailing*, **4** (2), 3–16.

Simpson, E. M. and Thorpe, D. I. (1996). A conceptual model of strategic considerations for international retail expansion. In *The Internationalisation of*

Retailing (G. Akehurst and N. Alexander, eds), pp. 16–24. London: Frank Cass.

Sparks, L. (1996). Reciprocal retail internationalisation: the Southland Corporation, Ito-Yokado and 7-Eleven convenience stores. In *The Internationalisation of Retailing* (G. Akehurst and N. Alexander, eds), pp. 57–96. London: Frank Cass.

Sternquist, B. (1997). International expansion by US retailers. *International Journal of Retail and Distribution Management*, **19** (4), 13–19.

Tordjman, A. (1995). European retailing: convergences, differences and perspectives. In *International Retailing. Trends and Strategies* (P. J. McGoldrick and G. Davies, eds). London: Pitman.

Tordjman, A. and Dionisio, J. (1991). Internationalisation strategies of retail business. Commission of the European Communities, DG XXIII, Series Studies, Commerce and Distribution, 15.

Treadgold, A. (1990/91). The emerging internationalisation of retailing: present status and future challenges. *Irish Marketing Review*, **5** (2), 11–17.

Treadgold, A. (1991). Dixons and Laura Ashley – different routes to international growth. *International Journal of Retail and Distribution Management*, **19** (4), 13–19.

Treadgold, A. and Davies, R. L. (1988). Forces promoting internationalization. *The Internationalisation of Retailing*, Chapter I, pp. 9–19. Oxford: OXIRM/ Longman.

Waldman, C. (1978). *Strategies of International Mass Retailers*. New York: Praegar.

Whitehead, M. (1991). International franchising – Marks and Spencer: a case study. *International Journal of Retail and Distribution Management*, **19** (2), 13–19.

Williams, D. E. (1992). Motives for retailer internationalization: Their impact. structure and implications. *Journal of Marketing Management*, **8** (3), 269–85.

Wrigley, N. (1997) British food retail capital in the USA – Part 2. Giant prospects. *International Journal of Retail Distribution Management*, **25** (2–3).

Wrigley, N. (1998) Market rules and spatial outcomes. In *Regions, Regulations, and Institution: Towards a New Industrial Geography* (T. Barnes and M. Gertler, eds). London: Routledge.

4

Retail brand marketing in the new millennium

Bill Webb

Introduction

The twenty-first century may see retail marketers, like cordwainers or fletchers, confined to the annals of history. For the present, they are still with us, although their average length of job tenure is less than 18 months and many experts predict that the writing is already on the wall. This chapter looks at the role and prospects for the retail marketing of consumer goods and services. It will not attempt a comprehensive review of the most recent marketing initiatives and techniques, as so much other contemporary literature has done, but rather look for a rationale for the continued existence of a distinct retail marketing function, and discuss what this might be. It will examine:

- Changes in the nature of consumer demand.
- The retail response to date.
- Conclusions for retail brand marketing.

It will concentrate on the UK, with occasional international references.

Marketing dominated commercial thinking in the second half of the twentieth century. The idea has predominated that the proliferation of product choice meant that successful retailers had to identify, measure and understand their 'market', and target a specific segment within it with a 'unique selling proposition', i.e. something that provided more 'added value' to that particular group of customers than any available alternative. This was a step on from the previous 'selling era', when retailers simply put on offer the products produced, ever more cheaply, efficiently and to higher standards, by modern, automated manufacturing plants, and waited for customers to form queues to purchase them. The three keys to success in retail marketing were famously said to be 'location, location and location', i.e. having your store near to where large numbers of your chosen customers live or shop. Many retailers maintained that, with shops in the right locations, there was no further need for marketing – the shops would do that for themselves. Some worked with other, additional, elements of the so-called 'Retail Marketing Mix' besides 'place' (location), i.e. product, price, people and promotion. This Anglo/American process became the textbook model for consumer goods marketing. It spawned numerous methods of identifying specific groups from 'ABC1s' to, more recently, 'Dinkies' and 'Yuppies'. It developed a plethora of persuasive tools and programmes from Tiger Tokens or Greenshield Stamps to, more recently, 'Computers for Schools' and 'reward' card schemes. It has been extended first into Western Europe and the old Commonwealth, and more recently into the developing countries of Eastern Europe, Asia and South America. It has supported the growth of a global consumer society beyond the wildest dreams of those charged with reconstructing shattered economies after World War Two. In whatever way retail marketing activities are classified (above/below the line, push/pull, advertising/promotion), they all have critical factors in common:

- They originate from the brand owner or distributor, and have the objective of attracting more customers to the brand or store.
- They assume that the potential customer knows less about the product than they do, and makes buying decisions within a limited and controlled market.

However, as any politician or athlete will confirm, it is just when everything seems to be sewn up nicely that some unforeseen change takes place which augurs a step change. One or two fundamental questions need to be asked at the outset:

- If the distribution of consumer goods and services is going to increasingly bypass physical stores, how will this impact a discipline based on the supremacy of locations?
- If these locations are 'reinvented', at least in part, for new roles, how relevant will retail marketing disciplines be to these objectives and activities?

- If customers are better educated, more cynical about media messages and totally capable of informing themselves on every aspect of their lives, what role will there be left for 'persuasion by communication'?
- How realistic will it be for most local brands to achieve competitive superiority in a truly global marketplace using traditional marketing methods?
- If the individual customer is at the centre of commercial activity, then no part of an organization will be able to opt out of the 'customer satisfaction' process. If marketing is 'everyone's responsibility' then it is no one's specific function. Does this explain why many successful retailers do not have a board level marketing director and also why there is such a rapid turnover of marketing directors elsewhere in the retail industry?

Once suppliers appreciated that they had to position, rather than just sell, their products, the concept of brand management developed, and with it, the idea that 'marketing' should orchestrate the other functions of a business. The 1970s and 1980s saw the growth of large marketing departments and the development of 'strategic' marketing plans by many British retailers. This author was himself appointed to the first marketing designated role in a leading fashion retailer in the early 1970s. During the course of the 1990s, we have seen a fragmentation of consumer markets and the introduction of new technologies which clearly transcend the remit (and often the understanding) of retail marketing departments. As a result, the marketing function has become increasingly sidelined. Emphasis has shifted from promoting the product to capturing and retaining the customer, and decisions on product range, pricing, shop design and so on are seen as too important to be left to the marketing department.

Furthermore, as the pace of change has increased, marketing's emphasis on research and strategy has often been seen as a constraint to innovation. The number of publicly quoted retail companies in the UK has also dictated a faster return on investment than a research-driven culture will allow as Sears, for example, found out under Liam Strong. A philosophy of 'learning by doing' has almost become 'de rigeur' for the retail industry, and even when disciplines are introduced it is accepted that they will have to be executed concurrently with the project rather than prior to its start, as traditionally happens in manufacturing industry. Transitory fashion and lifestyle influences are impacting many product sectors beyond the clothing industry. In fact, many would say that they have largely moved on from the clothing industry to influence purchasing decisions in the home and leisure sectors. These days, it is more profitable to be 'roughly right' and on time than 'precisely right' and too late.

Finally, stagnant consumer expenditure and increased competition in many areas has not helped. Expenditure on research, store design, marketing communications and especially the new loyalty schemes can be very high, and hard to validate. Marketing professionals themselves complain that traditional marketing tools 'no longer work' and have been slow to put in place robust

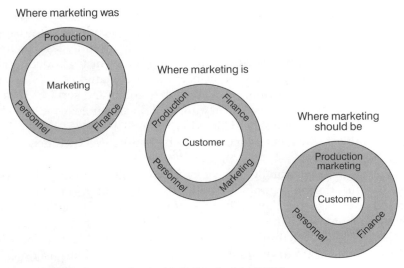

Figure 4.1 Marketing – as seen by the Marketing Society (1997).

measurement techniques which would have enabled them to defend their territory a little better. As profits came under pressure and the accountants and consultants moved in, it was not surprising that not only many retail marketing directors, but entire departments moved out.

These trends have been well recognized by the marketing profession itself (ironically, whose leading individual practitioners were, in the summer of 1998, awarded 'chartered' status). In July 1997, the Marketing Society surveyed its members, and under the title *The Profession: Keeping its Grip*, published a review of members' opinions, from which some of the preceding thoughts have been drawn (Marketing Society, 1997). It concluded with an impassioned plea for 'where marketing should be' – essentially a filter or interface between key organizational functions and the customer (Figure 4.1). What this role should involve or how it should be executed was not made clear. Can we justify this view in the context of the retail sector?

The new consumer

The existence of a mass market of homogeneous consumers was always something of a myth. However, in the early years of the 'consumer society', people were more than willing to trade off their individual preferences and personal service for a share of the cheap, high quality products coming on to the market. They needed to be informed about the products, have their features explained and be reassured about their appropriateness for their needs. No more. Except in a few specialist sectors, today's consumer is very different. The pace of social change is faster than it has ever been. UK society today is characterized by: a stagnant, ageing but healthier population; more but smaller families; more women working, but often part time; couples marrying later, and more often; incomes under pressure, but more windfall gains, especially from inheritance; more travel and demand for leisure time; less 'technofear' and widespread computer literacy; diminishing trust in traditional authority figureheads – to quote just a few of the better known examples. All these trends have relevance for the distribution of consumer goods and services, and hence for the future of retail marketing. They are well documented, especially by The Henley Centre, and will not be detailed again here.

Some significant insights which need to be highlighted include:

- Today's customers virtually defy classification – although the more complex they become, the more complex are the psychographic segmentation models created to categorize them. Shoppers today reflect the influences of the generation into which they were born, the lifestage they have reached (maybe for the second or even third time), their own income and lifestyle, the attitudes of their reference groups – and their own personality. Unlike past times, when there was peer group pressure to conform to a stereotype, today's consumer feels more than ever at liberty to 'be himself or herself' (although admitting to being a little insecure and exposed in this role). The result is that the customer of the new millennium is more individual than ever before. He or she wants control over his or her own life, and all the products and services that make it up. He or she is 'someone not anyone'. Today's family is no longer a 'unit', but a cellular base camp for individuals with their own phones, TVs and computers, front door keys, meal times (and content), dress styles, friends and values. No wonder the mixture is often volatile! No wonder the number of single person households has doubled in the past 25 years.
- There is growing evidence of customer rejection of mass products and cloned stores, in favour of something and some place which is 'right for me'. The rationale for much of the research-based marketing has long been the reduction of risk and the search for an acceptable 'common denominator' segment which can be targeted. It could therefore be said that marketing itself has acted as a brake on innovation, and has partly been responsible for customers turning away from traditional goods and services.
- The evidence for the growing individualism of today's shopper can be seen in the decline of many collective organizations from trade unions to political parties, religious bodies or retail co-operatives. Yet, at the same time, individuals express the need for security and solidarity by coming together in groups or 'tribes' – be they Arsenal Supporters, a local neighbourhood watch committee or a PC users' club. Brands too (such as Tommy Hilfiger, Prada or the British Airways Executive Club) can fulfil and exploit this need. This will be further discussed in a subsequent section.
- Shoppers also express their preferences in relation to their needs – home needs, leisure needs, work-related needs and 'self-actualization' needs. They exhibit different purchasing attitudes and behaviour according to which situation they find themselves in at any specific time. As Gavin Aldred, recently Managing Director of New Look, said, 'A customer is as likely to

buy a CD as one of our blouses. To be honest I've given up trying to fathom out why people buy what they do.' (Aldred, 1998).

- Levels of education are higher than ever before. Perhaps more important, there is the cumulative experience of two generations' exposure to marketing media, press, radio and TV. Shoppers have 'wised-up' to the various marketing strategies and programmes on offer. The media themselves delight in exposing any form of consumer 'exploitation' (especially by retailers or travel companies). Customers are also more willing to try alternative new, often global, providers if they feel they can get a better deal. Hence the growth of businesses like easyJet or Amazon.com.
- Shoppers are more confident than ever before in their capability to solve their own problems. They will write their own wills (on forms bought from W. H. Smith), treat their own ailments (with medicine bought from ASDA), select and book their holidays (on Thomas Cook's website), plan an instant dinner party (courtesy of Marks & Spencer) – and even select a new partner via the Internet. If there is something they cannot do then they go to an evening class – or seek help on the 'Net'. The Thatcher years engendered a culture of self-help in the UK which is unique, and which has endured well beyond her demise.
- For many people, incremental Time now has more value than incremental Money. Kurt Salmon Associates' 1998 Consumer Confidence survey reported that, given the choice, 53% of people would opt for more time over more money. Most people are striving to increase their personal time productivity in order to squeeze more activity and more experience into a finite (if longer) life expectancy. 'I want it NOW' has become the cry of today's consumer. Kids cannot understand why supper takes two minutes in the microwave when the package says 'instant'. In the food industry, Proctor & Gamble have invented the 20 : 20 rule – 20 minutes to shop for a meal and 20 minutes to prepare it. Retailers like Whistlestop and Harts grow by giving customers back their time in exchange for higher prices and margins. Starbucks famously sell a 'fifteen minute experience', rather than coffee and buns.
- In the furnishings sector, IKEA has swept all before it by offering instant fashion for the home, while Queensway, Maples and Waring & Gillow (now no more) continued to take customers' deposits and delivered a solution 6–8 weeks later. In fashion, much of the industry still demands orders to be placed six months in advance. Companies like Hennes & Mauritz and Zara are aiming to cut lead times from design studio to store display to just 15 days.
- When time runs out, people shift something to another time, making use of time that would otherwise be dead. They video late night films, sports events and educational programmes. They shop for groceries from their home or office and pick them up (or have them delivered) at their convenience. They buy their 'home meal replacements' ready prepared from the supermarket (EatZi's or Dean & Deluca amongst many others in the US, and now ASDA in Canterbury, or Albert Heijn in Haarlem in Europe). They buy Virgin Vie or Body Shop (and much more) from home sales

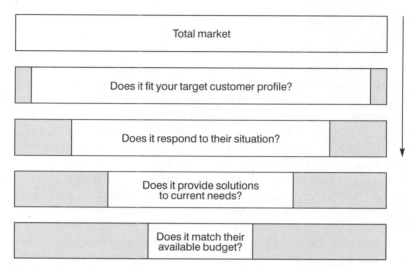

Figure 4.2 Brand targeting in the twenty-first century. *Source:* Wolny and Webb (2000).

representatives. They buy birthday presents at the Science Museum shop or the Manchester United superstore. Lifestyles have become a quest for solutions to fulfil multiple needs and desires simultaneously. As Peter Simpson, Commercial Director of First Direct, said in February 1998, 'The 9 to 5 society has gone, and is as dead as the proverbial Monty Python parrot. It is deceased, it is no more. There is a new definition of time' ('24 Hour Society' Conference).

● Because of the blurring of activities, people no longer perceive aspects of their life in discrete compartments. Eating in and eating out no longer retain their traditional significance. Sport, fashion and music all overlap – so that while the clothing retail sector stagnates, the sports sector explodes, largely by selling clothing. Markets can no longer be defined by product categories, but rather by multi-dimensional lifestyles, which present multi-faceted problems requiring new types of total solution.

So it is no longer enough to target goods and services at demographic or psychographic market segments. A template for determining the appropriateness of a product or service proposition is represented in Figure 4.2.

The retail response

As consumers increase the share of their spending devoted to education, health, leisure and entertainment, so they have decreased that devoted to traditional consumer goods – groceries, clothes, shoes, furniture and white electrical goods. Even in the innovative electrical leisure sector, falling prices have offset increased sales volumes. Partly, this is the result of saturated markets. An ageing population consumes less calories per head and has acquired a stock of durable items, leaving only a replacement market. Most households have so much 'stuff' that they no longer know what to use or where to store it. Hence the growth in charity shops and car boot sales. In the United States, a growth industry is personal 'lockups' where surplus items can be stored and brought out on a rotating basis. Partly it is because of the improved quality and life expectancy of many products, especially motor vehicles and clothing, which need replacing less frequently, and partly it is because of changing personal attitudes to possessions which are no longer deemed by many to be an indicator of personal success and status. As the American retail commentator Carol Farmer (1995) has written, 'we have entered the Less Decade'.

However, retailers, and retail marketers in particular, must also accept much of the blame for the performance of their sector. They have been guilty of the very mistake often attributed to Henry Ford – offering customers any colour they want as long as it is black. In the drive for centralized control, economies of scale and low operating costs, they have, with a few notable exceptions:

- Reduced the choice available to shoppers, both in terms of available products (too often identical in different stores) and shopping locations.
- Confused the customer with proliferation of similar products or products inappropriate to their needs.
- Irritated customers by de-listing favoured products on the basis of some new systemized management technique.
- Wasted the customer's time by locating key product categories in remote parts of the store, continuously changing the layout and product presentation, and slow payment processes.
- Explained away 'no-service' as 'self-service', and failed to invest in the calibre and training of store level staff who are in direct contact with customers.
- Created cloned stores and bland shopping centres which are virtually indistinguishable from each other.
- Offered products for sale that are consistently priced more highly than in other national markets (local cost structures and tax regimes notwithstanding).

As Burns et al. (1997) pointed out in a telling article, 'retail renewal' has become the critical issue of the decade. It is an indictment of the past performance of retail marketers, supposedly the customer's champion, that it is only now that some enlightened top managements have decided to truly focus on their customers that these issues have begun to be addressed. What these companies are doing will form the subject of the next section of this chapter.

Current retail initiatives

The pace of change in the UK retail sector continues to increase. Acquisitions, mergers, new ventures and bankruptcies are reported weekly. The UK is the target of a constant stream of new entrants from overseas, and our own retailers, with very mixed results, continue to expand into new territories. The small band of experienced senior retail executives continue to play musical chairs, and attempts to supplement their numbers from abroad, particularly America, have been largely unsuccessful. Analysis of these trends is outside the scope of this chapter, but from them is emerging, not only in the UK but in most markets, a radical new picture of how retailing will look as this century unfolds. For the present, this emerging picture is often described as being 'customer driven' or 'customer focused', but in truth, what we are witnessing is a major shift in power away from conventional retailers in favour of the final consumer. Clearly, this will impact the very nature of 'retail marketing'.

Retailers are responding to the new consumer at five levels:

- Corporate culture.
- Retail organization and management.
- Retail offer or 'proposition'.
- Means of delivery or executing this offer.
- Communications.

Culture

Marketing Week's citation for Tesco, winner of their 1996 'Brand of the Year', stated that 'the real lesson in Tesco's transformation over the past ten years is that a company can change its culture' (*Marketing Week*, 1997). That Tesco was able to metamorphose from a discount vendor of branded groceries to the polyfaceted solution to most of life's daily problems that it now is, is a tribute to the personal vision and leadership of Lord McLaurin, and those who are continuing his good work. Lord McLaurin realized that 'satisfying the customer' can only be achieved if those at the top have a personal and passionate appreciation of who their customers are and what the needs and desires are that their company aims to satisfy. International retailers such as Nordstrom (USA), Loblaws (Canada) or FNAC (France) have long realized that satisfying the customer is something which the best retailers are, rather than something which they do. In his book *Crowning the Customer*, Feargal Quinn (1990), Chairman of the Irish Superquinn Group, wrote 'the centre of gravity of a retail business should be kept as close as possible to the point where the action is – where the business meets its customers. If you are customer driven, then the most important place in the company is not the boardroom but the marketplace'. Like Lord McLaurin, Feargal Quinn is an advocate of 'MBWA' – Management By Walking About – spending time meeting, listening to and talking to customers.

Customer focus is not something which can readily be trained into, or imposed upon, a retail organization. It can only be established through a long-term and consistent example. Julian Richer of Richer Sounds believes that 'culture and people are interchangeable . . . A mission statement is not culture; culture comes from the heart' (Richer, 1995). At Richer Sounds, each sales receipt comes with a customer satisfaction counterfoil and assistants receive £3 for each 'excellent' rating (£4 if there is an additional favourable comment and £5 if a letter is received), but lose £3 for every report of 'poor' service.

So it has come to be realized by companies such as Richer Sounds, Carphone Warehouse and TGI Friday's that a truly marketing driven company does not put its customers first, but rather its own employees. If it fails to recruit, train, motivate and compensate the very best people then there is no chance that marketing and customer satisfaction objectives will be met. It has been demonstrated that staff loyalty and customer loyalty are closely linked in a virtuous (or vicious) circle. In an article in *Retail Week*, consultants Arthur Andersen (1997) reported that it costs £1500–2500 to replace a shop worker and 'three or four times that' for a supervisor or manager. Typically, retailers experience staff turnovers of 15–20% per year. John Ainley, Human Resources Director of W.H. Smith, states that every 1% of staff turnover costs the company £800 000 off the bottom line. As Julian Richer points out, theft and absenteeism are further costs which result from demotivated and disloyal staff.

Retail organization and management

Retail companies have changed the way they work, in order to respond more quickly and more precisely to changing customer demands. As Bernie Marcus of Home Depot is famous for saying, 'Being in stock of products that customers want to buy is by far the most important element of customer service'. The critical catalysts for this change have been:

- The development and application of new technologies.
- New management thinking, tools and skills.
- The changing relative cost of people, space and technologies.

During the past decade, we have seen the introduction of Quick Response and Just-in-Time techniques, Electronic Data Interchange, Efficient Consumer Response and Category Management. The application of these interlocking skills has varied from sector to sector, but they are all designed to achieve Bernie Marcus's famous dictum. They have been initiated largely by the financial and logistical experts, usually with little reference to the customer or their representative, the marketing department, so have featured 'efficient' rather more strongly than 'consumer response'. Like their forerunner DPP (Direct Product Profitability), they have tended to emphasize the profitability of the 'product' or 'category', often to the detriment of the holistic appeal of the total store or brand. Although they are at least a first step to organizing the store around consumer needs rather than supply-driven product brands, they have also contributed to what the French call the 'banalization' of retailing – the convergence towards a lowest common denominator, where customers complain about the lack of inspired, eccentric and personal products in most sectors – especially food and fashion stores.

As Figures 4.3 and 4.4 demonstrate, the structure of retail organizations has changed dramatically. Many layers of middle management have been stripped out as store-based technology has simplified merchandising, store operations and logistics. Functions and skills have become more specific, and many which were carried out 'in-house' are now outsourced. This includes many marketing activities from site research to database management. Buying, which was organized by product group to match suppliers' structures, is now more likely to be organized by category (fast food, mobile communications, etc.) or lifestyle (fashion, furnishings, etc.). Companies such as Tesco are starting to use their huge new customer databases (see below) to manage their businesses according to customer groups. The *Sunday Times* (1998) reported that Tesco is experimenting with dual pricing – charging lower prices in stores with catchment profiles of poorer shoppers.

In their mould breaking book, Peppers and Rogers (1993) illustrated how these changes are impacting the marketing function – with line management

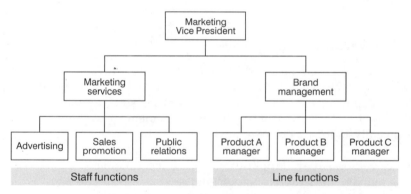

Figure 4.3 The brand management organization chart. *Source:* Peppers and Rogers (1993).

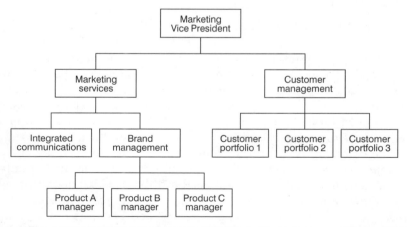

Figure 4.4 The customer management organization chart. *Source:* Peppers and Rogers (1993).

emphasis switching from the product to the customer (Figure 4.3). In this author's view, this analysis leaves unanswered the question of whether customer management can be carried out by the marketing function – an issue which will be explored in the conclusions of this chapter.

Proposition

'Proposition' describes the actual 'offer' of goods and services put forward by the retailer. Here too, there have been radical changes both at a conceptual level and in practical terms. Retailers are beginning to appreciate that markets are now better defined in terms of situations and needs (within budgets) than they are by demographic or psychographic descriptors. Thus, food shopping can be utilitarian (for basic needs), convenient (for emergencies and impulse) or stimulating (for entertainment or new ideas). Clothes shopping can also be segmented in a similar way according to intended use. Companies are starting to create and market their products and services as solutions to common lifestyle problems, rather than around product categories. In continental Europe, the leading French company, Carrefour, remodelled 15 of its largest hypermarkets as 'Universe' stores organized around solutions to needs early in 1998. Sales increases of 10–70% (by product group) have been achieved and conversion of the remaining 117 stores is now under way. Albert Heijn's latest store in Holland and Delhaize 'le Lion's' millennium outlet in Brussels (Belgium) are similarly laid out. In the UK, IKEA, Urban Outfitters, The Link and Tesco (yet again) are all examples. Even in Germany, companies like Ipuri and 'Lust for Life' (Karstadt) offer a lifestyle concept. This trend has major implications both for the methods of delivery of the proposition, and its branding and communications, which will be discussed below.

As Field (1997) has pointed out, stores are an expensive and inflexible means of distributing goods. As basic retail needs have become increasingly saturated, retailers have begun to extend their proposition into more and more new areas, including catering, financial services, health and education, and leisure. At the same time, the power and potential profit of retail activities has tempted many compelling non-traditional entrants into the sector – from museums and travel termini to sports venues and hospitals. What this suggests is that traditional definitions of retailing were constrained more by the methods of sourcing and distributing products than by a robust appreciation of the evolution of lifestyle needs. Customers' expectations of retailers have changed, and in particular, their definition of 'value' is changing. In the new millennium it is perhaps more helpful to conceptualize the market opportunity not only in terms of the traditional retail content of goods and services, but also in terms of leisure/entertainment and enrichment/self-actualization – things to make life fun and things to make life better.

Figure 4.5 illustrates the 'Concept Cube', which represents this picture. Although they will have to acquire new core competencies, retailers are better placed than many of the other organizations and institutions in the cube to move into and dominate the vacant top far right segment of the cube, because

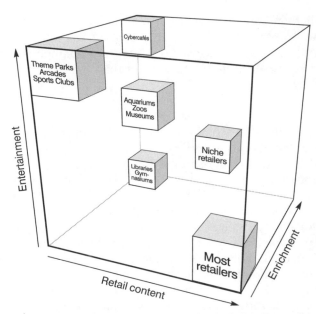

Figure 4.5 New retail brand market positioning matrix. *Source*: Sadleir, Tempus Entertainment (1996).

of their resources, commercial skills and closeness to the customer. There is already considerable evidence that they are extending the range of their offers into new activities:

- The proliferation of pharmacies, post offices and other services in supermarkets.
- The introduction of singles nights, weddings, political canvassing, etc. by ASDA.
- The holding of parties, art exhibitions, etc. by fashion stores, such as Jaeger and Selfridges.
- The opening of restaurants by fashion stores and book retailers (Books Etc, Borders, Waterstones) – and more recently by Boots.
- The development of HMR (Home Meal Replacement) offers along American lines by the new ASDA/Wal-Mart in Patchway (Bristol) and revamped Savacentre in Reading, and Sainsbury in the Cromwell Road, West London.
- The development of DIY workshops, tasting and cooking demonstrations, personal fashion shopping advisors and other educational programmes by leading retailers in all sectors.

When one operator or brand cannot achieve credibility across a sufficiently broad spread of activities, there is a trend towards forming strategic alliances to improve the quality and coverage of the total proposition. The introduction of branded concessions into fashion shops and department stores has long been an example of this. Recent times have seen a succession of link-ups between petrol retailers and supermarket operators for the same reason. The marketing rationale for this is to improve total overall operating competence and benefit from the collective specialist brand reputations. The downside is the dilution of the overall brand impact of the host store (or site) – does Total-Alldays have the same impact as Tesco Express?

Another tactic is for stores to purposefully group together with similar traders, thus enhancing the destination appeal of the location. Fashion stores always did this, but it is now common to find furniture or antique shops, DIY stores and electrical shops, and even superstores (as with Safeway and Tesco at Brent Cross) sited alongside each other. This strategy presumes that the overall local market catchment can be increased, as opposed to conventional analysis of finite product opportunity within a given geographical market.

A linked trend is for entities larger than individual stores to develop and market themselves on the basis that the appeal of the whole proposition is greater than the sum of the parts. Marketing a 'destination' can be simply a street (like St Christopher's Place, or Regent Street), it can be a shopping centre, or even an entire town. The highly successful Bluewater regional shopping centre in Kent developed a mission statement, detailed proposition and even a Brand Manual long before it opened. The City of Nottingham launched a civic reward card in October 1998 to promote the entire city. More and more UK towns and cities are appointing commercial managers (along the lines of German towns) to carry out this task.

Combining retail businesses with leisure, as suggested by the concept cube, is already under way, especially in the US. Examples are businesses such as Niketown, Planet Hollywood, The Rainforest Café, Disney and Warner Brothers stores, Viacom, Centex Life Solutions and many other so-called polysensual formats. As yet, there is little evidence that many of these formats cross the Atlantic profitably. European culture (and older populations) seem to demand more sophisticated concepts. However, retailers like Virgin and Boots in the UK, FNAC in France and Albert Heijn and Oininio ('Food for the Body and Soul'), both in Holland, are amongst the Europeans experimenting with these ideas.

The American futurist Faith Popcorn has identified 'fantasy adventure' as one of the key social trends in Western culture. People want the thrills and excitement of adventure without the time or money cost – or the personal risk or pain. This was previously only available at theme parks, like Disney World or Alton Towers, but can now be offered in shopping centres thanks to the enabling technologies of virtual reality. Tempus Entertainment pioneered this concept in The Mall of America, and a recent European example is the Opel Ride rally driving experience at the Geneva Motor Show. So Charles Revson's insight that he was marketing dreams rather than products turns out to have much wider relevance if we count vicarious experience as dreaming awake.

Delivering the proposition

Changes are also taking place very rapidly in terms of how the retail proposition is made available to customers. Not long ago, 'Location' enhanced by 'Retail Design' was said to be the key to retail success. Retail sales depended on the size and nature of the local 'market' and the quality of site within it. Now, as Tesco has stated, the emphasis has changed from share of the market to customer share – share of the customer's spending power that is. Retail marketing now has to make the proposition available to the customer wherever, however and whenever they find it convenient. The concept of 'lifetime customer value' has focused attention on alternative routes to market. Thus, Tesco now supplements its food-based superstores with hypermarkets (Tesco Extra, with an enhanced non-food offer), city centre convenience stores (Tesco Metro), convenience stores for the motorist (Tesco Express), Internet shopping on the Tesco website and a Tesco home delivery service. Other companies are following this lead with multi-channel strategies of their own. Sainsbury has opened a number of 'Local' stores and launched a new wholesale Sainsbury products offer for rural areas. Littlewoods now has stores, catalogues, Internet and DRTV retail offers.

Forecasts vary on the likely speed, coverage and growth of Internet shopping. All the experts agree that it is growing fast, from a very small base. Some experts such as Stern (1999) predict that the life cycle of many e-commerce operators, and the distribution channel as a whole, will be short. In the UK its total 'B2C' (Business to Consumer) value is still less than the annual increment in UK retail sales – so there need as yet be no 'losers'. Perhaps the most important impact is that it is one catalyst for the acceptance of non-traditional routes to market, by the new generation of shoppers. In total, all these new routes to market will have a major impact on the performance and profitability of traditional retail outlets. In the US, consultants Kurt Salmon Associates (1999) predict that all 'non-store' retailing will grow from 15% of retail sales in 1994 to 55% by 2010. Already, some 69% of US Internet browsers check out products online which they later buy in stores – and some 7% of on-line buyers return products to shops. Some important UK initiatives include:

- New mail order offers including 'specialogues' from traditional operators and initiatives from Arcadia, including the launch of Zoom! and the acquisition of Racing Green and Hawkshead, and launch of a Principles mail order catalogue.
- Introduction of new technology options by the leading mail order retailers, including CD-ROMs, Internet sites and the use of WAP phone technology.
- TV-based shopping, based previously on cable or the telephone, but with greatly enhanced potential thanks to digital TV.
- On-site automated shopping including vending machines such as the Belgian-based 'Shop 24' system or Video 24 in Hampstead. This also includes many experiments with kiosks of various kinds, from the abortive initiative at Heathrow Airport to the rather more successful use in Daewoo car showrooms.
- With more people based at home, the continued growth in party plan and home selling. Body Shop, Virgin Vie and Weekender are three recent entries into this sector.

- The growing number of manufacturers marketing direct to their customers rather than selling via traditional distribution routes. Examples are Nike, Levi's Swatch and Häagen-Dazs, now joined by Coca-Cola (in Las Vegas), Cadbury and Nestlé – who recently started marketing more than 250 products direct to customers in two test markets in Switzerland. As Wileman and Jary (1997) demonstrate, in fashion (or 'repertoire' retailing as they call it) there is a strong case for vertical integration as a driver for successful brand building.

Attention is also being put on adding customer value by the quality and manner of the delivery of the retail proposition, as well as the route to market itself. This means adding back the service factor. All the leading supermarket operators have beep recruiting packers people to carry out groceries to the car, and also adding service elements like baby change and toilet facilities. Safeway and Waitrose have introduced customer self-scanning in a selection of stores. Somerfield in partnership with IBM (and Delhaize in Belgium with Alcatel Bell) have experiments in progress whereby company employees can order via the Internet and have their groceries delivered to a secure locker in the company car park. A similar experiment, called Shopping Box, is under way on a wider basis in Munich. In a 1996 initiative, Marks & Spencer launched a new customer service drive to re-focus store staff away from company procedures in favour of acknowledging and serving customers – although this had little impact given the entrenched management cultures and processes at the time. The introduction of fitting rooms and counter service meat and deli departments also reflects the new awareness of the quality of the customer shopping experience – exemplified by their refit of their major store in Kensington High Street, London.

Communication

According to Grey Futures (1998), in 1997 some 90% of all consumer communication was one way – from the vendor to the customer. Grey projects that by the end of the year 2000 this ratio will have fallen to 60%. Facilitated by the explosion of various forms of e-commerce communication is turning into conversation, with customers willing and able to express their needs and views to retailers. Internet sites like letsbuyit.com and priceline.com demonstrate how fast and how far the balance of power has shifted in favour of the consumer. Some would argue that this is only reverting back to the pre-technology era when every grocer knew his customers personally. In an article in *Progressive Grocer*, Ryan Mathews (1998) talks about 'a grocer in Michigan who has one store and 26 computers so that he can get to know each one of his customers as well as his grandfather did'.

Instant realtime feedback is increasingly being generated via traditional 'bricks and mortar' retailers. The latest Albert Heijn store in Haarlem includes 'Supplier Hotlines' which customers can use to contact major manufacturers directly. Since April 1998, Tesco has been experimenting with an in-store TV information channel with the potential to be extended for interactive communication. However, the Grey Futures forecast highlights just how important direct marketing and the building of customer databases has become to retailers. This is undoubtedly the most important means by which retailers learn about their individual customers' spending behaviour patterns. The idea that retail marketing was largely a blunt instrument for informing and persuading customers en masse to buy things they never knew existed or believed that they wanted is no longer given much credence. Today's customers are too well informed and too streetwise to be taken in by messages which do not accurately reflect a retail brand's culture, offer and delivery performance. Rumbelows found this out to their cost with their 'We save you money and serve you right' campaign. (They did not and could not – profitably.) As the American retailer L. L. Bean is fond of saying, it is important to 'make sure the story is never better than the store'.

Both manufacturers and retailers have channelled a larger share of their communications budgets into 'below the line' promotion, as a means of talking to customers individually. This has meant:

- Introducing company branded card schemes of various types and sophistication. The early schemes were largely based on credit accounts, and some have been enduring and successful beyond their founders (Hepworth, now Next's, Club 24 scheme, for example). The launch of the Tesco Club card, and its role in helping Tesco overhaul Sainsbury, has been well documented. More recently, Shell Select and Boots have introduced cards with much more powerful chips replacing the traditional magnetic stripes. Boots shoppers can now obtain personalized promotions and discounts via their reward cards and a network of in-store kiosks.

- The initial rationale for these cards was that it is cheaper and more efficient to retain as many existing customers as possible, rather than continuously replacing them, especially given the current demographic age group profile. However, there is growing evidence that the proliferation of loyalty cards is doing little to change the fundamental habits of shoppers. Promiscuous shoppers are behaving just as they used to – only picking up the loyalty bonuses at each store they use. Loyal shoppers are simply claiming a discount.

- The Henley Centre (1998) has called this 'The Loyalty Paradox' and sees the current obsession with customer loyalty as merely the latest in a long line of retail panaceas – starting with Location, and including EPOS and Design, which have their relevance but in themselves cannot make up for shortcomings in the retail proposition. Operators increasingly claim that the real benefits lie in the construction of detailed customer profiles and databases, which enable them to fine-tune their assortments and promotions to more accurately reflect their customers' lifestyles and needs.

- Whilst initially flattered at receiving personalized letters from the local supermarket, customers are also finding the constant attempts to build 'relationships' rather irksome, especially when the other party misspells their name, sends them three copies of mailings, downgrades their status when separation or divorce reduces their spending, or connects them to unintelligible voice mail systems. As with people, relationships with stores or brands are discretionary and require the provision of genuine, desired benefits by both sides. Many of the owners of such brands still need to learn the sensitivities of relationship marketing.

- Tailoring communications much more precisely to groups or individuals. Tesco's *Club* magazine is published in five issues aimed at different lifestage customers. BT's 'Family and Friends' scheme is a good example of a promotion which retains economies of scale, yet is specific and relevant to each beneficiary. This approach has been called 'mass customization', and we should expect to see more individual tailoring of both products and promotions in the future. Wolny and Webb (2000) have identified the apparel industry as ripe for mass customization initiatives due to the specificity of consumer demand for fit and styling – as exemplified by Levi's 'Original Spin' programme.

- Coca-Cola is one company which has recently gone on record as saying that, within its overall brand personality, it must find ways of addressing different customers. Writing in *Adweek* (1998), their ex-Global Marketing Director, Sergio Zyman, explained that they no longer run one campaign, but 20 or more, so that the company can offer customers the choice of many different ways of relating to it.

- Communications strategies are becoming more flexible, with product and store brands being forced to be 'whatever different customers need them to be', when they are targeted at situations and needs rather than people.

- Making use of new media to allow customers to source information for themselves. The growth in retailer websites has been well documented. What is more surprising is the way in which they are being used. Steve Bowbrick (1998) of Webmedia, writing in *Design Week*, stated, 'Website owners have learnt that Internet users are sociable, confident and curious. They want to talk about their purchases to the retailer and to other shoppers, to compare notes and whinge about bad experiences. This is scary for retailers. Allowing customers to talk to each other – to compare deals and after-sales service, even to club together to get a better price is anathema to shop owners. The retail business model is actually dependent on ignorance.' He goes on to describe the sense of community generated by visitors to sites such as Garden Escape.com.

- On a wider basis, the availability of intelligent Internet search engines like Yahoo! or Excite enables customers to embark on active global searches for choice and value. New Internet services like y-bag.com will now even do this for them!

- Communications are increasingly focused on developing brand values rather than selling products. In their publication *Riding the Wave*, PriceWaterhouse Coopers (1997) wrote 'In the new world, if you haven't got a brand, you don't have a business.' Traditionally branding served a dual purpose – to act as a short cut to understanding a product or service proposition, and defining a system of values to which customers could relate. The tactical benefits of the former are being increasingly eroded, as customers judge brands on the basis of their own experience, but the strategic role of the latter is of growing importance. Virgin is a brand for the young and adventurous – whether in music, travel, fashion or financial services.

• Many retail brands are seeking to enhance their reputations by espousing good causes – what has been called 'Differentiation by Standing for Something'. The Body Shop was an early example of this. Current examples are fashion companies like Ann Summers supporting breast cancer charities, DIY companies protecting tropical rain forests, Habitat backing art galleries or Tesco running its highly successful 'Computers for Schools' programme. New retailers such as Plannet Organic and Fresh & Wild are exploiting small but growing segments of the food market. In Europe, companies like Migros and Auchan finance entire foundations dedicated to youth and education, whilst Obi runs a technical trade university.

• To be credible, brands must deliver against their promises, and increasingly be seen to be authentic – as is 'The Original Levi's Store' or 'Coke – The Real Thing'. This applies both to their physical proposition and any values that they espouse. Writing in the *Sloan Management Review*, Professor Herman Simon (1997) suggests that brands can experience a 'marketing hysteresis'. This means that their reputation suffers permanently from one major lapse in delivering core brand values – and recovery is only partial. He quotes the example of Shell and their conflict with Greenpeace over the disposal of redundant oil platforms. In the retail sector, Gerald Ratner's famous quip about his products being 'crap' is an example. Others could be the reaction to Benetton's shock advertising (especially in Germany), Hoover's transatlantic flights fiasco, or in a minor way, Levi's pulling its Dead Hamster campaign in the August 1998 or Esso's quick reversal of its price increase following the end of the September 2000 fuel blockade. Faith Popcorn (1992) talks about 'The Vigilante Consumer', and undoubtedly the guardians of brands (product or store) will need to be much more careful of protecting and delivering their promises, if they are not to be shunned by consumers. 'Best Value' is not the decisive store choice criteria for customers concerned about the fur trade, saving dolphins or trees, apartheid, dictatorships in Burma or Indonesia or child workers in India. Virgin trains (and clothing) for different reasons are high risk strategies for Virgin. The potential upside is great – on the one hand, because of the current abysmal repute of rail travel, and on the other because successful branding in the fashion and beauty sector elicits the greatest consumer emotional response of any branding. However, the potential impact of failure in either endeavour, and the knock-on effect on Virgin's total credibility, is very high.

• Businesses have found that alliances work better when the partners have roughly equal size and strength. So it is proving to be with customers. Mass markets were able to relate to mass producers and distributors. Now, many of the largest companies (including retailers) are losing market share, and it is evident that speed, flexibility, insight and attitude are at least a match for size. Avis was the first to exploit this with 'We try harder'.

- Many mainstream retailers too are taking steps to play down their corporate nature and respond to local communities with specific store designs, product assortments and communications programmes. There is clearly a balance to be achieved between the confidence and security of a successful brand, and the approachability of a local trader. Wal-Mart, the largest and most profitable retailer in the world, takes care to retain its small town, homey origins, both through its staff training and motivation and its communications. It could be argued that some of Sainsbury's difficulties stemmed from that company's psychological distance from its customers.

Conclusions

What can be concluded about the future shape and prospects of retail brand marketing? This chapter has suggested main conclusions, as follows.

1 Definitions of retailing are changing dramatically, and with them the organizational roles and skill required to operate retail businesses. Retail marketing will diverge quickly from physical 'shop' marketing.

2 Marketing has traditionally concerned itself with the removal of barriers, often self-imposed, to consumer satisfaction. It has been largely a compensation for deficiencies in the retail system – information, offer, delivery and communication. That is why it has sat so uneasily with those responsible for these functions. Step improvements in both supply chain efficiency and consumer demand generation will make most of the operational elements of marketing redundant within a generation. Mitchell (1997) maintains that changed circumstances have caused a 'paradigm crisis for marketing'.

3 As Fred Schneider of Arthur Andersen (1997) has written, 'We are moving from a world of consumer choice to consumer control'. Customers will be, already are, doing their own 'reverse marketing'. Let's call it 'specifying' for when that skill replaces 'marketing' in management and academic discussion. Infinite choice, in all aspects of the product and service supply chain, will be something required by consumers, not offered by distributors. Customers will be one part – indeed the driving force – in a multilateral data exchange embracing 'concept developer', manufacturer and distributor. SINFOS, an experiment by Rewe, Nestlé and Mars in Germany, is a first step in this direction.

4 For the present, as the Danish fashion company In-Wear (1997) wrote in its prospectus, 'The consumer market participants . . . may be divided into raw material suppliers, product producers, concept owners, wholesalers and retailers. The concept owners are the driving force in this process. They choose the materials and control the production and delivery process. In addition, they handle a large part of the marketing activities. Consequently it is the concept owners who create, maintain and develop brands, with the

effect that the value and goodwill belonging to the brand name is owned by the concept owner.' This means that both upstream manufacturing and downstream selling can be 'outsourced', with the value being attached to the 'needs solution concept'. Marks & Spencer is an outstanding example of a brand that has effectively eliminated any and all value attached to any of its suppliers.

5 Mitchell (1999) argues that customers will identify and select products according to their 'fitness for purpose', value and personal brand values congruity. Eventually, we should expect brands to become redundant, as individuals become their own brands, each and every one of us with our needs and desires individually addressed. In the interim period, the development and communication of brand values will be an ongoing requirement for 'consumer problem solution' businesses (retailers in today's terms), especially for new businesses and new products. This will apply very much more to those 'propositions' positioned against emotional needs (fun, leisure, personal support) than to those positioned against utilitarian or convenient needs, which will lend themselves much more readily to automated solutions. In this respect, the example of fashion marketing, rather than FMCG marketing, will have the most medium-term relevance.

As Professor Peter Doyle (1998) wrote in the Spring edition of *Market Leader*, the business of the future will need to do only three things: to identify opportunities for innovation; create networks which can deliver efficient, fast and marketable solutions; and build and sustain brand equity.

6 Organizations are clearly moving away from hierarchical structures and towards flexible, temporary, teams. Many members are from outside the organization, and may never actually meet other team members. Most retailer 'departments' will become redundant, and with them the functional directors who head them. As the current evidence makes very clear, the marketing function will be the first to be decimated. This will come as a great relief to those many retail companies who have not yet got round to creating one!

7 Only truly customer-oriented businesses will achieve long-term success. The top executives, company culture, and all operational management and staff will truly champion the needs of their customers. The importance of what marketing has been attempting to achieve for the past half century has transcended the abilities and remit of its practitioners. These organizations will be open and transparent to all stakeholders, and enjoy the automatic confidence and trust of their customers.

8 Key activities carried out under the banner of marketing will still need to be executed. These will largely concern the management of information and its transformation into knowledge. Currently, this falls under the remit of category management, but, as Peppers and Rogers (1993) pointed out, emphasis is moving quickly towards customer management. Most of these functions are being outsourced to experts, but organizations will need to execute them in a much more integrated manner, with a focus on customers and customer situations, than at present.

9 There is still little evidence that many retail organizations are managing to accumulate and progress their insights. Customers are learning much more quickly than retailers, which is why they are gaining control of the process – much as retailers wrested it from manufacturers 20 years ago. Possibly it is too late, but a key 'marketing' challenge for retailers in the new millennium will be how to effectively institutionalize a learning process.

References

Aldred, G .(1998). Quoted in *Retail Week*, 13 March.

Arthur Andersen (1997). Counting the cost. *Retail Week*, 24 July.

Bowbrick, S. (1998). Shop talk. *Design Week*, 16 January. London: Cetaur Communications.

Burns, K. B., Enright, H., Hayes, J. F., McLaughlin, K. and Shi, C. (1997). The art and science of retail renewal. *McKinsey Quarterly*, No. 2.

Doyle, P. (1998). Brand equity and the marketing professional. *Market Leader*, Issue 1.

Farmer, C. (1995). The less decade: dream or nightmare? *International Trends in Retailing*, **12** (1).

Field, C. (1997). The future of the store. *Financial Times*.

Henley Centre (1998). *Planning for Social Change*. London: Henley Centre.

In-Wear A/S (1997). *Danish Stock Exchange Listing Prospectus*. Copenhagen: In-Wear A/S.

Kurt Salmon Associates (1999). *Consumer Outlook*. New York: Kurt Salmon Associates.

Marketing Society (1997). *Shaping the Future – The Profession: Keeping its Grip*. London: Marketing Society.

Marketing Week (1997). Commentary on 1996 UK Marketing Award Winners, 17 April.

Mathews, R. (1998). Small guy – big heart. *Progressive Grocer*, 9 February.

Mitchell, A. (1997). Brand strategies in the information age. *Financial Times*.

Mitchell, A. (1999). When the customer finally is king. *Market Leader*, Issue 5.

Peppers, D. and Rogers, M. (1993). *The One-To-One Future*. New York: Piatkus Press.

Popcorn, F. (1992). *The Popcorn Report: Faith Popcorn on the Future of Your Company, Your World and Your Life*. New York: HarperCollins.

PriceWaterhouse Coopers (1997). *Riding the Wave*. New York: PriceWaterhouse Coopers.

Quinn, F. (1990). *Crowning the Customer*. Dublin: O'Brien Press.

Richer, J. (1995). *The Richer Way*. London: EMAP Business Communications.

Sadleir, W., Tempus Entertainment (1996). *Tempus Entertainment Unpublished Business Plan*. Phoenix: Tempus Entertainment.

Simon, H. (1997). Hysterics in marketing – a new phenomenon? *Sloan Management Review*, **38** (3).

Stern, N. Z. (1999). The impact of the Internet on retailing. *International Trends in Retailing*, **16** (2).

Wileman, A. and Jary, M. (1997). *Retail Power Plays – From Trading to Brand Leadership*. London: Macmillan.

Wolny, J. P. and Webb, W. S. (2000). Mass Customisation as an Individualised Value Delivery System. In *Retailing 2000 – Launching the New Millennium, Proceedings of the AMS/ACRA Conference*, Vol. IX. Columbus: American Collegiate Retailing Association.

5

The role of store image in the re-branding of Selfridges

Andrew J. Newman and Nick Atkinson

Introduction and core concepts

This chapter considers the independent fashion retailer Selfridges & Co. and how it developed a new branding strategy for a changing consumer market. Selfridges & Co. are a high quality fashion retailer catering for the upper end of the market. Together with Harrods department store, which is also based in the fashionable part of London, these two stores may be considered icons of British retailing. The following sections track the progress of Selfridges from its beginnings in 1909 to the start of the expansion programme in 1999. Today, the product range the store focuses on consists mainly of fashion branded goods. As these brands are available in their competitor stores, Selfridges had to create a point of difference in order to secure a profitable market position. We explain how Selfridges created that difference to compete in the market using three main areas of their strategy: buying strategy, customer service and creative services. A fourth and additional factor, store image, emerges as a vital part of the company's strategy in its attempt to realign the Selfridges brand.

Retail store image is critical to the success of a retail brand, and often makes the point of difference in the race for increased market share. Store image is the mental picture that consumers bring to mind when they think of the store or its name is mentioned. The image can be described as the overall look of a store and the series of mental pictures and feelings it evokes. For the retailer, developing a powerful image provides the opportunity to stand out from the competition and be remembered. Forms of advertising are designed to evoke these images, and ads are used extensively to *reinforce* store image.

In general, a store's image is the result or product of all retailing efforts. However, store layout, presentation, signage, merchandise and displays all change to reflect newness and excitement from week to week, season to season. These components must, however, always remain true to the underlying image. The actual components of image are extensive, and range from the internal and external architecture of the store to visual merchandising displays. Visual merchandising takes on several guises: store planning and design, store windows and floor displays, signage, space design, fixtures and hardware, decorative panels, and mannequins. The extent of the visual merchandising function is still evolving and changes constantly with the times. For example, the window displays of Victorian Britain became an intrinsic part of the fashion and the retail industry. By 1910, department stores had developed a floor plan that to this day remains the model for most large retail stores.

Background

Selfridges' original store was first opened in 1909 by Gordon Selfridge at 400 Oxford Street. The magnificent building was Britain's first ever purpose-built department store and was designed by the architect Daniel Burnham. Selfridge was an American businessman who wanted to export the North American retail experience (which even in the early 1900s was highly developed) to the UK. The Selfridge retail philosophy held that all customers were welcome in the store – a factor that was reflected in the wide range of merchandise and services available. For example, there was a safety deposit located in the basement. Merchandise ranged from general groceries and clothing to aeroplanes. In fact, the great atrium within the building had a Sopwith Camel aeroplane suspended from the ceiling. The atmosphere created by the internal and external features (Kotler, 1974) of the Oxford Street store was importance, and played a part in its success.

Over the nine decades that the store has been open, it has changed drastically in both the products stocked and the interior of the building. During the 1960s and 1970s, the interior was changed to match the changing tastes of the British consumer. In keeping with the modern style of the time, all of the original architectural features were covered up and false ceilings were fitted. This altered the general image and atmosphere of the store to appeal to the 1960s and 1970s consumer. Altering the design and layout of any retail store is a critical step and one that must be taken with care, as this will impact on the overall store image. This is the mental image (or picture) that enters the mind of the customer when they think of the store. Images of the store and of course its merchandise are used to create the retail brand.

The product range in the store was also tailored to a specific market of the time, mainly consisting of middle class, middle aged couples. These aspects of the store became static as the market moved and tastes changed, leading to comments in the press and other publications comparing Selfridges to the Grace Brothers store in a British television sitcom called 'Are You Being Served?'

Company profile

In the early 1990s, Selfridges still had its Grace Brothers image and profits were falling. The board of directors at Sears decided to make a large cash injection into the business that started a 7-year and £100m refurbishment of the London store. The image had to be brought in line with the thinking and styles of a new era. Retail provision and town and city centre developments in the 1990s were enjoying a renaissance, and a return to the more classical layouts and designs of the nineteenth century. City planners emphasized this with the use of street architecture and the refurbishment of old dilapidated buildings, which focused on nostalgic themes. The old was now in and the 1970s modernist architecture was definitely out.

In line with this, the Selfridges Oxford Street interior was restored and the false ceilings and façade that had been erected decades earlier were taken down to expose the building's original features. A central atrium was one of the main areas of restoration. This was updated with additions such as glass barriers around the edges, producing a more open aspect. The new layout provided the store, and the Selfridges brand, with a new image in keeping with the period and customers' expectations. Refurbishment provided the London store with an extra 7% selling space and led to an increase in sales and profits. By the end of July 1998, Selfridges & Co. (as it now called itself) had separated from its parent company Sears and had redefined its brand. The £100m refurbishment was nearing completion and a second department store was due to open in September that year. The company had a new vision:

> To be the best department store chain in Europe, in a unique and theatrical way, whilst maintaining operational efficiency and share-holder value.

Selfridges: now and in the future

Most companies look towards expansion, and Selfridges had only had one store for the 85 years since its founding. Selfridges' second department store was opened in September 1998 at the Trafford Centre in Manchester. The site was an important opportunity because Manchester is the financial centre of the North West. Moreover, the Trafford Centre location made it easily accessible by car and bus for the rest of the region, and so customer patronage was more or less assured.

At the time of opening, Trafford was Europe's largest shopping centre and cost around £650m to build. The centre contains shopping malls and an area with restaurants, bars and 20 cinema screens. The designers of the Trafford Centre set out to create an exciting building, which was tastefully decorated and offered high quality shopping. The aim was to produce a total shopping experience complete with dining facilities under one roof. Taking this experience one stage further, the designers created the Orient experience, which is modelled on an ocean-going liner with a spectacular ceiling that simulates from day to night and back again via dusk and dawn every hour. In addition to the range of high quality restaurants, including the first Rainforest Café outside London, customers have 280 retailers to choose from. Selfridges obtained the largest single retail site in the centre, strategically placed off an area called 'The Dome', which is the central part of the complex. The store also benefits from several external entrances. These are important as they give the impression externally that the mall is part of the Selfridges store rather than the opposite.

This move by Selfridges into a retail shopping mall heralded an important change in the company's location strategy. Probably the most significant risk from this new approach was to the company's image. Shopping at Selfridges has always been associated with the city of London and Oxford Street, so a degree of uncertainty existed as to how the Selfridges customer would receive such a dramatic change. The prestigious image of the company does not really go hand in glove with a mall type location, which tends to be associated more with high street names such as Top Shop and NEXT. For Selfridges *at* Manchester this question of image was high on the agenda long before roll out, or opening day.

The answer lay in the type of customers that the Manchester store hoped to attract. These were very different than the traditional London profiles and fitted in more with the new Selfridges location. Nevertheless, given the profile of the company, operating out of a retail mall, albeit a superior one with architecturally designed features, was a risky venture. An earlier decision by Selfridges to expand culminated in the opening of an outlet at Heathrow Airport in 1990. The main rival Harrods had already opened two stores at Heathrow and Manchester International Airport. These locations suit Harrods because their tourist trade makes up a large part of their turnover. Selfridges, on the other hand, had in place a new brand image, which was more appealing to the brand conscious and younger end of the market. Their Heathrow store did not fit in with this image and closed after just 2 years of operation.

Before opening Selfridges *at* Manchester, extensive market research was carried out to establish the level of brand awareness (Jobber, 1998). Selfridges mainly sells designer branded products and the intention was to provide the brands local consumers desired rather than pushing existing brands. Product ranges are altered to suit the consumer as part of the buying strategy. As discussed, a major feature of the Selfridges brand is the atmosphere created by the store, as this sets the scene for the customer and thus was crucial to the success of the new store.

The Manchester Selfridges has a third of the space of its London counterpart, so producing a carbon copy was never an option. However, in the space available, the company wanted to recreate the 'Selfridges experience'. In this rather different setting, the company chose to opt for a classical feel externally, and rely on the internal merchandise displays to provide the greatest impact. This visual merchandising plays an important part in projecting the image of the store, and was instrumental in creating the impact necessary for Selfridges *at* Manchester.

Visual merchandising comprises five main components: image, layout, presentation, signage and displays. Everything the retailer does within the store, such as how the layouts, presentations, signage and displays are developed, must fit into the required image. Even though there are many influences at work in the shopping experience, the look of the store counts the most in enticing customers through the doors. This is because people tend to sum up that initial in-store encounter in visual terms. For Selfridges *at* Manchester, the existing reputation and strong brand name served to reinforce the customers' visual experiences. Nevertheless, a major part of the customer experience when visiting the store was taking in the atmosphere generated by the interior and exterior layouts.

The Manchester Selfridges was a test for the company brand. Over the first financial year of operation, sales equalled £220 per square foot. The pre-opening costs of the Manchester store totalled £6.3m. Since then, sales have been increasing and in the second half of the Manchester store's first full financial year the store moved out of the red. Over the 6 weeks of the Christmas and Millennium period, up to 8 January, sales rose by 32% on the previous year. All this led to analysts expecting a doubling of Selfridges' pre-tax profits to £27m.

In the future, Selfridges expect to open their third store in the UK at the Bull Ring Centre, Birmingham (Sabbagh, 2000). This is expected to open in the autumn of 2003, with other sites in Glasgow, Newcastle and either Bristol or Cardiff likely. Another area of development is the hotel located next to the food hall entrance of the Oxford Street store. The hotel was opened in 1970 and at the moment is only graded as four stars, partly due to the lack of investment. The property is currently leased to Thistle Hotels, with expiry in 2001. Selfridges plan to build a 20-storey tower on the site, making it the tallest buildings in the country (Finch, 2000). This new development will be more than a shop and will work to reinforce the idea of the 'Selfridges experience', which is about leisure and enjoyment as much as it is about shopping. The company wants the landmark to be a great tourist attraction, with retail, residential and leisure areas.

Even though Selfridges has maintained its philosophy that their stores are aimed at all groups, they must retain an element of exclusivity for the consumer (McGoldrick, 1990). By limiting their operation to a small number of stores, Selfridges maintain their exclusive image.

Major competitors

In the fashion retail market, there is a great deal of competition (Tolman, 1974). Selfridges stock a wide range of fashion brands from high street brands such as Karen Millen to designer fashion labels such as Miu Miu and Prada Sport. For each brand or group of brands, Selfridges competes with small independent or chains of shops, whether they are own-brand outlets or boutiques. There are many department stores in London, such as Harrods, Harvey Nichols, Liberty's, Dickens & Jones and Fenwicks of Bond Street. These stores are all aimed at different markets, even when the majority of the product range stocked is similar. Another feature they all share, and one that is highly relevant here, is the upscale and affluent image similar in character to that of the London Selfridges. London is such a large market in terms of the number of consumers and the financial wealth in the area to support all of these stores. Two of the major competitors are now discussed.

Harvey Nichols

The flagship store is located in the Knightsbridge area of London, in close proximity to the Harrods department store. The store itself is five stories high with a large basement. This makes it approximately half the size of Selfridges' Oxford Street store. However, it shares the same type of store image, which is created with a mixture of internal furnishings, visual merchandising and its architecturally designed spaces. Harvey Nichols is known for the fifth floor food hall containing a sushi bar, licensed bar and restaurant. It is also well known as a result of the BBC comedy 'Absolutely Fabulous', which gained the store cult status.

Like Selfridges, Harvey Nichols has one other store outside London. This is located in the city of Leeds and was opened in the mid-1990s. From a retail and lifestyle perspective, Leeds has drastically changed over the past decade, with shops, bars, nightclubs and hotels moving into the area. Leeds and Manchester have a more contemporary and cosmopolitan feel, and have become quite 'trendy'. The store's internal decor and merchandising projects this image while maintaining exclusivity.

Contemporary thinking and trendy professionals with money to spend have opened up new retail opportunities. Both Selfridges and Harvey Nichols have capitalized on this social change. For instance, Harvey Nichols is rumoured to be interested in moving into a prime location in Manchester, where over the past 5 years the gentrification of city areas (old warehouses converted into prestigious city dwellings) has created a large number of loft style apartments. The occupants of these tend to be young professionals who are very brand aware, and the ideal customers for Harvey Nichols.

Harrods

Probably one of the most famous of all departments stores in the world and located in Knightsbridge, London, Harrods started life as a small grocery store on the same site nearly 150 years ago. It quickly grew and became the magnificent department store it is today. At one time the store was owned by the Glasgow-based House of Fraser chain, but its current owner is Egyptian millionaire Mohamed Al Fayed. Harrods name is often linked to the death of the owner's son Dodi Al Fayed with Princess Diana. In a recent survey of brand awareness carried out by the American market research company Interbrand, the Harrods brand was rated at number 41 in the 100 greatest world brands. In the area of fashion, there are numerous brands, all of which are considered exclusive with a small market and very high price. The Harrods customer can be simply divided into two broad categories: rich and tourists.

The term 'rich' is used to describe this Harrods customer group as a certain degree of wealth or credit is required to be able to shop in the store. Many international customers fit into this category and these people visit the store for its exclusive name. The types of products stocked are specifically aimed at this affluent market, and are mainly own-brand merchandise from Harrods shirts to oven gloves. Much of the own-brand merchandise is packaged in the famous green and gold colours. This theme runs through the store and composes the Harrods brand. The Harrods Knightsbridge store is a classic example of luxury retailing and has all the features of a traditional department store. Harrods is famous for its high quality image and atmosphere, which it owes mainly to the sumptuous internal features (including its merchandise) and external architecture. Like Selfridges, Harrods uses visual merchandising extensively to produce the high status and wealthy lifestyle images. These tend to be universally recognized – a factor which has created for Harrods a world famous brand.

Harrods has more stores across the world than Selfridges or Harvey Nichols, but none of these outlets are department stores. In the UK, Harrods have three outlets at Heathrow and Manchester airports. These outlets stock a very limited range of merchandise that in the Harrods tradition is predominantly branded material aimed at the high status tourist market. For this market, the airport is the perfect location due to the extended footfall and dwell time (this refers to the number of people passing by the store and the time they are obliged to spend in the vicinity). Outside the UK, Harrods runs outlets in the Far East and under license to local companies.

Selfridges: their framework for success

This part of the chapter looks at the buying strategy and the role of the buyer in Selfridges, and the adaptability of that role as the company expands. A major part of this expansion and re-imaging process has been the emergence of a strong merchandising team. These and other factors such as the Selfridges shopping experience, the creative services and the high status store image they produced have provided a framework for success. The following tracks these areas of the retail operation and explains how they have altered the Selfridges image.

Buying strategy

A key consideration in the Selfridges recovery was the buying strategy, and the role of the buyer. Buyers select and purchase stock on behalf of the company for resale. Fashion buying may vary between retailers depending on whether the merchandise is own-brand or branded such as designer label products. At Selfridges, the merchandise is made up solely of branded 'designer labels' with no own-brand items on sale. Buyers therefore purchase garments from a set range produced by designers such as Hugo Boss.

Buyers

The brands and the products chosen by buyers have a great impact on the retailer both financially and with respect to the retailer's brand image. A positive effect will produce profits for the company and reinforce their brand image. To ensure a positive outcome a new strategy is produced for each season. This process begins a year before the merchandise will appear on the shop floor, and involves predicting which key brands and styles will be popular for the following season. Two methods are used to achieve this: (a) buyers visit the designer shows in New York, Paris, London and Milan; and (b) they observe trends in textile, design and new technologies. This is used to produce a fashion directive for the following season.

Buyers use this information along with their personal experience of evolving trends and previous sales figures to produce a strategy for the areas they are responsible for. It is important to ensure that, when buying the individual collections, the overall look is consistent with the trend. For example, in Selfridges' Contemporary Menswear department brands change frequently and lines *must* be 'cutting edge' to be truly contemporary. The objective is to seek the next big brand and to stock it exclusively. Selfridges & Co. achieved this with the launch of Miu Miu Menswear, a diffusion brand from the large Italian fashion house of Prada, in the spring of 1999. This added value to the Selfridges retail brand and the retailer gained 'kudos' and (lifestyle) publicity for being the exclusive stockist.

Menswear is split into four main areas: contemporary, casual, formal wear and accessories. For the purposes of buying and merchandising, each of these is further reduced into distinct product areas.

This buying strategy is similar for the Selfridges stores in both London and Manchester, and whether in areas of fashion or homeware. To provide a focus, we will consider Casual and Contemporary Menswear and the merchandising that is undertaken in these areas. Concentrating on this segment of the merchandise (and the store) allows us to look in greater detail and so helps the reader to understand what has taken place and why.

Merchandising

Merchandisers and buyers closely interact and work together in teams based around the various departments. In Menswear, a planning manager oversees the strategy for all four departments, but takes no part in the buying function. Each department has a buyer manager and a separate buyer. Menswear, for example, is divided into two teams: Casual-Contemporary and Formal-Accessories. As the department's merchandise is usually complementary, pairing is a cost-effective method of dealing with diverse ranges.

The three primary issues for the merchandiser are space, budgets and stock levels. As retail space is always at a premium, the merchandiser must use the space as effectively as possible. This task is more often than not numerically driven as the merchandiser employs previous sales figures and recommendations from the buyers to allocate space in the departments for different brands. As the allocation of space impacts on the store's image and atmosphere, decisions of this type are critical and made with precision. Using a space plan, sometimes called a Planogram, the allocation of merchandise is carefully determined by variables such as brand, price, lifestyle and gender. The role of the merchandiser is thus crucial to the success of the store's performance.

It is the merchandiser's role to allocate funds for the purchase of stock (each brand carried) from the departmental budget. Considering the space allocated, and the amount spent on stock, merchandisers set performance targets for each brand. Merchandisers are also responsible for stock control, and set and adjust model stock levels based on sales performance. As departments are obliged to achieve overall margins for a season, merchandisers must work closely with buyers.

There are two factors affecting the buying strategy at Selfridges: commercial and creative. The commercial side is vital for the company to be financially viable in order to give the shareholders a return on their investment.

For the company to be successful, both the commercial and creative aspects of buying strategy must be fulfilled. Creativity plays a large role in reinforcing Selfridges new brand image. This is especially true in high profile departments such as Contemporary Fashion. The following briefly discusses the four areas that make up the Contemporary Menswear Department.

Contemporary is the cutting edge of fashion and concerned with the current season's trends. It is subdivided into three classes, the first being contemporary collections, which has the greatest space allocation. Brands include Dries Van Noten, Neil Barrett and Dolce & Gabbana. These are mainline catwalk collections (designer's premier collection), more exclusive and therefore carry a higher mark up. Contemporary sports, including designer denim from Versace Jeans Couture and D & G Jeans, are diffusion lines. Other mainline themes appeal to a broader market, with a lower price tag to match. There is also a third class known as 'urban spirit' or 'streetwear', which portrays a young street image for followers of this trend. Brands in this area include Carhartt, Firetrap and cult labels such as Evisu and Confused. A large part of the contemporary collection remains the same year on year.

We now consider the second area of change and element of Selfridges' strategy, which we have termed 'the Selfridges experience'.

The Selfridges experience

Selfridges' brand identity depends on many factors, including its store image, the high class brands it stocks and the design of its stores. The two factors comprising merchandise (brands) and store design help to construct the store's image. Selfridges aim to be the best in Europe and to help achieve this aim they have created a distinction in the service they provide. Interior and exterior designs project the luxury upscale images that the Selfridges customer has come to expect. Shopping at Selfridges is more than just buying items, it is an exceptional experience for the customer (Nelson, 2000). The personal contact provided by the sales staff (or associates) helps to achieve this.

Personal selling

Sales associates are key to maintaining brand effectiveness, as they are the 'face of the company' and everything they do will reflect upon the image of Selfridges. They are the front line employees who make contact with the customer and provide the service expected when shopping at Selfridges. For Selfridges' customers, front line employees are an important part of the overall image of the store and, as such, are a crucial element of the brand. We can see therefore that contact personnel are an important component of image.

To foster the quality impressions necessary, the company funds a scheme designed to maintain high levels of customer service, which focuses on personal development and performance. Commission-based incentives motivate staff to increase sales, but do not always lead to good customer service.

Personal shoppers

This takes the idea of one-to-one service to the next level. Conceived in the US, this new customer service practice uses personal shopping suites and a team of personal shoppers who specialize in fashion or interiors. This service allows the customer to relax with a drink while the personal shopper shops for them. Records of the customer's details, e.g. tastes, clothing sizes and budget, are in place for future visits. The personal shopping service is free of charge and all the customer pays for is the product they purchase or services they consume. In the London store, the personal shopper will help the customer to produce a menu for a special occasion. Selfridges' chefs then prepare the food that is then delivered to the customer when required.

It is important to attract the types of customers into the store that reinforce the brand identity. TV celebrities and football players are regular customers, and these facts are reported widely in the press. Such events maintain and enhance the image of the Selfridges company, which is then linked in the customer's mind to the rich and famous. The in-store social environment is thus combined with the physical characteristics (i.e. layout and design) to support brand identity and encourage customers to buy more.

As we discussed, the type of customer varies between the Manchester and London store locations. This is important as customer profile is linked to brand image, and what attracts one type of customer may not necessarily attract the other. In general, the Selfridges customers have similar characteristics, but differ in a number of ways.

London

The Oxford Street site has been open for over 90 years and the market has changed quite dramatically since it first opened. Today, the store attracts a younger and more affluent type of person. Selfridges now views itself as a store for all customer types, but the stock, store design and atmosphere are predominantly aimed at a younger, more fashionable market. The customer base in the London store can be divided into two distinct groups: locals and tourists. These can be socially classified as ABC1 using the ACORN (A Classification of Residential Neighbourhoods, 1993 – produced by CACI Information Services Ltd based on the 1991 Census data) model (Table 5.1).

Table 5.1 An adaptation of the ACORN 1993 model (based on the 1991 Census data, produced by CACI Information Services Ltd) for Selfridges' London store

Grouping	
A	• Wealthy achievers, suburban areas • Affluent greys, rural areas • Prosperous pensioners, retirement areas
B	• Affluent executives, family areas • Well-off workers, family areas
C	• Affluent urbanites, town and city areas • Prosperous professionals, metropolitan areas • Better off executives, inner city areas

The majority of Selfridges' customers fall into the B and C categories in the ACORN model, due mainly to the appeal of the brands sold in the stores. This grouping is also attracted by the store design and atmospherics that specifically target the profiles who shop at the Oxford Street store. The earlier refurbishment programme ensured that the decor and layouts matched customers' expectations, both local and tourist. The latter form a major customer group who come from all over the world and consider London's leading department stores a major tourist attraction. Whilst Harrods with the green and gold lifestyle symbols remains the first stop for tourists, Selfridges is becoming more popular with its distinctive yellow and black trade mark.

Manchester

Selfridges' second store is quite different in size, make up and customer profile. Firstly, Manchester does not enjoy the level of tourist trade that exists in London. However, since its opening, the Trafford Centre, where Selfridges is situated, has gained in popularity and people have started to visit the centre from all over the country. In part, this is the result of the attention it has received from the British television daily documentary programme 'Shopping City'.

Research had identified four key groups of customers which, as in London, fell into the ABC1 categories using the ACORN model. These groups were identified as follows: Affluent country set, young families, young affluents, and village people. The last group does not fit into one or the other category but all categories and is therefore not specified in Table 5.2.

Selfridges targeted these groups when the Manchester store opened in 1998. We can see from the tables that London and Manchester customers share similar characteristics. Customers in London generally have higher disposable incomes than Manchester. This differential, and the fact that tastes in fashion and popular trends in Manchester differ, has presented some important challenges to the Manchester store management.

Selfridges aim to distinguish themselves from the competition through providing an innovative customer service style that is tailored to individual customer needs. This means moving away from the cultural and social imperative that the more customers spend the better the service they receive.

Table 5.2 An adaptation of the ACORN 1993 model (based on the 1991 Census data, produced by CACI Information Services Ltd) for Selfridge's Manchester store

Grouping	
Affluent country set A	• Working empty nesters with high disposable incomes • Women in this group tend to work part time and are married to wealthy professional men • They live in the rural outskirts of large cities
Young families B	• Young professionals who intend starting a family in the near future or are with young children • They live in suburban areas on the edges of Manchester and although they do not have the highest disposable income they like the finer things in life
Young affluent(s) C	• Generally graduates, young professionals or middle management • Single or living with their partner, no children and a high disposable income • They live in the city as urban space as a residential area

The personal shopping service has helped to move the company away from this ethos. If Selfridges wished to build a brand that provided for everybody then the levels of service must be the same for all customers.

Creative services

The repositioning of Selfridges required many changes to the structure of the company. Two important functions and drivers of these changes are brand marketing and creative services. The latter oversees the running of promotions, advertising and window displays. Their task is to work with the visual merchandising to create the Selfridges atmosphere, which involves dressing mannequins and rearranging floor layouts. By definition, this also involves managing or tuning the internal atmosphere of the store, and maintaining the brand image. Designs and colour schemes target the customer profiles and help to create the renowned atmosphere of the store. It is these cues that customers respond to when browsing and choosing merchandise, and when they think of the Selfridges name. One of the most important changes surrounded the company logo and the colours used on the all-important carrier bags. From the plain blue on a white background, the new logo declares 'Selfridges & Co.' in solid bold black on a yellow background. These and other visual cues can be grouped into three distinct and overlapping areas: architecture, visual merchandising and promotion. All three are created so they fit in with the new brand image.

Architecture

A store's exterior and interior look is often referred to as the architecture, and comprises aspects such as building materials, architectural style, colours and textures. As discussed in an earlier section, today's trends require that original architecture is restored and contemporary designs employed to enhance it, rather than mask it. The Selfridges London store is a remarkable piece of architecture. Working with exciting designers and architects, the fabric was refurbished to help create the new brand image. Internally, Ladies' Contemporary Wear, for example, is built round the principle of a gallery and clothes are displayed as pieces of art. An internal feature called 'Design Lab' presented a new concept that encouraged experimentation with a clinical look in pure white. Outside the Selfridges Oxford Street building, the plan is to clean and restore the façade as part of the final stage of the store refurbishment. The store will then be wrapped in a giant canvas (by the artist Sam Taylor Wood) featuring a number of celebrities. Such internal and external displays are vital and reinforce the overall image of the retailer, which is associated with upbeat lifestyle symbols. External window displays and internal arrangements of merchandise are an important and integral part of this effect.

Visual merchandising

As discussed, visual merchandising comprises five components: image, layout, presentation, signage and displays. Everything you undertake within the store, such as how you develop your layout, presentation or signage, must fit into the image you choose to create. At Selfridges, the visual merchandising team is responsible for the ever-changing merchandise arrangements and displays of the two stores.

The Manchester store was built with flexibility in mind, and style and layout of the interior can be readily altered. Wall-mounted fixtures can be rearranged with ease and walls painted. Selfridges has found that wood effects are now unsuitable for their stores because the style created through the use of wood does not reinforce the brand image. For the past decade, pale woods have been the height of fashion, but tastes change. To keep the look up to date requires flexibility as fixtures that look dated have a detrimental effect on the brand image. Plaster walls mean that a quick change of colour is possible. For example, when bright colours are in fashion the walls are painted white. White complements bright colours and allows brand names to stand out. Research suggests that colour affects buyer behaviour in retail environments (Bitner, 1992) and can lead to higher conversion rates. Separate teams design and create the displays in the store windows.

Stores have become famous for the windows that they create. Harrods and Bloomindales, for example, have made great impressions in the past. With the recent exception of Harvey Nichols, inspiring window displays have been in short supply. Window displays may be classed as art not just as promotional tools. The message behind these windows is not a simple issue, and displays have been influenced by many different styles over the years. One Selfridges' technique is to place products in a scene rather than just placing them on display. Window displays then appear similar to a magazine lifestyle shoot. Similar window displays using live models appeared on the opening day of the Manchester store. Selfridges have been able to use their window displays as a method of defining the new brand image and the continued reinforcement of that image.

Promotion

Selfridges have never needed to advertise, as their customers were aware of the store and what it offered. After refurbishment and the complete repositioning of the company's image, it was necessary to tell the public what changes had been made (Spitzer, 1982). In Manchester, the location of Selfridges' second store opening, most potential customers were unaware of what the store now had to offer. Moreover, as these customers had different profiles this fact had to be taken into consideration.

An advertising campaign reinforced the 'everybody is welcome' philosophy and to explain the diverse range of brands available in the store. New adverts are 'more intelligent'. There are four different images in the campaign, all similar to one another in style. As before, the adverts all show the diversity of products available and the bright contemporary image represents the style of the brand. Selfridges adopt campaigns for each season to keep pace with changing consumer needs and secure customer loyalty. Regular promotion keeps the brand fresh and alive in the mind of the customer, making it more attractive than the competition.

Summary

In summary, this chapter set out to explain the methods used to re-energize a famous fashion brand. With such an important brand name as Selfridges, which has a worldwide reputation, images about the nature of the in-store merchandise stocked and the type of customers who shop in the store were already firmly placed in the mind of the consumer. The key aim of the re-branding exercise was therefore to change that perception, and re-position the store in the customer's mind. Selfridges accomplished this by targeting the three areas that most influenced their business: buying strategy, customer service and creative services. However, the increasing importance of the Internet and home shopping may well alter Selfridges' future strategy, and the areas of the business they target.

Internet shopping has global appeal and is likely to enjoy an increasing share of the British retail marketplace over the next decade. For the retailer of fashion and luxury brands, the Internet offers some intriguing possibilities and demands new approaches. For example, how can fashion retail websites offer the tactile information that consumers tend to use when purchasing high quality fashion garments? More importantly, does the purchase of expensive fashion brands necessitate the right type of atmosphere, which an Internet-based site can only hint at? Apart from the colours and general layout, all websites offer similar interfaces. That is, the entry or doorway into virtual stores is much the same. Similarly, the manner in which the goods or merchandise are collected for purchasing usually takes the form of a shopping basket. New approaches may be needed to accommodate the luxury fashion market, with websites that offer mood-inducing properties consistent with the retailer's image. For this to work, the retailer's website must become an integral part of the brand, and offer comparable levels of excitement and experience for consumers.

References

Bitner, M. J. (1992). Servicescapes: the impact of physical surroundings on customers and employees. *Journal of Marketing*, **56** (April), 57–71.

Finch, J. (2000). Selfridges proposes new London landmark. *The Guardian*, 17 February.

Jobber, D. (1998). *Principles and Practice of Marketing*, 2nd Edn. London: McGraw-Hill.

Kotler, P. (1974). Store atmospherics as a marketing tool. *Journal of Retailing*, **49** (Winter), 48–65.

McGoldrick, P. J. (1990). *Retail Marketing*. London: McGraw-Hill.

Nelson, F. (2000). Selfridges is aiming higher. *The Times*, 17 February.

Sabbagh, D. (2000). Selfridges moves into Birmingham. *Daily Telegraph*, 17 February.

Spitzer, H. (1982) *Inside Retail Sales Promotions & Advertising*. New York: Harper & Row.

Tolman, R. (1974). *Fashion Marketing and Merchandising*. Bronx, New York: Milady.

6

Store environment of fashion retailers: a Hong Kong perspective

Alice W. C. Chu and M. C. Lam

Introduction

To survive into and through the next decade, the retail store environment should be better designed, and focused on continuous improvement so as to provide a desirable store environment where consumers want to be during shopping.

Many apparel retailers realize that the design of store environment is an important element of marketing strategy; retailers strive to develop consumer-oriented store environments, which have been identified as a potential competitive advantage. They strive for a differential advantage on variables that are most likely to be store-choice factors as determined by the expectations of consumers in the target market. No wonder many fashion retailers spend millions of dollars periodically designing and refurbishing their stores, because the central challenge lies in understanding the needs of consumers, and hence providing the store environment that appeals to consumers' needs.

With rescheduling of spending priorities and amounts in clothing, consumers are changing the amount of time spent on shopping. Recent research showed that the average time people in the US spend shopping has been declining; the cardinal rule among fashion retailers has been to try to keep customers in the store as long as possible. In this connection, retailers should provide the store environment that makes shopping convenient, relaxing and fun, instead of merely providing racks of clothing for consumers to choose from in the store (Reda, 1997). Otherwise, consumers can use their limited time for other leisure activities which are more enjoyable and satisfying if they find shopping is boring.

Regarding the situation in Hong Kong, it is becoming increasingly difficult for apparel retailers to differentiate their stores solely on the basis of merchandise, price, promotion or location. Hong Kong has been well known internationally as the sourcing centre for most fashion retailers overseas. With the advance in production skills and quick response techniques, clothing styles are easily copied once they have proved to be successful in the retail market. In addition, Hong Kong is just a small city where shops are clustered together; shoppers can easily buy their clothes at a reasonable price by just doing comparison shopping of the nearby stores. Since Hong Kong customers still rank shopping as their favourite pastime, a retailer should provide a retail environment which can lure these customers to enter. Thus, the unique environment offered may be influential to the consumer's store choice decision (Darden et al., 1983). Furthermore, a store's environmental design is particularly important for retailers when the number of competitive outlets increases, or when product entries are aimed at distinct social classes or lifestyle buyer groups. In a study of department store image in Hong Kong and Shanghai, it was revealed that a store's atmospheric design is one of the elements which develop a 'sense of prestigious and high quality' (Chan and Leung, 1996). This indicated that store environment affects the store choice of customers in the upscale market segment.

The purpose of this chapter is to review some of the basic concepts on retail store environment and how Hong Kong consumers react to the retail store environment. A research finding on several Hong Kong casualwear chain stores is included. Results show that social factor in store atmospherics is relatively important compared with other factors such as ambience and function. This is not to say that physical facilities and aesthetic elements are not important in a fashion store environment, rather it indicates that fashion shoppers in Hong Kong are more sensitive to the presence of personnel in the store.

Background

Some retailers can perform well in the competitive fashion retail industry, while some are merely struggling for survival. The reason is that the successful retailers really understand what is the real meaning of 'value' in the consumer's mind. However, many retailers wrongly assume that value means price. Value is the total experience, it means the benefits received from purchasing. Those benefits include pleasant store environment, good sales-people service, convenience and quality merchandise. Clearly, price is not equivalent to value, it is just part of the value (Berry, 1996). It implies that not all purchasers are price conscious; some of them are willing to pay more to those stores where the store has nicely displayed merchandise, has a tidy and clean shopping floor together with good customer services, or simply a favourable overall store environment.

Much research has shown that at a time when retailers are finding it difficult to obtain a competitive advantage on the basis of price, promotion and store location, store environment becomes an opportunity for market differentiation (Ward et al., 1992; Kenhove and Desrumaux, 1997). An appropriate store environment catering for the needs of consumers makes for a pleasurable shopping experience. Some researchers found that consumers stayed longer in a shop with a pleasant environment and spent more money than originally planned (Donovan et al., 1994). Keller (1987) also pointed out that many consumers make decisions at the point of purchase, so the store environment can affect people's purchasing behaviour. Most shoppers have shared the experience that, irrespective of the merchandise offered, some stores are more attractive than others, some stores induce a feeling of relaxation, while others may make one feel uncomfortable, or even irritated. Consumers tend to buy more things and spend more money when in a positive rather than a negative store environment. In addition to affecting store patronage choice, a store which has a favourable environment can also achieve a higher customer loyalty (Darden et al., 1983), as well as affecting perceived store image (Lindquist, 1974; Zimmer and Golden, 1988).

The importance of the store and its environment becomes evident when one realizes that 70–80% of customer purchase decisions are finalized when consumers are in the store inspecting the merchandise (Schlossberg, 1992). An appropriately designed store environment where there is good merchandise and services offered can be a powerful means for providing a pleasant shopping experience for consumers, and enables the retailer to obtain a competitive advantage over its competitors. This is the reason why store environment is becoming an increasingly important issue in retail marketing management and retail marketing research. In the past, many retailers took their customers for granted; they merely provided generic goods without much emphasis on store environment. Nowadays, drawing customers into the store and providing a place where they can browse comfortably is the latest strategy which retailers and brand owners are using to enrich consumers' shopping experience.

The consumer's definition of value changes over time, and it can be affected by their past purchase experiences and individual factors such as innate personal needs. Thus, continuous enquiry about the consumer's needs and expectations in the store environment is required. Consumer satisfaction is a function of the closeness between expectations and the store's perceived performance. If the store environment falls short of consumer expectations, the consumer is disappointed; if it meets consumer's expectations, the consumer is satisfied.

In other words, if the perceived store environment can meet their expectations, consumer satisfaction results. Consumers who are satisfied with a retailer may tell an average of five other people, whereas dissatisfied consumers will talk to two or three times more people they meet (Waldrop, 1991), and may never return to the store again. Obviously, the key element to the success of a retailer lies in their ability to identify and define their consumers, and hence cater to their preferences and needs in a distinctive manner (Berman and Evans, 1995).

Store environment

Store environment is critical to a retailer, because it directly affects consumers' total shopping experience. It is also a determining factor in affecting consumers' store choice decision for shopping. Hence, the management of the physical environment is considered as an important element in contributing to a retailer's financial success and a valuable shopping experience for consumers (Eroglu and Machleit, 1993).

The concept of 'atmospherics' was first introduced by Kotler (1973), where a store's atmosphere is defined as the effort to design buying environments to produce specific emotional effects in the buyer that enhance purchase probability. In-store environmental stimuli are positively related to the level of pleasure experienced in the store (Tai and Fung, 1997). Positive store environmental elements can induce a positive experience with the store, and finally contribute to a pleasant response of consumers.

Donovan and Rossiter (1982), using the Mehrabian–Russell environmental psychology model (Mehrabian and Russell, 1974), specified that a store's environmental stimuli can affect the consumer's emotional states of pleasure and arousal, which further affects approach or avoidance behaviours in purchasing. Pleasure refers to the degree to which the consumers feel good, happy, satisfied and joyful in the store environment. Arousal refers to the degree to which consumers feel in control of, or free to act in, the environment. Baker et al. (1992) indicate that, when ambient cues interact with social cues, it can affect consumers' emotional states of pleasure, while social cues influence arousal in the store environment.

More recently, Darden and Babin (1994) indicated that store environment has an emotion-inducing capability. A positive emotion-inducing store can contribute to a consumer's pleasurable shopping experience; stores with courteous and friendly personnel are associated with high levels of pleasure. On the other hand, overcrowded stores are associated with low levels of pleasure.

An elaborate positive store environment can be an effective tool to evoke a consumer's emotion of pleasure or arousal. A positive store environment helps to foster goal attainment, more consumers in a pleasant store environment can easily achieve their goal, and hence attain a pleasurable shopping experience (Spies et al., 1997). Shoppers reporting relatively high pleasure, for example, also report correspondingly high customer satisfaction (Dawson et al., 1990). Thus, there is an important interaction between store characteristics, consumer's mood and satisfaction.

As Parasuraman et al. (1990) noted, consumers compare tangibles of a store with what they think a store should look like. Satisfaction with the store can be increased by minimizing the gap between customers' perceptions and expectations. When expectations were not met, consumers experienced disconfirmation (Churchill and Surprenaut, 1982) and consequently dissatisfaction. If the perception matches the expectations, the customer is satisfied. If the performance exceeds expectations, the customer is delighted and highly satisfied.

Satisfaction can help consumers to identify that a store is worthy of their loyalty. Shopping tends to be a leisure activity and consumers want the shopping experience to deliver something emotional or pleasurable to them (Bromley and Thomas, 1993). Successful retailers need to identify and respond to consumers' expectations (Smith, 1997). There is no doubt that shoppers nowadays want to gain enjoyment and satisfaction when spending their precious time shopping; retailers should therefore acquire a better understanding of consumers' expectation regarding a store's environment.

Store atmospherics

The influence of retail store environments on consumer perceptions and behaviour is a topic that has received relatively little attention since Kotler (1973) introduced the concept of 'atmospherics'. Many researchers became aware of the importance of store environment in creating a differential or competitive advantage in the retailing industry. Researchers started to study a store's influence on shopping behaviour. Consumer satisfaction with the store is greater in a pleasant store environment; customers spontaneously spent more money on merchandise they simply liked if the store environment was pleasant (Spies et al., 1997). Other marketing scholars and practitioners have focused their investigations on the influence of specific atmospheric elements, such as music, social factors or lighting, on shopping behaviour, and the degree of consumer satisfaction and loyalty (Bellizzi et al., 1983; Baker et al., 1992).

Some researchers shifted emphasis to the sensory information of store environmental cues relating cognitive or affective states which can affect shopping behaviours and consumers' product perception (Gardner and Siomkos, 1985). More recent study shows that ambient and social elements in the store environment are more likely to affect consumers to make inferences about merchandise and service quality, and these inferences, in turn, influence store image (Baker et al., 1994). Baker (1986), in her research on the store atmosphere, has developed a three-category framework of store environment, namely store ambient factor, store design factor and store social factor, for evaluating store atmospherics.

Store ambient factor

The ambient factor refers to the background characteristics of the environment that tend to influence consumers at a subconscious level (Campbell, 1983). This includes elements such as temperature, lighting, music and scent (Ward and Russell, 1981; Wineman, 1982; Milliman, 1982; Yalch and Spangenberg, 1990).

All of these elements can profoundly affect how people feel, think and respond to a particular store establishment, and exist below the level of customers' immediate awareness. As a general rule, ambient conditions influence the five senses (Zeithaml and Bitner, 1996). According to Davidson et al. (1988), the ambient factor is felt more than it can be seen and measured.

Ambient conditions are especially noticeable to consumers in extreme circumstances. Undesirable ambient conditions can cause dissatisfaction if the attention of consumers is heightened. For example, a store where the air conditioning has failed, and the air is hot and stuffy, will heighten a consumer's awareness, and dissatisfaction may result. Instead of taking more time to shop, consumers who feel uncomfortable may hurry to make their intended purchases and leave the store (Botlen, 1988).

Background music that is soothing can create a pleasurable atmosphere (Milliman, 1982). Also, soft lighting can create a more pleasant and relaxing mood than using bright lighting (Meer, 1985). Noise that is too loud may make a shopper feel annoyed, and the glare of lighting may lower the consumer's ability to see and cause physical discomfort. Just like noise, unfavourable scent can actually drive consumers away from the store. All these ambient elements can influence whether people stay in or enjoy the store environment.

Store design factor

The design factor refers to a store's environmental elements that are more perceptible in nature than ambient factors. These elements can be aesthetic and/or functional in nature (Marans and Spreckelmeyer, 1982).

Functional elements in stores include layout, comfort and privacy. Aesthetic elements include such factors as architecture, materials, colour and merchandise display; they can contribute to consumers' pleasure in shopping (Baker, 1986). Layout is functional in nature; it helps to route consumers through the entire store in search of merchandise. A wide and uncrowded aisle can also create a better atmosphere than narrow and crowded ones.

Merchandise displays can also be an important aid in helping consumers to make purchase decisions (Dunne et al., 1990). Some apparel consumers regard the dressing room and its facilities as major elements in store selection (Berman and Evans, 1995). As the trend of the store environment becomes more minimalist, the emphasis on the fixtures and fittings will become obvious (Zachary, 1998). Merchandise fixtures help to show the merchandise to consumers, as well as playing a secondary role of aesthetic function. Also, an attractive floor might have considerable aesthetic appeal to consumers (Diamond, 1993).

The design factor is at the forefront of consumers' awareness; it is more visible and perceptible than the ambient factor as consumers can evaluate more easily what they see. The design factor serves as a facilitator in aiding the performances of both employee and consumers in the store, because a well-designed and functional store can help people to be orientated and to find their way. Consumers can more easily locate and obtain the required merchandise/services (Bitner, 1992). It also helps to improve efficiency and user satisfaction (Greenland and McGoldrick, 1994), and encourages people to browse and look into every corner rather than just standing in the store. If consumers can easily satisfy their goals, the feeling of a pleasurable shopping experience will be enhanced.

Store social factor

The social factor involves people who are present in the store environment. Russell and Snodgrass (1987) note that the number, type and behaviour of both consumers and salespeople are included as elements of the social factor.

Inadequate salespeople can make consumers feel annoyed when they are required to wait for service. Salespeople's performance can also greatly affect consumer (dis)satisfaction. Consumers will evaluate salesperson services based on the personal expectations that they bring to the service encounter (Crosby and Cowles, 1986). As consumers' expectations increase, they expect salespeople to have a deeper product knowledge, and to be reliable and responsive to consumers' needs (Kotler et al., 1996). Frontline employees are assumed by consumers to be not only salespeople, but also consultants (Lovelock, 1991).

In a clothing store, consumers may ask salespeople for suggestions on merchandise selection. Conversations between salespeople and consumers frequently occur in the retail environment (Harris et al., 1995; McGrath and Otnes, 1995). A positive impact of the conversations between consumers and salespeople can achieve consumer satisfaction, which has been well researched and documented (Bitner et al., 1990; Harris et al., 1997).

Research has revealed that one of the three most important factors influencing repeat purchases at a new store was 'helpful personnel' (Schneiderman, 1997). Good salesperson service is about providing the consumer with an efficient, positive and enjoyable purchasing experience (Livingstone, 1997). Similarly, attractive appearance and pleasant behaviour of salespeople can greatly enhance the service experience (Baker, 1986).

The social factor has also been investigated in terms of other consumers in the store, which is exemplified by research on crowding (Harrell et al., 1980). The number of consumers inside a store can have an impact on the shopping experience. Overcrowded stores are associated with low levels of pleasure of consumers (Darden and Babin, 1994).

A consumer in a crowded store finds shopping less enjoyable (Andreoli, 1996). Within a crowded environment, consumers restrict themselves to interacting with salespeople, are less likely to engage in exploratory shopping and will postpone any unnecessary purchase. The behaviour of consumers also affects the experience. A store with ill-mannered consumers would deter shoppers from coming into the store.

A crowded store can also lead to avoidance behaviour, because shoppers perceive that crowdedness can restrict task performance within a store (Stokols, 1976). Mackintosh et al. (1975) found that respondents performing an experiment in overcrowded conditions described themselves as 'tense' or 'confused', whereas positive feelings such as 'pleased' or 'relaxed' were found in less crowded conditions. This showed that physical density and crowdedness may influence consumers' level of satisfaction (Harrell et al., 1980).

Store environment is the overall aesthetic and emotional effect created by the store's physical environment; it is the total sensory experience created by the store. Today's shoppers, regardless of their shopping motives, are more attracted by safe, attractive and comfortable shopping environments. Therefore, a store environment should be tailored to the psychological and physical needs of consumers by creating a focused collection of sensory impressions and shopping experiences (Sullivan, 1992).

An appropriately designed store environment is about providing the consumers with a positive, efficient and enjoyable purchasing experience. Darden and Babin (1994) indicated that store environment has the capability of inducing an effect. A good mood-inducing store will lead to a good shopping experience, which will contribute to positive effects on shopping intentions (Swinyard, 1993).

Store design in the 1980s, with the emphasis on opulence, image and consumption, seems to be outdated (Goldman, 1991). The biggest challenges faced by today's apparel retailers is integrating fashion elements into the lives of consumers and finding ways to make the shopping experience both efficient and entertaining (Reda, 1997).

Retailers now delight in learning more about their target customers than ever before in providing a store environment which can please every possible demand. They want store designs to be flexible enough to respond to changes in merchandise and consumer demographics, as well as being functional and beautiful (Lewison, 1994). Since most store designs are being 'tailored' for this new generation of shoppers, continuous investigation into consumers' needs in the store environment is required.

Current study on the importance of store environment to consumer's casualwear fashion store choice decision in Hong Kong

Importance of store environment to consumer's store choice decision

Using Baker's three-category framework, research was conducted in 1998 in Hong Kong to explore the importance of store environment to consumer's store choice decision. More than 90% of respondents in Hong Kong agreed that store environment is important in affecting their store selection.

Based on the result obtained, the social factor is most important in allowing consumers to have a pleasurable shopping experience. The design factor was perceived as second and the ambient factor third.

Relative importance of elements of the three factors

For the ambient factor, the tidiness of the store was regarded as the most important element in maintaining good ambient conditions. Other remaining elements – lighting, music, scent, temperature and noise level – were of less concern.

For the design factor, most respondents regarded store size as the most important element. The next most important element was also related to size – the size of the fitting room.

For the social factor, a large proportion of respondents considered 'service manner of salespeople' as the most important element in this category. 'Number of people in the store' was also considered as important.

Consumers' expectations on store environment

Nine expectations on store environment, labelled as (1) comfortableness, (2) number and nature of people, (3) recognition by identifiable salespeople, (4) courteous and friendly salespeople, (5) spacious environment, (6) non-irritating environment, (7) minimalist environment, (8) fixtures and displays, and (9) merchandise suggestions, were found.

'Comfortableness' refers to the size of the fitting room, chair availability inside the fitting room, aisle width, clear merchandise arrangement, noise level, temperature and tidiness of the store.

'Number and nature of people' refers to the number and types of customers, as well as the adequacy of salespeople. This includes not only the variables related to the number of consumers and salespeople in the store, but also the nature of shoppers. Shoppers expected that other customers in the store would not be ill-mannered.

'Recognition by identifiable salespeople' suggests that salespeople should wear clothes with similar style and colour, provide proper greetings and wear a name badge. By greeting and saying goodbye to consumers, salespeople can give consumers a feeling that they are recognized and also give them a sense of respect.

'Courteous and friendly salespeople' shows that the attributes of friendliness, courtesy and responsiveness of salespeople are applied.

'Spacious environment' refers to large store size, chairs for resting, large signage and modern window displays.

'Non-irritating environment' of the store refers to store lighting, music and scent.

'Minimalist environment' refers to the background colour (light) and theme colour of the store (white).

'Fixtures and displays' illustrate that merchandise is displayed with hanger appeal, and the use of wooden fixtures was expected by the respondents.

Subsequently, a cluster analysis was employed to see which of the nine expectation dimension(s) was (were) important to each cluster. The largest cluster, comprising a total of 61.3% of respondents, indicated that consumers have a high expectation regarding the social factor.

Most popular casualwear chain store

In order to obtain additional information of consumers' expectations on store environment, respondents were asked to rank four casualwear chain stores in Hong Kong in terms of the most satisfying store environment. The four stores were: (1) Bossini; (2) Esprit; (3) Giordano; (4) U2.

Table 6.1 illustrates that over 70% of respondents were mostly satisfied with the store environment of Esprit. The second most favourable store was U2, with over 50% of respondents ranking this as the second best store environment among the four stores. The third ranked store was Giordano, with a total of 42.8% of respondents rating the store environment in third position. The fourth was Bossini; respondents were comparatively less satisfied with this store environment, with over 55% of respondents ranking it as the least satisfying of the four stores.

Favourable store environment and pleasant shopping experience

A majority of respondents agreed that a favourable store environment could lead them to have a pleasant shopping experience. Over 99% of respondents considered that a favourable store environment could achieve a pleasant shopping experience. Less than 1% of respondents denied that store environment could lead them to have a pleasant shopping experience.

Table 6.1 Ranking of the store environment among four stores

Ranking	Bossini (%)	Esprit (%)	Giordano (%)	U2 (%)
1st	4.8	74.3	9.3	11.6
2nd	16.1	8.2	26.0	50.7
3rd	24.0	7.2	42.8	25.0
4th	55.1	10.3	21.9	12.7
Total	100	100	100	100

Conclusion

The results of this study suggest that store environment is relatively important in affecting consumers' store choice decision when comparing it with other factors such as store location, merchandise assortment and product price. This implies that not all consumers are price conscious; they are willing to select the store for shopping, or just going into the store for browsing if there is a desirable store environment.

According to Zeithaml and Bitner (1996), a well designed and functional servicescape can give consumers a pleasant experience. The present study shows that the majority of respondents agreed that a satisfying store environment could create a pleasurable shopping experience. It is quite clear that the social factor was most important to consumers in leading them to have a pleasurable shopping experience, in comparison with the ambient and design factors.

As noted by Darden and Babin (1994), stores with courteous and friendly personnel correlated with high levels of pleasure to the consumer. This result shows that the 'service manner of salespeople' is the most important element of the social factor in affecting their perception of a pleasant shopping experience, with the social factor regarded by respondents as the most important factor in their having a pleasurable shopping experience.

On the other hand, tidiness of the store was the most important element of the ambient factor, whereas store size was the most important element of the design factor in leading consumers to have a pleasurable shopping experience. Apparently, the ambient and design factors were comparatively less important than the social factor in the consumer's mind. Nevertheless, this does not mean that the above two factors can be ignored; we can only say that these two factors were relatively less sensitive to consumers in helping them to achieve a pleasurable shopping experience.

The results also show that consumers' expectations on the store environment could be further divided into the following nine dimensions: (1) comfortableness; (2) number and nature of people; (3) recognition by identifiable salespeople; (4) courteous and friendly salespeople; (5) spacious environment; (6) non-irritating environment; (7) minimalist environment; (8) fixtures and displays; (9) merchandise suggestions. The results further show the detailed dimensions of consumers' expectations on the store environment. The result of cluster analysis indicated that most of the respondents had expectations regarding the social factor. This implies that salespeople should be rich in product knowledge, and hence that they can be assured of providing quality service, as well as giving individualized suggestions on merchandise selection for each consumer. As Berry (1996) noted, consumers nowadays are concerned with respectful service offered by retailers; they expect salespeople to treat them like royalty, with courtesy, a friendly service attitude and a welcome on their arrival.

More specifically, a satisfying store environment can lead consumers to achieve a pleasant shopping experience. Store environment stimuli can affect consumers' emotional states of pleasure (Mehrabian and Russell, 1974). It is certain that a positive store environment can be an effective tool in evoking the consumer's emotion of pleasure.

Recommendations

Among those areas which consumers would like stores to further improve is the social factor – the service manner of salespeople. This also proves that consumers definitely regard the social factor as relatively more important than the other two factors, and they also have higher expectations in this area. The result supports respondents' concerns on the social factor of a store's environment.

Management of casualwear chain stores will not be surprised to learn that the social factor contributed greatly in achieving consumers' pleasant shopping experience. A desirable store environment can be an important element of achieving a pleasant shopping experience. This influence is likely to be especially pronounced for the social factor of the store environment. Effective retailers can seek a competitive edge in providing a unique store environment that the consumers want, to satisfy their needs and enhance their shopping experience.

The results also indicate that both the ambient and design factors are perceived as less important by consumers. Marketers should be more concerned with the social factor of the store environment, especially the service attitude of salespeople. Hence, it is suggested that casualwear chain stores could provide a desirable store environment by paying more attention to the social factor. As such, special care should be taken with regard to the service manner of sales personnel.

On the other hand, whether there is an adequate number of salespeople on the shop floor can be directly controlled by the retailer. An appropriate number of sales personnel helps to provide a responsive service to consumers. An inadequate number of salespeople will keep consumers waiting for service, and consumer dissatisfaction will result. However, too many salespeople would be wastage. Retailers need to clearly identify the amount of salespeople required to maintain a frontline operation.

Particular care should also be taken by retailers of casualwear chain stores on the expectation of 'recognition by identifiable salespeople' as consumers appreciate a sense of respect by the salespeople when they enter and leave the store. 'Courteous and friendly salespeople' implies that consumers have a high expectation regarding the attitude of sales personnel. Since quality service from friendly, courteous salespeople with an appropriate service attitude does not simply happen, retailers are advised to take particular care to develop a 'service culture' within their organizations. This can enhance the employee's recognition of their responsibilities of customer service. Apart from the development of service culture in the organization, motivation can also be an effective means to achieve this aim. Undoubtedly, financial motivation, including bonuses and commission, is an important means of encouragement.

Particular care should also be taken by the retailers in training the salespeople to be more effective in their interpersonal encounters with consumers, since salespeople are required to be 'friendly and courteous' to consumers. Also, the findings show that consumers expect suggestions on merchandise selection from salespeople. It is suggested that retailers should place emphasis on continuous training of their employees, especially in the areas of being 'courteous and friendly' and having 'expertise' on the products they sell.

Provision of expert sales help can be achieved by enriching the product knowledge of salespeople. Once the salespeople possess sufficient knowledge of their merchandise, the limitations and strengths of the merchandise can be recognized by the salespeople. This enables the salespeople to be highly responsive to all kinds of consumer needs and problems, and assess the value of the merchandise, as well as offering individualized suggestions on merchandise selection. Hence, salespeople with sufficient product knowledge can make more accurate individualized suggestions on merchandise selection based on the different needs of consumers.

In order to provide individualized suggestions on merchandise selection, retailers should not overlook the listening skills of frontline employees. Salespeople who fail to be a good listener fail to understand consumers' concerns, needs, wants and preferences, and in turn fail to give consumers appropriate suggestions on merchandise selection. To fulfil the expectations of consumers, retailers should take particular care in training salespeople to be good listeners.

Although it is suggested that the store manager pays more attention to the social factor of the store environment, the ambient and design factors should not be neglected. A store can have excellent salespeople to deliver high quality service, but if the store plays unfavourable loud music, without much air conditioning and space, the overall shopping experience will be affected. Instead of staying longer in the store, consumers will leave the store as quickly as possible. Therefore, the three factors should be well co-ordinated so as to achieve a desirable result.

This study provides a new insight into the relative importance of the three environmental factors, the level of importance of the store environment in affecting consumer's store choice decisions and their expectations on store environment. The study suggests that the social factor is potentially useful in leading consumers to have a pleasant shopping experience. Therefore, during the refurbishment of the stores, retailers should set aside some financial investment to enhance the social factor of the store environment.

To conclude, fashion retailers that plan to refurbish their stores need to determine in advance the concerns, preference and expectations of the target customer regarding store environment. The better the understanding of the consumer, the better the targeted result of the refurbishment can be obtained. Store environment is just like the packaging of a product; if the package is desirable or attractive to consumers, it can largely enhance the saleability of merchandise. The 1990s were 'value driven'. Retailers are no longer taking consumers for granted; they should maximize the benefits received by consumers. Consumers want a good return on the financial investment they make in their purchasing. One of the most important benefits is a desirable store environment. Consumers, especially those for fashion and clothing, want to have a pleasant shopping experience within the store environment where they can browse and inspect merchandise freely.

References

Andreoli, T. (1996). Hassle-free service the key to repeat biz. *Discount Store News*, 6 May, p. 64. Also see: Goldberger, P. (1997). The store strikes back. *New York Times Magazine*, 8 April, 45–9.

Baker, J. (1986). The role of the environment in marketing services: the consumer perspective. In *The Services Challenge: Integrating for Competitive Advantage* (J. A. Czepeil, C. A. Congram and J. Shanahan, eds), pp. 79–84. Chicago, IL: American Marketing Association.

Baker, J., Levy, M. and Grewal, D. (1992). An experimental approach to making retail store environmental decisions. *Journal of Retailing*, **68** (Winter), 471–95.

Baker, J., Grewal, D. and Parasuraman, A. (1994). The influence of store atmosphere on customer quality perceptions and store image. *Journal of Academy of Marketing Science*, **22** (Fall), 328–39.

Bellizzi, J. A., Crowley, A. E. and Hasty, R. W. (1983). The effects of colour in store design. *Journal of Retailing*, **59** (Spring), 21–45.

Berman, B. and Evans, J. R. (1995). *Retail Management: A Strategic Approach*. Prentice Hall.

Berry, L. L. (1996). Retailers with a future: the new value equation. *Chain Store Age*, October, 4D–6D.

Bitner, M. J. (1992). Servicescapes: the impact of physical surroundings on customers and employees. *Journal of Marketing*, **56** (April), 57–71.

Bitner, M. J., Booms, B. M. and Tetreault, M. S. (1990). The service encounter: diagnosing favourable and unfavourable incidents. *Journal of Marketing*, **54** (January), 71–84.

Botlen, W. H. (1988). *Contemporary Retailing*. Prentice Hall.

Bromley, R. and Thomas, C. J. (1993). *Retail Change: Contemporary Issues*. UCL Press.

Campbell, J. M. (1983). Ambient stressors. *Environment and Behaviour*, **15** (3), 355–80.

Chan, K. K. and Leung, Y. L. (1996). *A Study of Department Store Image In Hong Kong & Shanghai*. Hong Kong Baptist University, Business Research Centre, Papers on China Series CP96015.

Churchill, G. A., Jr. and Suprenaut, C. (1982). An investigation into the determinants of customer satisfaction. *Journal of Marketing Research*, **19** (November), 491–504.

Crosby, L. A. and Cowles, D. (1986). A role consensus model of satisfaction with service interaction experiences. *Creativity in Services Marketing: What's New, What Works, What's Developing, Proceedings Series*, pp. 40–3. Chicago, IL: American Marketing Association.

Darden, W. R. and Babin, B. J. (1994). Exploring the concept of affective quality: expanding the concept of retail personality. *Journal of Business Research*, **29**, 101–9.

Darden, W. R., Erdem, O. and Darden, D. K. (1983). A comparison and test of three causal models of patronage intentions. In *Patronage Behaviour and Retail Management* (W. R. Darden and R. F. Lusch, eds), pp. 29–43. New York: North-Holland.

Davidson, W. R., Sweeney, D. J. and Stampfl, R. W. (1988). *Retailing Management*. John Wiley.

Dawson, S., Bloch, P. H. and Ridgway, N. M. (1990). Shopping motives, emotional states, and retail outcomes. *Journal of Retailing*, **66** (Winter), 408–27.

Diamond, E. (1993). *Fashion Retailing*. Delmar Publishers.

Donovan, R. J. and Rossiter, J. R. (1982). Store atmosphere: an environmental psychology approach. *Journal of Retailing*, **58** (Spring), 34–57.

Donovan, R. J., Rossiter, J. R., Marcoolyn, G. and Nesdale, A. (1994). Store atmosphere and purchasing behaviour. *Journal of Retailing*, **70** (Fall), 283–93.

Dunne, P., Lusch, R., Gable, M. and Gebhardt, R. (1990). *Retailing*. South Western Publishing.

Eroglu, S. A. and Machleit, K. (1993). Atmospheric factors in the retail environment: sights, sounds and smells. In *Advances in Consumer Research* (L. McAlister and M. L. Rothschild, eds), Vol. 20, p. 34. Provo, UT: Association for Consumer Research.

Gardner, M. P. and Siomkos, G. J. (1985). Towards a methodology for assessing effects of in-store atmosphere. In *Advances in Consumer Research* (R. Lutz, ed.), pp. 27–31. Chicago, IL: Association for Consumer Research.

Goldman, D. J. (1991). Classic designs return amid economic uncertainty. *Stores*, January, 130.

Greenland, S. J. and McGoldrick, P. J. (1994). Atmospherics, attitudes and behaviour: modelling the impact of designed space. *The International Review of Retail, Distribution and Consumer Research*, **4** (1), 1–16.

Harrell, G. D., Hutt, M. D. and Anderson, J. C. (1980). Path analysis of buyer behaviour under conditions of crowding. *Journal of Marketing Research*, **17** (February), 45–51.

Harris, K., Baron, S. and Ratcliffe, J. (1995). Customers as oral participants in a service setting. *Journal of Services Marketing*, **9** (4), 64–76.

Harris, K., Davis, B. J. and Baron, S. (1997). Conversations during purchase consideration: sales assistants and customers. *The International Review of Retail, Distribution and Consumer Research*, **7** (3), 173–90.

Keller, K. L. (1987). Memory factors in advertising: the effect of advertising retrieval cues on brand evaluations. *Journal of Consumer Research*, **14** (December), 316–33.

Kenhove, P. V. and Desrumaux, P. (1997). The relationship between emotional states and approach or avoidance responses in a retail environment. *The International Review of Retail, Distribution and Consumer Research*, **7** (4), 351–68.

Kotler, P. (1973). Atmospherics as a marketing tool. *Journal of Retailing*, **49** (Winter), 48–64.

Kotler, P., Swee Hoon Ang, Siew Meng Leong and Chin Tiong Tan (1996). *Marketing Management: An Asian Perspective*. Prentice Hall.

Lewison, D. (1994). *Retailing*. Prentice Hall.

Lindquist, J. D. (1974). Meaning of image. *Journal of Retailing*, **50** (Winter), 29–38.

Livingstone, N. S. (1997). Service tips included. *Fw*, May/June, 56–7.

Lovelock, C. H. (1991). *Service Marketing*. Prentice Hall.

Mackintosh, E., West, S. and Saegert, S. (1975). Two studies of crowding in urban public spaces. *Environment and Behaviour*, **7** (June), 159–84.

Marans, R. W. and Spreckelmeyer, K. F. (1982). Measuring overall architectural quality. *Environment and Behaviour*, **14** (November), 652–70.

McGrath, M. A. and Otnes, C. (1995). Unacquainted influencers: when strangers interact in the retail setting. *Journal of Business Research*, **32**, 261–72.

Meer, J. (1985). The light touch. *Psychology Today*, September, 60–7.

Mehrabian, A. and Russell, J. A. (1974). *An Approach to Environmental Psychology*. Cambridge, MA: MIT Press.

Milliman, R. E. (1982). Using background music to affect the behaviour of supermarket shoppers. *Journal of Marketing*, **46** (Summer), 86–91.

Parasuraman, A., Berry, L. L. and Zeithaml, V. A. (1990). Guidelines for conducting service quality research. *Marketing Research*, **2** (December), 34–44.

Reda, S. (1997). Apparel retailers focus on improving shopping experience. *Stores*, March, 38–9.

Russell, J. A. and Snodgrass, J. (1987). Emotion and the environment. In *Handbook of Environmental Psychology* (D. Stokols and I. Altman, eds), pp. 245–81. New York: Wiley.

Schlossberg, H. (1992). Marketers told to get customers involved and 'take back the store'. *Marketing News*, 13 April.

Schneiderman, I. P. (1997). New retailers' old tricks. *Women's Wear Daily*, 9 September, 10.

Smith, T. (1997). Integrating the cultures. *SEN: The Magazine for Retail Ideas*, May, 33–4.

Spies, K., Hesse, F. and Loesch, K. (1997). Store atmosphere, mood and purchasing behaviour. *International Journal of Research in Marketing*, **14**, 1–17.

Stokols, D. (1976). The experience of crowding in primary and secondary environments. *Environment and Behaviour*, **8** (March), 49–86.

Sullivan, L. R. (1992). Appealing to the technophiles. *Forbes*, 27 April, 52–4.

Swinyard, W. R. (1993). The effects of mood, involvement, and quality of store experience on shopping intentions. *Journal of Consumer Research*, **20**, 271–80.

Tai, H. C. S. and Fung, A. M. C. (1997). Application of an environmental psychology model to in-store buying behaviour. *The International Review of Retail, Distribution and Consumer Research*, **7** (4), 311–37.

Waldrop, J. (1991). Educating the customer. *American Demographics*, September, 44–77.

Ward, J. C., Bitner, M. J. and Barnes, J. (1992). Measuring the prototypicality and meaning of retail environment. *Journal of Retailing*, **68** (Summer), 194–220.

Ward, L. M. and Russell, J. A. (1981). Cognitive set and the perception of place. *Environment and Behaviour*, **13** (September), 610–32.

Wineman, J. D. (1982). Office design and evaluation: an overview. *Environment and Behaviour*, **14** (May), 271–98.

Yalch, R. and Spangenberg, E. (1990). Effects of store music on shopping behaviour. *Journal of Consumer Marketing*, **7** (Spring), 55–63.

Zachary, S. (1998). Into the age of honesty. *SEN: The Magazine for Retail Ideas*, January, 17–18.

Zeithaml, V. A. and Bitner, M. J. (1996). *Services Marketing*. McGraw-Hill.

Zimmer, M. R. and Golden, L. L. (1988). Impressions of retail stores: a content analysis of consumer images. *Journal of Retailing*, **64** (Fall), 265–93.

7

The process of fashion trend development leading to a season

Tim Jackson

Research design

Primary research for this chapter consisted of six in-depth interviews with key informants drawn from major fashion companies (Promostyl, Marks & Spencer, Courtaulds, Line, Selfridges and Au Studio). The interviews were conducted November/October 1999 and September/October 2000. Interviews were tape-recorded and transcribed. Each interview typically lasted about 1.5 hours. The interviews were informed by a set of questions that were sent to the interviewees in advance of the meeting. This was done with the aim of gaining quality information from respondents and allowed further probing to take place during the time allowed for face-to-face interviews. Additional material was gleaned from two respondents who were unable to take part in the interviews. These two people were journalists from the *Woman's Journal* and *Company* magazine, where factual responses were provided in a written reply to the questions.

What is fashion?

There is a need to define the term fashion, as this chapter is primarily concerned with the sequence of events that form a process through which trends in fashion clothing and accessories emerge. Perna (1987) defines fashion as 'an expression of the times'. This broad interpretation fits well with the modern consumer society in which many aspects of people's lifestyles are vehicles for reflecting social status and success. This is especially pertinent to products and services that are highly visible when being used, such as mobile phones, clubs, bars, cars and clothing. Polhemus and Procter (1978) recognized this when they pointed out that the term 'fashion' 'is often used as a synonym of the terms "adornment", "style" and "dress"'.

Although the term fashion therefore has a very wide frame of reference, the fashion industry tends to be focused on those businesses involved in the design, production, sale and promotion of clothing, accessories and footwear. Indeed, clothing is the most common vehicle used to express fashion issues in the media. Barnard (2001) refers to the need for people 'to be social and individual at the same time' and that 'fashion clothing are ways in which this complex set of desires or demands may be negotiated'. Additionally, the bi-seasonal changes in fashion clothing have led to the evolution over many years of a structured sequence of trade shows servicing the various stages of pre-season fashion garment development. Consequently, this chapter will focus on the specific events that contribute to fashion trends in clothing, while recognizing that a similar process applies to the development of other 'fashion' products.

Fashion trends

Fashion trends provide an insight into the style and colour direction that future fashion products will take in their final form. The notion of a fashion trend will vary according to the kind of business using it, in particular where they are in the clothing supply chain and what their information needs are. For example, yarn producers are more concerned with trends in colour than garment silhouettes, as their business operates at the very early stages of the supply chain. However, a buyer for a fashion retailer needs to be aware of the complete range of trend information relevant to the fashion product category they are responsible for. Also, there are long-term trends that underpin future designs, such as a move to less structured garments or performance fabrics, and short-term trends usually associated with a particular season, for example a particular print.

A fashion garment possesses various attributes that can be manipulated to reflect changing fashions. Each attribute is potentially able to reflect a very strong fashion trend in its own right.

- Colour
- Fabric

- Print
- Silhouette
- Styling detail
- Trim.

In the recent past, a fashion garment would sell, all things being equal, if it were the 'right' colour. By the same token, a fashion range would suffer if it did not contain colours that were the right shade for a season. Now it is not so important to have the right shade so long as a version of the 'on-trend' colour is included in a season's range. The early 1990s saw many consecutive seasons of neutral tones in womenswear, with an explosion of bright and pastel colours occurring in the mid-1990s. The break in the neutrals began with pink and proceeded through lime, orange, yellow and blue through to the millennium.

Although trends in fashion are reflected through a variety of design elements, it is believed that customers respond to colour first. There are a number of reasons for this, including strong social and cultural semiotic associations that are learned and, more simply, because a colour is obviously noticeable as it covers the surface of the product. Where fashion products are black and white or neutral, it is increasingly common for colour to be used in the packaging or visual merchandising of such products. However, fashions may also be strongly reflected through fabric qualities (e.g. performance related, shiny, sheer), fabric patterns, product silhouette, product styling, trims and packaging.

Fashion trends may vary in longevity, with a particular 'look' crossing many seasons. This could be a colour, a fabric attribute (e.g. transparent) and a garment shape (e.g. skirt length). It could also be a focus on a part of the body such as the midriff, which may generate a variety of designs utilizing different garment shapes (e.g. low slung hipster pants or tops that are short in the body). Stone (1990) writes of 'rules' where a fashion emphasis concentrates on a part of the body, for example the legs or midriff, until the interest or variety of looks is fully exploited. Through varying emphases and interpretations, this may take a number of seasons. Buyers will also want to milk a particularly successful shape or style, and this can also extend the longevity of a fashion trend.

Fashion seasons

When examining fashion trends, the issue of fashion seasons emerges as a context in which the trends can be understood. The term 'season' refers to a period of time during which fashion products are sold. The specific period of the selling time associated with a season will vary according to the nature of the fashion business. For example, a fabric manufacturer will sell fabric for production of Spring/Summer merchandise many months before the Spring/Summer retail selling season begins.

Historically, there have been two clearly defined and traditional fashion seasons, which are Autumn/Winter and Spring/Summer. Easy (1995) explains that retailers have organized themselves around consumer demand that has traditionally been influenced by weather patterns. Although factors other than simply the weather are increasingly driving the make-up of fashion product ranges, these seasonal terms are still used because they are firmly ingrained in our culture. Changes to the nature of a fashion season arise partly from changes in consumers' lifestyles. For example, once very seasonal merchandise such as swimwear, traditionally sold from March to July, is now also sold in December and January to accommodate demand from people on winter holidays to the sun.

Seasons and user occasions

As consumers' lifestyles have changed, so fashion retailers have needed to buy more quickly and keep ranges focused on what consumers want at particular times of the year, as opposed to buying to satisfy two large periods of demand. In marketing terms, it could be said that the retailers are 'buying' to satisfy specific consumer 'user occasions'.

User occasions are situations when consumers develop a need for a product either as a result of their attitudes and lifestyle activities or because of a specific event/occasion. Some reflect traditional occasions like beachwear in summer and party outfits for New Year, but increasingly consumer demand is pushing retailers to rethink product ranges around changed consumer behaviour. For example, smart-casual outfits for the office are demanded to balance the need to accommodate a 'dress-down' professional work culture with after work socializing.

With a fashion season having to accommodate traditional demand, such as party dresses at Christmas, with lifestyle fashion occasions, the traditional Spring/Summer and Autumn/Winter seasons have inevitably become fragmented.

A more common fashion retail approach to seasons is given in Table 7.1.

Table 7.1 The changing fashion retailer seasons in the UK

Sub-season	Period
Early Spring	January/February
Spring (Events – e.g. Valentine's Day)	February/March
Early Summer (Holiday)	April/May
Summer	May/June
Summer Sale	June
High Summer	June/July
Transitional Autumn	July/August
Back-to-school (where appropriate)	August
Autumn	September/October
Party wear	November
Christmas presents/Transitional Spring	December
Winter Sale	December/January

Although the structure of a season may have changed and the boundaries between seasons become blurred, a new fashion season presents a fashion business with opportunities to freshen its stores through new stock. Frequent changes create the perception of 'newness' and provide retailers with an opportunity to monitor the performance of early product deliveries. Fast selling styles can be 'repeat ordered', making the rest of the season more profitable. However, no one is certain which particular trend is going to take off until the season begins to sell.

Since fashions are fast moving and subject to many influences, it is difficult for a designer to predict and accurately interpret the 'fashion look' for a particular season. As such, the fashion designer and buyer must interpret a range of information and then adapt the key looks for their market.

Retailers' research

Fashion retailer buyers ultimately determine the look of most fashion apparel, accessories and footwear sold to consumers. Their decisions about the look and fashionability of products are influenced by a variety of events and activities. Many fashion retailers use the design teams of their suppliers to work on product designs. A small design team working for the retailer guides these designers, but it is usually the fashion retail buyer who finally selects the product designs for the range. Buyers work closely with their designers, garment technologists and merchandisers during the early stages of range development, sharing ideas and information. Historical sales data provide some trend information relating to 'best and worst' selling styles, colours, sizes and price points. However, early fashion ideas come from a synthesis of influences that emerge from a variety of additional sources, including the following:

- Overseas trips to fashionable shopping locations in foreign cities to buy or photograph samples for 'inspiration'.
- Research of competitor stores for information on new styles, pricing and packaging.
- Research from 'out-of-season' shows providing trend ideas ahead of time.
- Trawling through a variety of specialist fashion and style magazines.
- Customized forecasting services/trend books (e.g. Promostyl).
- On-line forecasting services, such as Worth Global Style Network (WGSN) and style websites such as 'Style.com'.
- Specified textile shows such as Premiere Vision (although knitwear designers and buyers may also attend earlier yarn shows such as Pitti Filatti).
- Specified product shows such as 40 degrees.
- Ready-To-Wear shows.

The above represents a variety of information sources commonly used by designers and buyers throughout the range development process. Retail buyers will simultaneously be analysing 'best and worst' historical sales data with merchandisers to determine the commercial balance of core and new fashion looks in the range.

New technology has resulted in some trips becoming less necessary as on-line forecasting services, such as WGSN, provide comprehensive, global visual information. This information includes summaries of store window displays in foreign shopping locations, speedy coverage of the latest yarn, textile and product shows, and trend summaries under men's, women's and children's wear categories.

Other fast on-line styling services include Style.com, Vogue.com and Elle.com, all of which post photographs from the Ready-To-Wear shows almost as they are happening. The sites also provide invaluable 'behind the scenes' views of hair styling, make-up and the images from fashion parties after the shows.

Role of fashion forecasting

Trend forecasting agencies offer fashion designers objective and early guidance about the changes in fashion colour, fabric and shape. Forecasters explain the global influences on fashion and suggest how to reflect the changing mood of fashion from a colour, fabric and styling perspective. The task of interpreting how the changing world is likely to impact on consumers' desire for fashion will be handled differently by retailers. Some will use trend managers to give direction to their designers, although most fashion retailers use some kind of fashion forecasting service to find out how future seasons' trends are evolving. Some retailers, however, prefer to research and interpret the trends themselves to maintain their originality.

The process

Forecasters reflect the earliest views on trends some 18 months in advance of a season. At this stage, colour is a crucial consideration for yarn mills that need to know what the needs of fabric weavers and knitters will be. It is also the focus of discussion among others who have an interest in very early trend decision-making. An illustration of the sequence of decision-making is shown in Table 7.2 and reflects the wide range of varying and specialist inputs that contribute to a season's fashion look. Fashion forecasters combine the views emerging about colour and fabric from the early yarn and fabric trade shows with their own socio-economic and cultural analysis. Major trends in lifestyles, attitudes and culture, in particular music, sports, cinema and television, are used to predict changing consumer demand.

Trend forecasting businesses

French companies based in Paris have traditionally dominated fashion trend forecasting. Although a number of the larger ones are still French and based in Paris, many with satellite offices around the world, a number of new niche

Table 7.2 Key decision-making stages in the development of a fashion season for Spring/Summer 2001

Date	Event	Textile shows	Garment shows
May 99	Fashion forecasters plan colour		
June 99	**British Textile Colour Group** (BTCG) meets **Intercolour Group** meets – Paris **BTCG** representatives return to review		
October 99		Premiere Vision (AW 00/01) incorporating **Indigo** S/S 01	
November 99		**Filo Yarn** – Milan (mainly weavers)	
December 99		**Expofil** yarn show – Paris	
January 00		**Pitti Filatti** yarn show – Florence (mainly for knits)	
January 00	**Promostyl** conference at The Wallace collection		
February 00		**Tissu Premier** fabric show – Lille	
March 00		**Prato Expo** fabric show – Florence	
March 00		**Premier Vision** – Paris	
July 00			**Pitto Uomo** Menswear – Florence
August 00			**40 degrees** Casualwear – London
August 00			**Herren Moda–Inter Jeans** – Cologne
Sept/Oct 00			Designer **Reader-To-Wear** shows
January 01			Designer **Couture** shows

forecasters have emerged offering their own specialist combination of products and services. Some of the better known trend forecasters include:

- Sacha Pacha
- Peclers
- Trend Union
- Line Creative Partners Ltd
- Au Studio
- Promostyl.

Promostyl is an international trend forecasting business with a global client base, offering both a customized consulting service to clients as well as a range of trend books for each season. Their trend books provide detailed forecasts about colour fabric and styling for various market sectors, including womenswear, menswear and childrenswear. The books also provide a quick and relatively cheap global overview of major evolving trends. With fashion affecting more and more products from cars to household plants, Promostyl has a wide client base that goes beyond fashion clothing companies.

Tapping into the changing external environment

Social and cultural changes are major determinants of emerging fashions. However, they are themselves affected by other drivers of change that include globalization of world markets and the accessibility of more sophisticated communications technologies. The latter has provided people with faster and wider access to more ideas and influences from other cultures and societies, driving demand for wider choice in fashion products. The days of a few large retailers producing predictable looks for predictable seasons Spring/Summer and Autumn/Winter are long gone.

Figure 7.1 identifies some of the major drivers of change influencing fashion trends in the late 1990s. The model provides an indication of the

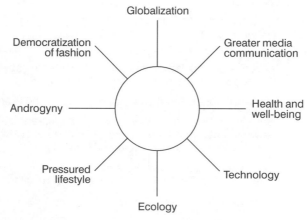

Figure 7.1 The drivers of fashion change. *Source:* Jackson and Shaw (2000).

diverse range of factors impacting on fashion design, rather than representing a complete list of all possible factors.

Although 'globalization' has impacted on the fashion industry in many ways, including sourcing and the spread of international fashion brands, some fashion retailers have suffered through not taking into account the differences in demand of micro markets. C&A withdrew from the UK market after struggling to sell ranges that did not take account of the different UK fashion tastes.

Promostyl refers to the 'democratization of fashion' to explain the growth of previously ultra-exclusive brands like Prada and Gucci into mass market acceptance. This is increasingly common as consumers mix brands from different market levels to achieve an individual and affordable look that includes an element of luxury.

Technological innovations in fibres and fabrics

Frequently, the development of a completely new product is the result of a particular functional need, like a 'trainer sock' or a 'body', but often it is driven by the benefits offered by a new fabric. Specialist forecasters like Line Creative Partners (UK) make the point that technology is changing the range of benefits that designers can build into garment products through the textiles used in construction. As more functions and properties are integrated into their structures, textiles can provide a new range of benefits for garments, including greater protective capabilities, body enhancing qualities and the benefits associated with 'smart textiles' like Amicor, from Courtaulds.

Table 7.3 shows that not all product improvements are derived solely from the development of new fibres, as innovation can occur across the entire textile development process.

Table 7.3 Textile developments

Textile level	Development
Fibre	Amicor – a modified acrylic with anti-bacterial capabilities that is designed to eliminate odour and skin irritation
Yarn	Improved cotton spinning processes producing a softer handle
Fabric	Gore-Tex fabric which uses a hi-tech membrane sandwiched between outer and inner layers of fabric to allow skin to breathe whilst protecting against wind and rain
Finish	Chemicals added to woven fabric to provide crease resistant benefits – e.g. Teflon finish to provide dirt resistant effect
Colour	Development of vegetable dyes/fox fibre–natural coloured cotton

Source: Jackson and Shaw (2000).

The importance of shows

Buyers and fashion designers are able to predict what is likely to be 'in fashion' through a combination of influences, including reviewing important textile and style magazines, the specialist services of forecasting trend agencies, and visits to textile and garment fashion shows.

Range of shows

The word 'show' is given its widest possible interpretation here to refer to the range of organized textile and fashion garment trade shows, operating over the 16 months preceding a season. Trade shows, whether yarn, fabric or product, have a basic function which is to sell products. The use of these shows for prediction is often a secondary function, although many clearly exploit this aspect. At a basic level, yarn mills sell to fabric weavers and knitters, who sell to garment manufactures and retailers. Fashion buyers may buy direct from fabric or product manufacturers depending on whether they are sourcing on a CMT or factored basis. The different needs arising from the fashion clothing supply chain have resulted in a sequence of yarn, fabric and product trade shows and Ready-To-Wear fashion shows evolving over the years.

Visitors vary according to the nature of the show. A yarn show will attract a range of people, including fabric manufacturers, some retail buyers and designers, although the mix will be more weighted to people involved in fabric production than garment design and buying. Fashion trade press cover the shows, informing those buyers and designers, for whom the shows are too early, of the major trends that are emerging.

The fabric shows perform a more balanced role with great emphasis on the sale of fabrics, but with more retail designers and buyers attending as the products on show have greater direct relevance to garment design and the shows are that much closer to the season.

Garment shows are much more diverse, ranging from the product trade shows through to the high profile Ready-To-Wear Designer shows like London Fashion Week and then the exclusive Couture shows.

Lead-times

Lead-time refers to a period of time between specified events. In this case it is used to refer to the period of time prior to a season that a particular show is being held. As a general rule of thumb, fabric shows are held approximately 10 months before a season and garment shows approximately 5 months before a season. The beginning of a season is January for Spring/Summer and August for Autumn/Winter. However, the Transitional Spring ranges are in store late December with Early Spring in January.

The sequence of trade and fashion shows

Table 7.2 (page 128) shows the sequence of fashion trend evolution, using the season Spring/Summer 2001 as an illustration. The same sequence is mirrored for Autumn/Winter at different times. Not all the events or shows are directly relevant to fashion retail designers and buyers, as many shows have particular specialisms and audiences. However, like pieces of a jigsaw they all contribute to an evolved 'fashion look' for a season.

National and international colour bodies

In the UK, the process really begins with the British Textile Colour Group (BTCG) meeting, where around 25 representatives of a range of companies from different industry sectors, including car, retail and forecasting, meet to discuss colour and views on factors likely to affect the season's fashion trends. Two representatives are selected to attend the Intercolour Group meeting, which is traditionally held in Paris, but occasionally moves to other countries. Here, the equivalent representatives from many countries around the world, including Europe, Asia and the Far East, meet to exchange views on the likely development of trends and especially the development of colour. The UK representatives then return to the UK for a review of the global position with the rest of the BTCG.

Premiere Vision

The next early sign of trends for the season emerges in the Indigo exhibition, held as part of the Autumn/Winter 'Premiere Vision' (PV). Although the Autumn/Winter exhibition is showing for a different season, it incorporates the Indigo show of textile prints within it. Held in Paris twice a year, March for Spring/Summer and October for Autumn/Winter, PV represents an accurate view of colours and fabric trends approximately 10 months ahead of a season. It is regarded by many to be the 'first sight' of colour and fabric trends for much of the European fashion industry, and is still one of the most important shows in the calendar.

Within the two vast exhibition halls, approximately 850 European weaver–exhibitors show their fabric ranges to 45 000 visitors over the 4 days. The presentation of key trends on display within the vast exhibition is the result of the combined views of a European Concertation, a body of 65 fashion experts who identify the current trends emerging from around the world, and the PV Fashion team. Colour palettes and key theme statements are signed around the exhibition summarizing the trends, and there is an audio-visual show, which provides an overview of the season at intervals throughout the day. Those visiting who are not trained designers but are trying to obtain a feel for the particular season's trends should realize that PV is not a garment show and so should expect to gain mainly fabric and colour information.

Although PV is an important show, there are other fabric shows like Tissu Premier that are providing earlier insights into colour and fabric trends. Tissu, in particular, is considered a good earlier source of trend information, even though it is not so large and has fewer fabric categories.

Product shows

Continuing the sequence, specialist product trade shows are held after the fabric shows. These shows are segmented according to broad sector, like menswear or womenswear, and by specialist product category, like sportswear or lingerie. There are many international product shows such as ISPO (sportswear), Pret a Porter (womenswear) and UK-based product shows including Pure and '40 degrees'. The 40 degrees show is aimed at buyers of young branded fashion who are seeking directional labels for men and women. The shows are good indicators of colour, fabric, styling and new products.

Designer Ready-To-Wear and Couture shows

The Ready-To-Wear garment shows really provide the last opportunity for fashion retailers to incorporate styling changes or overlooked 'must have' items in their ranges. The shows are held in New York, London, Milan, Paris and Tokyo, and provide the influential fashion media with an opportunity to review and promote the particular season's trends and provide publicity for the designers.

The final set of shows reflecting the season's trends are the Couture shows that are held in Rome, London and Paris in January for Summer and Winter. The summer shows held in January have little immediate impact on high street fashion, as Early Spring stock is already in the stores with Summer already being shipped. However, these made-to-measure garments are dominated by occasion wear, including 'after-six' evening wear and ballgowns, many of which are often worn by celebrities at events that carry major media coverage, such as the 'Oscars'. The extensive coverage of celebrities attending high profile events, often given outfits to wear by leading designers, means that new design ideas receive enormous exposure. Frequently, the design themes that emerge seem too forward for most people, but they often have a long-term influence upon future seasons.

Final stage of trend development

The final 'fashion look' for a season is therefore the result of a process of development that combines the evolved views of textile and product trade shows, forecasters, designers, buyers and Ready-To-Wear shows. Like a collage, the final picture emerges after the various layers have come together. Up to the Ready-To-Wear shows, the proposed new looks for a season have not been subject to broad media scrutiny and so are mostly unknown to the end user consumers. Even though these shows have an impact on some last minute high street fashion buys, their major impact is mainly on reflecting the final views on trends close to season. Crucially, the media coverage of these shows is another important dimension in the trend development process as it highlights fashion trends that fashion editors believe will be strong for the forthcoming season. Such 'authoritative' coverage of the media, focusing attention on aspects of fashion, including 'must-have' looks, colours and products, influences consumers' acceptance of hot trends for a season. As Packard et al. (1983) state, 'Price levels do not indicate fashion, acceptance is the key'.

Magazine coverage of Ready-To-Wear shows

The extensive coverage of the Ready-To-Wear shows by the fashion media provides consumers with their first authoritative views of the new season's looks. This coverage occurs at different times and with different degrees of authority. For example, press and television journalists report headline stories emerging from the shows on a daily basis, whereas the influential monthly women's magazines report in detail some months after the shows. The coverage occurring during the shows tends to be news focused, ranging from stories centred on radical designs to the use of celebrities in fashion shows. As there is little reported analysis of trends during the September/October period of the shows, the consumer does not have a clear picture of what the key fashion themes will be until the New Year.

Trend coverage

Significant and structured 'trend' coverage of the shows is principally delivered to the consumer through the pages of the monthly women's magazines, including *Vogue, Elle, Marie Claire, Cosmopolitan, Company, Woman's Journal* and many more. Table 7.4 shows the relationship between the timing of the Ready-To-Wear shows and the monthly magazines' issue deadlines.

As these magazines work on three-monthly lead-times, the earliest practical coverage of the September/October shows is in the January issue. The December issues are too focused on Christmas and the completion of the current year to address next season's trends. Furthermore, advertisers in the magazines want to keep Spring/Summer images close to the relevant selling

Table 7.4 The relationship between the timing of Ready-To-Wear shows and monthly magazine issue deadlines

Month	Ready-To-Wear Fashion Shows	Monthly Magazine Deadlines	Retailer Promotion
September 00	New York London	December issue 00	
October 00	Milan Paris	January issue 01	
November 00	Tokyo	February issue 01	Press samples arrive Press days
December 00		March and April 01 issues	

periods. Although some Spring/Summer trends are featured in the January issues, with each magazine doing things differently, the major trend coverage will come in subsequent issues. This is because fashion editors tend to wait for the first signs of Spring/Summer samples, generally arriving in November, before producing significant features.

These 'photo' or press samples are couriered ahead of the rest of production to enable fashion retailers to promote the range. Some magazines will feature a special Spring/Summer trend supplement in a fixed month, commonly April, with other magazines allowing the trend coverage to trickle out across issues from January onwards to stimulate interest.

Obviously, the interpretation by fashion editors of what the major colours and styling features are for a season has an impact on consumers' belief of what is fashionable. 'Must have' colours, styles and products are promoted through the magazine features and consumers are educated into an acceptance of what to wear that season. In addition to the specific trend coverage of the Ready-To-Wear shows, the magazines include specific fashion features that focus on a particular aspect of the season. This could be based on an occasion, such as 'holidays', or on a strong fashion theme such as a denim look. Many of these features will include photographs of the season's products that are to be in the stores at the time the magazine is published.

In order to take advantage of such opportunities, many fashion retailers hold 'press days' during which fashion journalists and editors preview the forthcoming ranges. This exposure provides magazines with relevant material to shoot for their fashion features and benefits retailers by giving them crucial publicity. Retailers provide fashion journalists with 'look books' containing photographs of important products in the new ranges and many of the monthly magazines select items from the 'books' to shoot for their own features. As the season unfolds, so the media in all its various forms features particular looks over the months, maintaining the 'newness' of the fashions and interest from consumers. Efficient buying departments are able to respond to fast emerging 'hot trends' that supplement the rest of the range.

References

Barnard, M. (2001). *Fashion as Communication*. Routledge.

Easy, M. (1995). *Fashion Marketing*. Blackwell Science.

Jackson, T. and Shaw, D. (2000). *Mastering Fashion Buying and Merchandising Management*. Macmillan.

Packard, S., Winters, A. and Axelrod, W. (1983). *Fashion Buying and Merchandising*. Fairchild Publications.

Perna, R. (1987). *Fashion Forecasting*. Fairchild Publications.

Polhemus, T. and Procter, L. (1978). *Fashion and Anti-fashion and Anthropology of Clothing and Adornment*. Thames & Hudson.

Stone. E (1990). *Fashion Merchandising: An Introduction*. Gregg Division, McGraw-Hill.

8

Innovation management in creating new fashions

Beatrice Le Pechoux, Trevor J. Little and
Cynthia L. Istook

Introduction

Each apparel manufacturer's new collections of garments and accessories are
created to satisfy a predicted target consumer demand. These demand
predictions are based on target market research and past sales analysis,
and input from experienced product merchandisers, designers and buyers.
The collections are influenced by trends observed in apparel and related
industries (textile, shoes, accessories, home furnishings, etc.), and/or other
industries (such as entertainment, sports, music or automotive), as well as
wider environmental movements (cultural, social, technological, economical,
etc.). All these elements combined help determine the concepts and themes
for the new season. Relevant materials, colour palettes and silhouettes are
developed and selected accordingly. Trims and details may be added as
further embellishments. These former and latter design elements are co-
ordinated and grouped into product lines that meet cost, production and
delivery time requirements.

The apparel design process involves gathering and analysing information on fashion trends, markets and past line sales, and editing ideas for successful combinations of fabric, style and price. These ideas are the result of creativity. The discussion of the role of creativity in today's textile/apparel industry applies to the world's highly developed economies in general, which are entering a new stage of development. For centuries, this growth was based on increases in productivity. However, 'this expansion trajectory is now perceived as unsustainable' (Andersson, 1997). Quantitative growth must be replaced by improvements in quality. 'Wealth creating innovations ultimately substitute knowledge for energy or materials. Knowledge accumulates exponentially, with every innovation creating the opportunity for a greater number of innovations' (Petzinger, 2000). As products are becoming more varied and complex, creativity rather than productivity is becoming the key to business success and survival. In the new knowledge-based economy, Petzinger (2000) concludes 'creativity is overtaking capital as the principal elixir of growth'. Despite the importance of creativity for product differentiation, creativity regarding textile or apparel designers, design teams and the design process has not been widely investigated.

Most of the models reviewed describe the creative process as a problem solving system. Alexander (1977) recognized that in the architectural design process some problems occur over and over again, in a given environment, with a core (generic) solution. From that observation, he was the first to develop a pattern language for a design process, where each pattern describes a problem/solution combination related to a specific context. The patterns are formulated in such a way that they can be used in different sequences and numbers, many times over, without ever doing it the same way twice. Therefore, the output can always be unique and new, thus defined as creative.

A pattern language for the apparel design process could channel creative efforts and enhance communication between design team members by providing them with a common language for creative fashion design.

Mapping the creative design process

The design process generally includes all the steps involved from generation of ideas and concepts to prototype development of the end product (Secor, 1992). It is a multidisciplinary science that requires teamwork and collaboration between various corporate functions. Marketing and sales information are particularly important in the initial phase of the process. Design, material and process knowledge is necessary to follow through to the next phases and ultimately create new products.

Textile/apparel design processes in the literature are covered from both a theoretical and empirical point of view. Since market and production constraints need to be integrated into the process, a combination of skills and therefore a collaboration of various corporate activities and functions are required. Theoretical models and empirical descriptions attempt to capture the creative design process to make it more tangible for all the design team members and management. The following figures show the product design and development processes from different points of view.

Figure 8.1 shows a theoretical model of the apparel design and development process (Carr and Pomeroy, 1992). Similarly to Carr and Pomeroy's model, Sadd (1996), of KSA, identifies five steps to product development: consumer research, design/concept development, sampling, specification development and finally pre-production sampling. This whole pre-production phase is critical to achieve successful product sell through. Here, we will focus on the

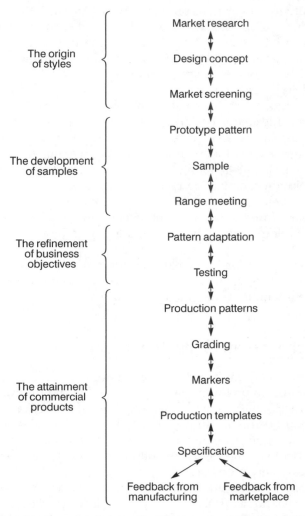

Figure 8.1 The process of apparel design and product development. *Source*: Carr and Pomeroy (1992).

'origin of styles' phase, which will always be referred to as the creative design or conception phase for the purpose of clarity.

The following models focus more on this conception phase. The first one is based on a case study run by Gaskill (1992) in order to profile the functional activities performed by two speciality retailers carrying 100% private label merchandise. Having previously observed that retailers were increasingly involved in the process of product design by setting up specialized product development divisions, the objective was to differentiate them by creating unique products that catered to their target consumer's specific preferences. Resulting from the study, the Retail Product Development Model (Figure 8.2) shows the sequence of events that take place throughout the creative apparel design process, along with its internal and external influences. This model stops at the line presentation phase.

Product development model

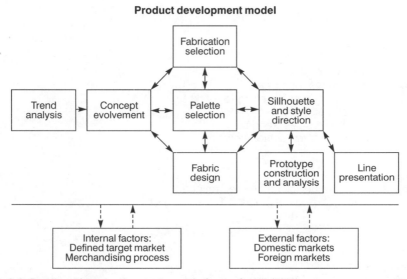

Figure 8.2 Retail product development model. *Source:* Gaskill (1992).

Recently, Gaskill, along with Wickett et al. (1999), conducted a new study to support and develop this initial Retail Product Development Model. One of the objectives of these authors was to validate Gaskill's original model by testing it across a broader range of speciality stores. In developing their data analysis tools, they created a guide providing the researcher with a detailed outline of the pre-determined activities included in the product development content areas. Table 8.1 includes the most detailed description of the creative product design process found in the literature. This process can be divided into two basic phases. Initially, information is probed for orientation ideas regarding moods, themes, concepts and product types. In a second phase, all these data are digested and translated into product ideas combining silhouettes, materials and colours.

Table 8.1 Activities guide for apparel product development

Trend Analysis
Sources of trend inspiration:
- Shopping domestic markets
- Shopping international markets
- Media (magazines, television, mail order catalogues)
- Fashion support services (trade shows, fabric libraries, styles services, runway shows, colour services)
- Anywhere
- Internal sources (employees, sales tracking information)
- Competition

Employees involved in search for trends:
- Buying area (buyers, general merchandise managers)
- Design team
- Product development manager
- Fashion director
- Chief executive officer
- Merchandising manager
- Product manager

Concept Evolvement
How decision on concept emerged:
- Perceptions gained from travelling to markets
- Evaluation of overall trend information
- Assessment of past sales trends
- Information gained from fashion services
- Instinct

Palette Selection
How seasonal colour decisions are determined:
- Based on information gained during Trend Analysis

Source of colour information:
- Colour services
- Historical colour data
- Colour testing results
- New 'emerging colour stars'
- Purchased garments
- Trends
- Yarn samples
- Colour swatches
- Colour shows

Fabrication Selection
Criteria used in selecting product fabrication:
- Structural fabric characteristics (performance, quality, appearance, draping ability, weight, hand)
- Seasonal theme or timing of the line
- Aesthetics
- Marketplace trends
- Part sales history
- Fabric price
- Perceived customer benefits
- Textile mill availability

Fabric Design
Source of fabric design:
- Original designs (prints/plaids) created by the company
- Both pre-developed designs and original designs
- Pre-developed designs from fabric companies

Source of fabric design ideas:
- Books and magazines
- Fabric services (fabric libraries, print services, design services, forecasting services)
- Fabric samples
- Fabric mills
- Market trends
- Textile studios

Silhouette and Style Directions
Sources of silhouette and styles:
- Original designs
- Branded merchandise ('knock-offs')
- Both original designs and knock-offs

Silhouette and style inspiration provided by:
- Marketplace (domestic and international)
- Current trends
- History (past successful basic style blocks)

Line Presentation
Line presentation incorporated:
- Prototype samples
- Sketch-boards
- Computerized renderings
- Storyboards
- Paintings
- Pictures
- Swatches
- Fabrications

Line decisions based on:
- Saleability judgements
- Testing results
- Perceived customer reaction
- Cost
- Selling history
- Co-ordination with other apparel groups
- Marketplace trends
- Other (newness, variety, lead-time, quality, colour, instinct)

Intervening Factors
Internal factors:
- Needs of the defined customer base
- Sales trends
- Input from employees
- Analysis of store performance
- Specific garments being developed

External factors:
- Fashion trends
- Domestic and foreign markets
- Competition
- Media, quota restrictions and fabric capability

Source: Wickett et al. (1999).

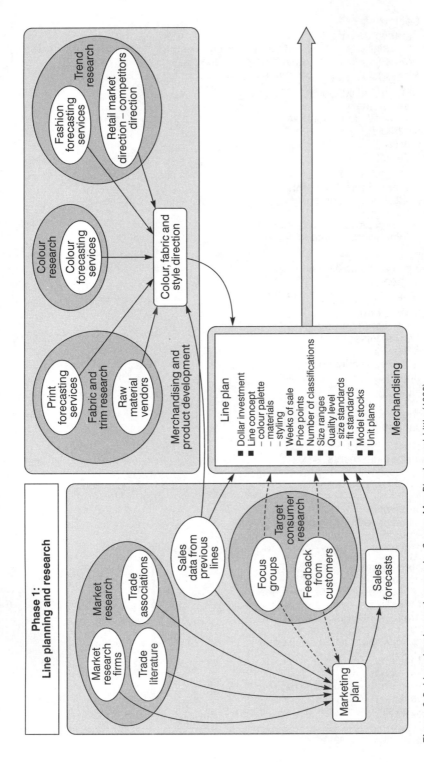

Figure 8.3 Line planning and research. *Source:* May-Plumlee and Little (1998).

Early phases include trend analysis and concept evolvement. Influences come from both external and internal sources, both from the environment and personnel related to the design process directly or indirectly. This first step involves identifying the product styles and categories that are most in demand in the target market. A brief among design team members will usually initiate the process by defining 'the garment type, age group, purpose, climate and price range which designers should aim at' (Carr and Pomeroy, 1992). Market research is critical to 'starting off right' by capturing the market pulse and direction. The design team needs immersion in 'all current means of communication of fashion ideas' (Carr and Pomeroy, 1992): fashion shows, textile/apparel trade shows, recent technological innovations, colour and fabric libraries, store visits, opinion of buyers, market data services, trade press, product offer from the competition, etc. Cultural, social and political events should also be considered.

The second phase includes palette selection, fabric construction and surface design selection, and silhouette and style directions. These activities are related to more tangible design elements utilizing design principles and skills, along with material and process knowledge to combine them effectively. At this final stage of the creative design process, sketches should include overall silhouettes and details such as collars and pockets, and eventually surface decorations such as pleats or fringes.

Figure 8.3 was taken from a larger model that covers the whole product design and development process for apparel. This 'phase 1' depicts the creative design process of apparel up to the line plan. Figure 8.3 illustrates the various types of research information that can be pulled from the environments, and how they integrate the marketing, merchandising and product development processes to establish a line plan.

At the corporate level, Knox (1989) shows (Figure 8.4) how design interfaces with other company activities providing creative, technological and commercial input in a total market environment. He stipulates that two-way relationships exist between the three types of inputs to develop products that can satisfy future market requirements (Knox, 1989).

Knox then breaks each of these three major fields into groups of activities that directly interface with the designer. In Figure 8.5, he shows how creativity has multi-faceted relationships and affects all areas of company strategy.

Since typically 80–90% of a product's life cycle cost is determined during the pre-production stages, careful planning is a necessary support to successful effective and efficient product design (AICPA, 1998). Inefficient product design can create bottlenecks for improved product quality and time to market. Ineffective product design can lead to poor quality or non-sellable designs. The starting point to successful product design is in the market and trend analyses.

Companies need to set up a research system that enables them to anticipate demographic changes and how lifestyles and expectations of the target market segment are influenced, to 'create a critical path analysis so that the right thing happens at the right time' (Robinson, 1987). Manufacturers seek shorter

Analysis of designer requirements

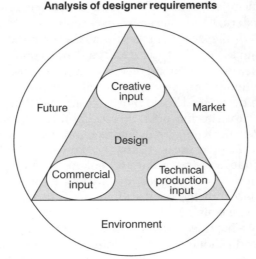

Figure 8.4 Design relationships. *Source*: Knox (1989).

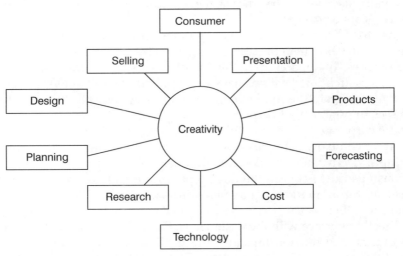

Figure 8.5 Creativity and design activities. *Source*: Knox (1989).

product development, sourcing, production and delivery cycles. This task is particularly complicated for apparel due to the high number of Stock Keeping Units (SKUs), the need for constant change, and working on at least three seasons and several lines at a time (Remaury, 1996). Development of new apparel products suffers from low success rates and difficulty in compressing time cycles. Currently, management focus is set on reducing the latter while increasing the former. Compressing time cycles at this stage is crucial to meet calendar deadlines and avoid losing market shares (AAMA, 1991).

Shah (1987) believes that 'timing', i.e. getting new styles to the streets at the precise moment the consumer is susceptible and ready for that design message, is related more to market intelligence and understanding the consumer than speed and technology. Though a combination of all three elements really seems key to reaching perfect timing, we agree that design team efforts should particularly focus on and build on this market intelligence. Forecasting is considered critical in apparel and all fashion-related industries. McPherson (1987) suggests that merchandise planning, which translates marketing objectives into specific product lines, can help control potential losses and rapidly take advantage of favourable sales trends.

Marketing and design

Marketing is a two-phase process, which consists of identifying market needs and satisfying them (Carr and Pomeroy, 1992). To reach these objectives, companies need to constantly interact with suppliers, competitors, industry analysts and especially customers to avoid being 'future shocked' (Dammeyer, 1994). 'Now we must invest in consumers . . . Figures alone are not enough: we must understand attitudes, interests, and preferences' (Robinson, 1987).

Identifying market needs

Identifying and understanding market needs is a complicated task, which still needs to be mastered. Currently, most consumers are not satisfied with their shopping experiences. According to Kurt Salmon Associates' 1996 Annual Consumer Pulse Survey, 68% of the apparel shoppers know what they are looking for but 49% claim being unable to find it (KSA, 1996). They seek instant gratification. Satisfying them has become retailers' top concern. Having pushed back in the pipeline some of their actions, they are increasing their operation costs for developing systems to better understand and target their customers, hence increasing responsiveness.

Retailers have shifted their focus from return on investment (ROI) to return on customers (Tandem Corporation, 1997). Instead of trying to increase the number of individual transactions, they now want to increase the value of long-term customer relationships by supplying many 'right' products to one customer rather than one average product to as many customers as possible. The main idea is to increase loyalty, attract old customers back and target new ones more efficiently.

To better focus on specific target consumers, companies develop market segmentation approaches. Initially, market segments were based on product category and simple demographics of the target consumer (such as age, sex, income level and geographic location). In today's intensely competitive environment, products have become increasingly specialized and complex, multiplying the number of definable market segments and blurring the borders between them. To deal with the increasing complexity of market segmentation, marketing has evolved into a new field called 'micro-marketing', which focuses on pinpointing narrow local markets to target customers more efficiently. Based on multi-variable segmentation, micro-marketing requires collecting a wide variety of data incorporating detailed demographic data, as well as consumer information on psychographics, lifestyles and family life cycles, activities, interests, opinions, purchasing and consumption profiles, media used, etc. (Pitt, 1997; Brown, 1997). The information may be based on individual consumers or on households (Carr and Pomeroy, 1992).

This detailed micro-data collected will be used to segment and locate target groups, plan relevant marketing mix, map product potential usage and help customize assortments. As a matter of fact, management focus is shifting from product to category (McCann, 1997), also known as 'consumption constellation' (Solomon and Englis, 1998), taking into account interaction between, rather than within, product categories to offer creative buying incentives and promotional products on a store-to-store basis. This knowledge is particularly relevant to develop different lines of apparel and accessories that may lead to bundled purchases.

Electronic commerce via the Internet will enable manufacturers to directly communicate with and supply consumers, while monitoring and analysing the information each customer is individually pulling down from the World Wide Web. Micro-marketing will become possible on a one-on-one basis. This next stage is already being called 'relationship marketing' (Brown, 1997). The Internet will thus greatly contribute to collecting data on the consumers in addition to that collected through current and past POS and marketing tools such as frequent user programmes.

Response to market demand

Once market needs have been identified and interpreted, response can be given to these defined consumer demands through a mix of marketing elements. The traditional marketing mix factors known as the '4 P' (Kotler and Armstrong, 1994) are product, price, promotion and place. As shown in Figure 8.6, this mix is centred around the target consumer and helps articulate the whole marketing strategy cycle from analysis and planning to implementation and control stages. Product refers to the items and services offered by a company to its target market. Price refers to what will be charged for the purchase of the product. Place refers to where the product will be sold. 'Promotion includes all the efforts of a company to establish the identity and enhance the demand for specific brands and designer name products or to encourage buying from certain retailers' (Jarnow and Dickerson, 1996).

Several authors have given different definitions of the marketing mix, which always include the notions of product, price, place and promotion, while classifying design as a category in itself (Rigamonti, 1987; Carr and Pomeroy, 1992; Robinson, 1987; Jarnow and Dickerson, 1996).

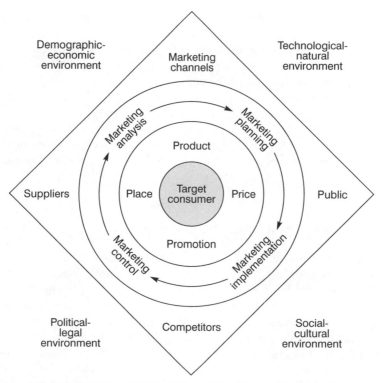

Figure 8.6 Factors influencing marketing strategy. *Source*: Kotler and Armstrong (1994).

Micro- and macro-environments

The marketing environment includes all the opportunities and threats that affect a company's ability to reach its 'goals in developing and maintaining successful business relationships with its target customers' (Jarnow and Dickerson, 1996). For companies to survive they must 'want to change', and this change should be based on knowledge of three main categories: the customer, the market and society. This knowledge can help interpret what lies behind the statistics gathered in market research.

Figure 8.6 shows two types of environments in the inner diamond and the outer square. The micro-environment is closest to the company, affecting 'its ability to serve its target market'. It includes marketing channels, suppliers, competitors and public, such as 'the financial community, the media and the general public'. The macro-environment refers to the larger societal settings in which the company operates. Though there may be a supra-environment that affects all individuals all over the world, note that the environments referred to here may vary from one geographic location to another. Keeping track of the pertinent environments is crucial, especially for a company that designs its product line in New York, sources it in various foreign countries and sells it to global markets.

The marketing of fashion goods is not an isolated process (Rogers and Gamans, 1983). Socio-economic trends prevail and need to be interpreted. Social, political, environmental, technological and even legal events are interrelated to the fashions of a country and shape what will be bought and sold, in both an 'overt and subliminal' manner. Forecasting is based on observation and analysis of all these factors, their potential synergies and correlations, to help determine what influences they may have on future consumer behaviour and fashion (Robinson, 1987). The following section will identify how environmental influences interrelate with consumer wants, fashion cycles, brand image and style, thus influencing the design of new products.

The complex environment of design

Fashion permeates all the environments of the apparel design process. Rogers and Gamans (1983) define fashion as 'any form, custom, usage or style during a particular time that is socially accepted'. 'Fashion is everywhere. We wear it; we use it; we ride in it; we look at it; we read it; we listen to it. Society is permeated with fashion.' The list of possible demographic and social influences on fashion is enormous (Shah, 1987) and dynamic. 'Fashion can never stand still' (Rogers and Gamans, 1983). Therefore, fashion changes with everything that is happening around us and is strongly dependent on time and context. Global and local conditions create an atmosphere that triggers feelings, attitudes and pressures among the consumer population that require change. Therefore, any industry that is related to fashion must understand the constantly shifting consumers' inner emotions at the fastest pace possible. 'It is largely psychological motives that encourage the growth, change, and perennial quest for newness in fashion' (Rogers and Gamans, 1983). Burns (1998) concludes that fashion can be studied either as an object or idea, or as a process of change. 'Although the term "fashion" is often associated with dress and adornment, "fashion" can be related to any object or phenomenon that changes over time based upon individuals' preferences.'

All these contextual and individual factors that affect a person's or a group's selection of what they want their appearance to be, interact with fashion. As with dress, fashion both integrates social factors and is itself a social phenomenon. 'The cyclic changes of fashion currents are cultural factors which in turn influence culture itself' (Entrada, 1998). Rogers and Gamans (1983) examined fashion in a marketing context. They insist that the fashion cycle must be considered when creating a marketing mix and that market positioning and fashion image are interrelated.

Fashion cycle

Fashion is both a product and a stimulus of changing consumer needs and wants through time. Therefore, fashion is evolutionary. 'Acceptance of the new requires a rejection of the old and a period of time before it is embraced by a substantial number' (Packard, 1983).

Figures 8.7 and 8.8 show the process of fashion acceptance and the effect it has on various elements of the marketing mix during the life cycle of a garment style (Packard, 1983). The various stages describe the product's life cycle on the marketplace once it has been designed and developed: introduction, growth, maturity and decline. Today, the introduction stage is increasingly intertwined with the product design and development processes, which integrate continuous market information and consumer feedback. Fashion innovators will adopt the style initially. Opinion leaders and early conformists follow and contribute to increasing the popularity of the style. In the maturity stage, the style becomes widely accepted by mass-market consumers, followed by late fashion adopters at the beginning of the decline stage. Finally, 'fashion isolates'

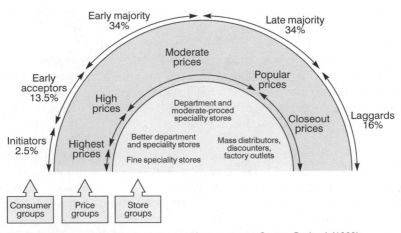

Figure 8.7 Fashion acceptance: consumers, prices, stores. *Source*: Packard (1983).

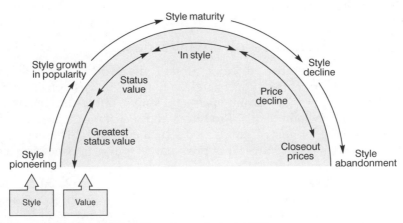

Figure 8.8 Product life span of fashion. *Source*: Packard (1983).

and/or laggards will adopt the style once it has already become obsolete (Kaiser, 1990). Traditionally, these consumer groups were associated with specific types of income levels, social status and lifestyles, as can be determined from the associated price and store groups shown in Figure 8.7. Based on the literature reviewed, these consumer group definitions, based on the trickle down theory of fashion leadership, are no longer restrictively associated with the value, price and store groups defined in Packard's figures.

Style and brand image

Because of their aesthetic component, images have always been important in fashion. 'Dress stimuli' are generally of visual format, such as photographs, drawings, films, video or live encounters (Damhorst, 1990). The visual aspect of clothing is more crucial than ever in today's multi-media 'visual society', where fashion and marketing both focus on image, and where consumers of fashion have become 'consumers of illusion' (Entrada, 1998). Visual images have become more powerful, speaking to a greater number across the globe; aesthetics are critical. Fashion not only focuses primarily on brand image, but fashion has become a mass media in itself. Since 'a picture is worth 1000 words' and is understood internationally, designers who have managed to efficiently market their image have commanded influence and made huge profits in various market categories. Re-targeting or re-launching an image can stimulate total market demand and expand the life cycle of their products and/or their brand(s).

Robinson (1987) believes that since fashion transcends people's lifestyles, distinct brand image and style should transcend corporate culture and structure. To establish a company style, the aim of the business must first be clearly identified, including the target customer, product type and price level. To be successful, the style then needs to be 'consistent'. Building an image can be accomplished with successful marketing and promotion, available time and money, and complete adherence of all company members to the chosen and well-defined style and image.

Environmental sources of creative design

There are now a number of cities around the world considered to be inspirational fashion centres (Rogers and Gamans, 1983). Fashion centres serve as a focal point for new styles and ideas, and spread out to the consumers via retail buyers and fashion media. Producers and distributors meet in order to move the resulting promoted goods to the final consumer. The experts, who populate these fashion centres, interpret market pulse into new styles and predictions.

Perna (1987) illustrates how the fashion industry is activated by various 'gears' which turn in perpetual motion (Figure 8.9), requiring any fashion-related company to be plugged into the multiple check points of the fashion information network (Figure 8.10). Shah (1987) claims that it is actually a small

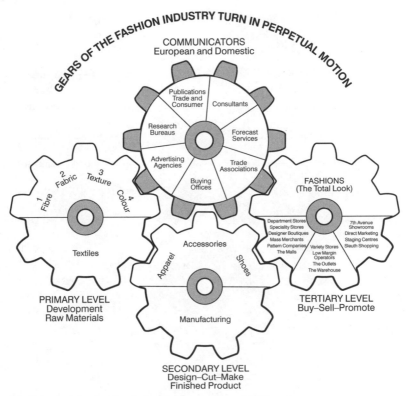

Figure 8.9 Gears of the fashion industry. *Source*: Perna (1987).

group of people who work for trend services or put together exhibitions like Premiere Vision who make fashion. Not only do they research and rationalize all the information, but also 'they co-ordinate their fashion accordingly and they have the muscle and influence to pass on these ideas in a pure and more personalised format to their own clients, magazines, etc.'. According to him, this is what makes Paris the styling centre rather than the individualistic Italy.

According to Kurt Salmon Associates' vision of textiles markets in the new millennium, the consumer who has developed a strong sense of individuality, making him or her loyal to only his or her wants, will play an active role in the apparel design process. The industry activities will be redistributed into a 4-D model: designers, developers, distributors and displayers. The first, second and fourth Ds will become 'co-designers' in a virtual network which will ultimately integrate the consumer as well. Consumers will test new designs, colours and sizes via the Internet and in-store direct consumer response. They will actually activate demand when and where they choose. New forms of competition will arise from the potential gain of successfully editing this massive information (Smith, 1995).

It appears that both the consumer and the designer are creative. The designer in the styles imagined, the consumer in the selection and combinations applied.

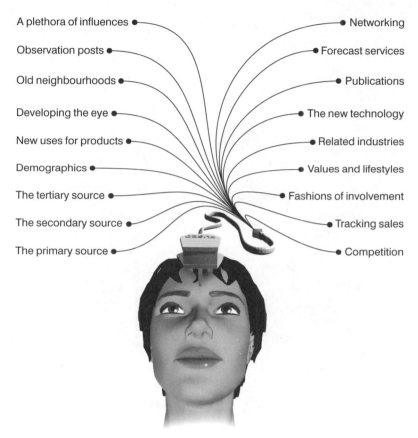

A plethora of influences ●

Observation posts ●

Old neighbourhoods ●

Developing the eye ●

New uses for products ●

Demographics ●

The tertiary source ●

The secondary source ●

The primary source ●

● Networking

● Forecast services

● Publications

● The new technology

● Related industries

● Values and lifestyles

● Fashions of involvement

● Tracking sales

● Competition

INFORMATION NETWORK –
are you plugged into the check points?

Figure 8.10 Information network. *Source:* Perna (1987).

Consumers are potential wearers and/or viewers. These three categories of people (designer, wearer and viewer) influence each other in their personal critical evaluation of a certain way to dress (Figure 8.11). All three are individuals who are part of a specific environment interpreting appearance and dress as forms of expression using all their five senses (Kaiser, 1990). Consumer behaviour and design creativity are affected by multiple factors. Fashion is both a consequence and an inspiration to the interaction between consumers and designers, where aesthetic traits are extremely relevant and changes occur at a rapid pace. Companies must therefore be able to mine available data for adequate information on consumer preferences in design, and establish differences in relation to competitors through creative design that incorporates continuously updated market intelligence.

The model presented in Figure 8.12 shows the various levels of contexts, embedded within one another and defining the perception of clothes. The model attributes a title at each level along with a few non-exclusive examples

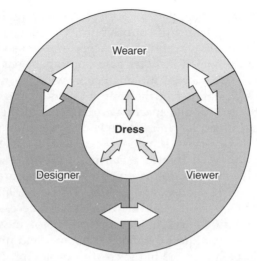

Figure 8.11 Critical framework for evaluating dress. *Source*: adapted from Bryant and Hoffman (1994).

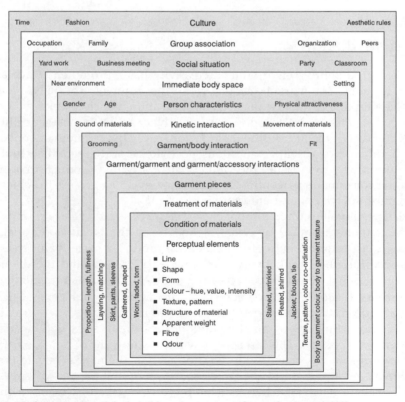

Figure 8.12 Contextual model of clothing sign system. *Source*: Damhorst (1990).

of factors influencing that specific context level. The inner layers refer specifically to the complete dress appearance. Clothing, including garment pieces, materials and all perceptual elements are embedded in the larger context of appearance, which includes garment to garment and/or accessory combinations. These are viewed in conjunction with the wearer's body and personal attributes as defined in the central layers of the model. The outer layers represent the micro- and macro-environments of the user, referring to his or her roles and identities. Immediate body space and 'social situation in which a person is observed provides a context for viewing his or her appearance, which may be framed in terms of group associations. Culture provides a larger framework for interpreting that appearance according to aesthetic rules, historical context, and fashion' (Kaiser, 1990).

Identifying the linkages within and across contexts is necessary to understand the similarities and differences in the assignment of meaning to clothing. Defining the contexts that affect the target consumer and understanding their interactions should be integrated in the creative design process because of the impact they have on the consumer's perception and selection of dress elements. The processes explained in this model help understand the dynamics that lie behind fashion and product life cycles, as well as the creative design process. The success of new products builds on the success of previous products.

Creative design

In today's competitive environment, creativity has a prominent place as it is what differentiates market leaders from the runners up (Sheasly, 1996). Creative thinking is the raw material of innovation, which enables a company to do things better, more cheaply, more effectively and more aesthetically (Bati, 1994). If creativity is indeed the main factor that helps differentiate one brand from another, two essential questions need to be addressed. The first is to figure out a way to measure the value of creativity in a product according to the target consumer's perception. Second is to develop a process to achieve this value most effectively and efficiently.

Creativity involves three components: *skills*, *newness* and *value* (Young, 1998). These components make up what is known as the creative product. It is difficult to distinguish between 'the creative product's social value versus its intrinsic value, the simplicity versus complexity criteria, and the distinction between creative achievement, creative skills/abilities/talent, and creative dispositions' (Kato, 1994). Eysenck (1997) distinguishes four general fields of creativity: product, process, person and environment. After briefly reviewing the multiple definitions of creativity and design, these terms will be analysed in a marketing context. This last section will show how the dimensions of value and newness are associated with the product and the market, while the skill component relates more to the process, the environment and of course the person or team who can achieve such a product successfully deemed creative by the target consumer.

'The target consumer could be an individual or a group of individuals (target market).' Both the designer and the consumer interact with a greater circle denoting culture. In the outer circle, the FEA design criteria are interrelated in various ways depending on the target consumer and use situation. They may be complementary or contradictory, dominant or negligible. The authors suggest pairing the three types of criteria to assess their relative importance. Functional criteria include fit, mobility, comfort and protection. Expressive criteria refer to values, roles, status and self-esteem. Aesthetic concerns deal with art elements, design principles and body/garment relationship. All these criteria could be determined and evaluated using the contextual model of clothing sign system presented in Figure 8.13.

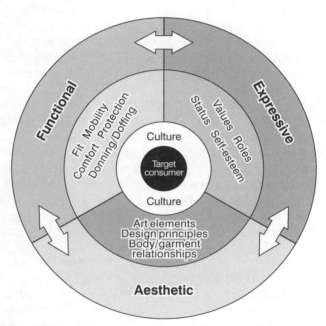

Figure 8.13 FEA consumer needs model. *Source:* Lamb and Kallal (1992).

According to Kato (1994), Besemer and Treffinger's (1981) evaluative criteria defined previously as novelty, resolution, and elaboration and synthesis, can be assimilated with the design criteria of the FEA model. Functionality relates to utility features, which are part of the resolution criteria. Expressiveness is one of the elaboration and synthesis criteria, which refer to 'the particular style the product transpires'. Finally, Kato contends that aesthetics in Western society include such notions as originality and uniqueness, which are classified as novelty criteria.

As stated previously, there is no one formula to creativity. 'Creativity always goes beyond any definition of it', because 'creative behaviour always goes beyond any codification of it' (Young, 1998). It all starts within a person. Tools, models and technology can only support the creative system, but it initially depends on a special blend of inner qualities (Ditkoff, 1998). Creativity results from synergistic interaction of intellectual, intuitive and emotional intelligence (Myers, 1998). Therefore, the creative mind combines a complex combination of various abilities, knowledge, skills, traits and needs.

By definition, creative output should be a surprise outcome, but according to several authors the process leading to successful creative design is predictable. Based on skill, knowledge, inspiration, motivation, experience and problem solving techniques, designers seek something new by creating change or finding new solutions to old and new problems. The design process transforms ideas into reality and occurs from conception of an idea until the development of a workable solution (van Praag, 1987). LaBat and Sokolowski (1999) believe that by following a structured process it is possible to develop a project in an orderly fashion so as to ensure maximum product design effectiveness and efficiency. It is also useful in establishing realistic timelines and providing a means of communicating the work process of the design team among its members and anyone who may be interested, such as other department managers (marketing, sales, sourcing, etc.) or even the CEO.

Most research done on creative design processes focuses on the cognitive approach. Several models have been developed to capture the sequence and associations of divergent and convergent thinking stages logically used to solve identified problems. 'Divergent thinking involves thinking in different directions or drawing from a wide range of options, whereas convergent thinking focuses on and synthesises toward one right answer' (Kato, 1994).

Jones (1981), for instance, describes the three stages of industrial design as divergence, transformation and convergence. The first stage requires the designer to actively research the entire problem without many constraints. The following stage of transformation 'requires that a pattern be imposed on all the information gathered ... The pattern must be precise enough to lead to a solution, but broad enough to reflect the realities of the situation'. This stage is the most creative, requiring 'high-level creativity, flashes of insight, changes of set, and inspired guess work' (Jones, 1981). Convergence then reduces the range of options after application of all the required criteria and constraints. According to LaBat and Sokolowski (1999), industrial design processes are most similar to textile design processes because designers in both cases have to 'combine in-depth knowledge of the physical nature of materials and processes with keen awareness of the aesthetic sense of the object'.

Kato (1994) stresses that little research exists on the implementation stage and that most of the research on evaluation deals with evaluating the finished product. How the designer conducts the evaluation is neglected, even though it is an integral part of this individual's creative progress. Kato also highlights that incubation is not addressed in the creative process models applied to apparel design. Many authors contend, however, that time is essential to nurture and stimulate idea generation and thus activate the creative process (Turner, 1991; De Bono, 1992; Guilford, 1950; Kim, 1990). In her doctoral thesis, Secor (1992) confirms that designers complain about having 'too little time to create'.

Design follows a visual thinking pattern (Kato, 1994; Finke, 1997), which comprehends 'ideas in parallel rather than one after the other: shapes, colours and textures as an integrated whole rather than separately' (Carr and Pomeroy, 1992). 'Because apparel is multi-dimensional and experienced through sight, sound, and touch, apparel designers may be particularly sensitive to these sensory modalities as they create apparel.'

Design creativity is a multidisciplinary science on several levels, especially now that much of the creative process is done in teams including designers, stylists, merchandisers and sometimes even buyers. Design creativity interacts with fashion and trends of the times, with the style of the designer, design team and/or company, as well as with the target consumer's needs and wants. Design creativity is personal to the creator's inner qualities or the creative team's synergies.

In their 1992 publication, Lamb and Kallal asserted that any design project requires market intelligence for analysis of FEA criteria of target consumer needs (Figure 8.14): 'success is judged by how well these needs are met in the final product'. However, after comparing their 1992 model with industry practice (Kallal and Lamb, 1993), they realized they had neglected a different category of criteria relative to merchandising and retail needs of the retail customer. Based on their field study, they collected the following criteria cited by selected apparel companies: ability to retail, brand image, calendar, company success, competition's past performance, costing and availability of resources and skills, line plan, past product performance, product quality, product sell-through, and response to market changes. Therefore, they revised their

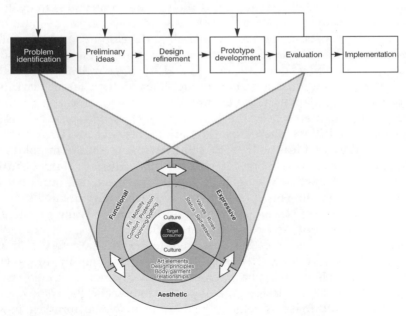

Figure 8.14 FEA design process framework. *Source*: Lamb and Kallal (1992).

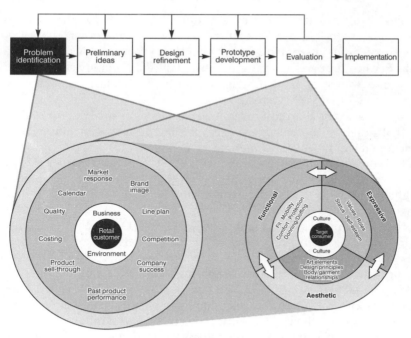

Figure 8.15 Product development framework. *Source*: Kallal and Lamb (1993).

framework, shown in Figure 8.15, to illustrate that the apparel manufacturer actually caters to two customers, the final consumer and the retailer.

Lamb and Kallal (1992) contend that their model contributes to evaluating products in the marketplace and can thus be considered 'as part of the merchandising function, specifically planning, developing, and presenting a product line'. The FEA model can be used to define new problem solving projects for developing seasonal concepts and styles, as well as to evaluate the suitability of existing products and product lines on their target markets and their potential for adaptation to new target market segments.

Figure 8.16 illustrates how the textile product design process has been delineated into distinct phases by the various researchers. Designers must pursue free flow of ideas with both short-term and long-term solutions in mind. Each season they must design products that satisfy the target consumer or even maybe attract new market segments, while making sure that these products correspond to, perpetuate and/or rejuvenate the company's style and brand image. They must also try to develop new and existing products in a way that will optimize their respective life cycles.

The creative exploration is the least well-defined stage, referred to as the 'creative leap' by Watkins (1988) or 'black box' design by Jones (1981). However, Jones believes this phase can be described, if not explained, in detail and communicated to all design process participants. This 'glass box' approach to design, as he calls it, is a systematic, visible and analytical approach in which sub-functions and links between functions are mapped out, and where patterns

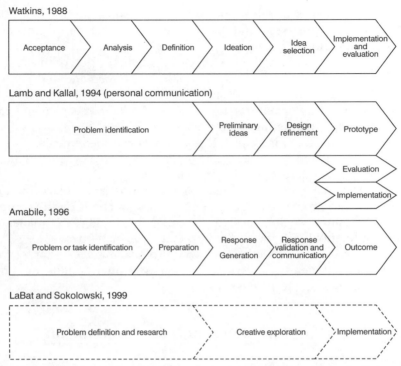

Figure 8.16 Comparing the phase of creative design process models. *Source:* Le Pechoux (2000).

are imposed on all the information gathered in the initial stage of the design process. The models reviewed fail to focus on this initial stage, its components and its dynamic structure. A pattern language could provide the tool to map out and move through the archetypal model of this creative process (Le Pechoux, 2000).

Future innovation management practices

The current state of knowledge in the area of creative fashion design teaches us that the dynamics of the industry are a complex system of interactions in the turbulent and unpredictable climate of the *fashionsphere*. Managing innovation poses significant challenges for the practitioners. The knowledge available can be synthesized as follows (Le Pechoux, 2000):

● In the textile and apparel product design and development models reviewed, design emerges as a multidisciplinary science, which is most generally achieved through teamwork.
● Marketing strategy models place design as an integral component of the marketing mix.
● The target consumer is always at the centre of the *fashionsphere*, guiding and constraining the design process and output.

- Consumer-related issues deal with defining personal profiles, social influ-ences, decision processes and the impact of context and perception on product evaluation.
- When fashion is analysed in a marketing context, it becomes a major environmental factor influencing both the consumer and the companies related to textile and apparel design.
  - Fashion affects a product's life cycle and all of the elements of the corresponding marketing mix.
  - Fashion is subject to multiple global sources and movements.
  - Each brand name has a style and image associated with it, which will evolve to a certain extent with overall fashion trends.
- Fashion is a major external source of inspiration and constraint for the creative design process. The design process also depends on the company's internal resources, such as design professionals, design team management and co-ordination with the company's marketing activities.
- The design process aims to create a product that satisfies a target market demand. Consequently, buyers and target consumers define the creative value of the product to be designed.

Developing a pattern language for innovation management

Research (Le Pechoux, 2000) shows that the creative apparel design process can be greatly improved through the development of a generic pattern language by developing a set of interrelated patterns that describes the initial creative phase of the apparel design process. Using the product development, marketing strategy and creative design process models presented earlier in this chapter, along with the internal and external factors that influence these processes, it is possible to build an archetype of this creative process that will incorporate all of the following:

- Focus on the creative phase of the apparel design process.
- Definition of the design and marketing components within that phase.
- Identification of the links between these components and the various stages of the process.
- Dynamic structure based on these links.
- Consideration of environmental factors.
- Evaluation method of the created output.
- Combination of logical thinking, 'educated' processes and sensory 'naive' processes.

The pattern language developed articulates the dynamic structure of the archetype. Patterns describing the links between all the components and stages of the creative apparel design process have been established (Le Pechoux, 2000). The pattern language enhances the understanding of the creative design process and provides a common language for all design professionals practising a 'glass box' approach. However, it can be foreseen that this pattern language can be used to develop a software tool, customized to the needs of design team members, which will help channel creativity in apparel design and optimize the process. Different design teams developing unique styles could use the pattern language describing apparel design creativity. Their creativity will depend on their own interpretation of each individual pattern, and their selection and sequence of patterns composing their personal language. They may even add some patterns of their own making to this language. As prescribed by all pattern language experts, patterns developed by one design professional should be shared with others in order to speed up the process of establishing a comprehensive pattern language for apparel design, and thus benefit the whole apparel design community and its related industries.

References

Alexander, C. (1977). *A Pattern Language: Towns, Buildings, Construction*. Oxford University Press.

Amabile, T. M. (1996). *Creativity in Context*. Oxford: Westview Press, Harper Collins.

American Apparel Manufacturers Association (AAMA) (1991). The impact of technology on pre-production activities. *TAC Report: The Impact of Technology on Apparel*, pp. 63–8. Washington: AAMA.

American Institute of Certified Public Accountants (AICPA) (1998). Product lifecycle management. *Center for Excellence in Financial Management Business Management Issues*. AICPA/CEFM Publication <http://www.aicpa.org/cefm/plcm/index.html>.

Andersson, A. E. (1997) Creativity, complexity and qualitative economic development. In *The Complexity of Creativity* (A. E. Andersson and N.-E. Sahlin, eds), pp. 139–51. Dordrecht: Kluwer Academic.

Bati, A. (1994). Ideas. *Textile Horizons*, **14** (3), 48–50.

Besemer, S. and Treffinger, D. (1981). Analysis of creative products: review and synthesis. *The Journal of Creative Behavior*, **15**, 158–78.

Brown, A. (1997). Micro marketing, relationship marketing. *Class Notes*, Ch. 10 <http://www.udel.edu/alex/chapt10.html>.

Bryant, N. O. and Hoffman, E. (1994). A critical framework for exploring the aesthetic dimensions of wearable art. In *Aesthetics of Textiles and Clothing: Advancing Multi-Disciplinary Perspectives, ITAA Special Publication No. 7* (M. R. DeLong and A. M. Fiore, eds), pp. 84–96. Monument, CO: International Textile Apparel Association.

Burns, L. D. (1998). *Fashion Theory* <http://osu.orst.edu/instruct/aihm577/fthome.html>.

Carr, H. and Pomeroy, J. (1992). *Fashion Design and Product Development*. Oxford: Blackwell Scientific.

Damhorst, M. L. (1990). In search of a common thread: classification of information communicated through dress. *Clothing and Textile Research Journal*, **8** (2), 1–8.

Dammeyer, M. A. (1994). Marketing research: pinning down change. *Industrial Fabric Products Review*, **71** (3), 22–3.

De Bono, E. (1992). *Serious Creativity – Using the Power of Lateral Thinking to Create New Ideas*. New York: Harper Business.

Ditkoff, M. (1998). Qualities of an innovator. *Personal Creativity* <http://www.thinksmart.com/articles/MP_3-4-2.html>.

Entrada, J. J. (1998). *Fashion: A Cultural Communication of Image* <http://home.earthlink.net/~entrada/writing/Fashion.html>.

Eysenck, H. J. (1997). Creativity and personality. In *The Creativity Research Handbook* (M. A. Runco, ed.), Vol. 1, pp. 41–66. Creskill, NJ: Hampton Press.

Finke, R. A. (1997). Mental imagery and visual creativity. In *The Creativity Research Handbook* (M. A. Runco, ed.), Vol. 1, pp. 183–202. Creskill, NJ: Hampton Press.

Gaskill, L. R. (1992). Toward a model of retail product development – a case study analysis. *Clothing and Textile Research Journal*, **10** (4), 17–24.

Guilford, J. (1950). On creativity. *The American Psychologist*, **14**, 444–54.

Jarnow, J. and Dickerson, K. G. (1996). *Inside the Fashion Business*. Upper Saddle River, NJ: Prentice Hall.

Jones, C. (1981). *Design Methods: Seeds of Human Futures*. New York: John Wiley.

Kaiser, S. (1990). *The Social Psychology of Clothing – Symbolic Appearances in Context*. New York: Macmillan.

Kallal, M. J. and Lamb, J. M. (1993). Linking industry practice with apparel design education. In *Lectures and Writings from the International Conference on Fashion Design*, 25–27 May 1993 (H. Sillanpaa-Suominen and M. von Knorring, eds), pp. 253–8. Helsinki: University of Industrial Arts Helsinki UIAH, the Department of Clothing and Fashion Design.

Kato, S. L. (1994). An investigation of the creative process and application to apparel design models. In *Aesthetics of Textiles and Clothing: Advancing Multi-Disciplinary Perspectives, ITAA Special Publication No. 7* (M. R. DeLong and A. M. Fiore, eds), pp. 48–57. Monument, CO: International Textile Apparel Association.

Kim, S.H. (1990). *Essence of Creativity, A Guide to Tackling Difficult Problems*. New York: Oxford University Press.

Knox, S. (1989). Design management. *Textile Horizon*, February, 59–61.

Kotler, D. and Armstrong, G. (1994). *Principles of Marketing*. Englewood Cliffs, NJ: Prentice Hall.

Kurt Salmon Associates (KSA) (1996). *KSA Annual Consumer Pulse Survey Results*. KSA Publications.

LaBat, K. L. and Sokolowski, S. L. (1999). A three-stage design process applied to an industry–university textile product design project. *Clothing and Textile Research Journal*, **17** (1), 11–20.

Lamb, J. M. and Kallal, M. (1992). Conceptual framework for apparel design. *Clothing and Textile Research Journal*, **10** (2), 42–7.

Le Pechoux, B. (2000). A pattern language describing apparel design creativity. Textile Technology and Management Ph.D. Dissertation, College of Textiles, North Carolina State University, Raleigh, NC, USA.

May-Plumlee, T. and Little, T. (1998). No-interval coherently phased product development model for apparel. *International Journal of Clothing Science and Technology*, **10** (5).

McCann, J. M. (1997). The evolution of marketing systems. *Generation Marketing Insights* <http://www.duke.edu/~mccann/mwb/12partnr.html>.

McPherson, E. M. (1987). In *Apparel Manufacturing Management Systems* (H. L. Needles, ed.). New Jersey: Noyes.

Myers, N. (1998). What is this thing called 'Heart Intelligence'? *Personal Creativity* <http://www.thinksmart.com/articles/MP_3-1-1.html>.

Packard, S. (1983). *The Fashion Business – Dynamics & Careers*. New York: CBS College Publishing.

Perna, R. (1987). *Fashion Forecasting – A Mystery or a Method?* New York: Fairchild.

Petzinger, Jr., T. (2000). There is a new economy out there – and it looks nothing like the old one. *The Wall Street Journal*, 1 January, sec. R, 31.

Pitt, T. (1997). 'Advanced' target marketing. *Segmenting and Targeting Markets*, Ch. 6 <http://www.pcola.gulf.net/~tonypitt/mk6.htm>.

Remaury, B. (1996) L'évolution de la fonction produit/collection. In *Repères Mode & Textile 96*, pp. 178–88. Paris: Institut Français de la Mode.

Rigamonti, A. (1987). Second-generation marketing in the textile industry. In *World Textiles: Investment Innovation Invention*, pp. 229–48. The Textile Institute. Papers presented at the Annual World Conference, 4–7 May 1987, Como, Italy.

Robinson, H. (1987). Fashion: the way forward. In *World Textiles: Investment Innovation Invention*, pp. 249–58. The Textile Institute. Papers presented at the Annual World Conference, 4–7 May 1987, Como, Italy.

Rogers, D. S. and Gamans, L. R. (1983). *Fashion – A Marketing Approach*. New York: CBS College Publishing.

Sadd, D. (1996). Structuring product development for higher profits. *Bobbin*, October, 68–73.

Secor, L. C. (1992). *Computer Usage in Apparel Design and its Effect on Styling and Creativity*. UMI.

Shah, D. R. (1987). Timing: the key to success. In *World Textiles: Investment Innovation Invention*, pp. 269–82. The Textile Institute. Papers presented at the Annual World Conference, 4–7 May 1987, Como, Italy.

Sheasly, W. D. (1996). The essence of creativity. *Chemtech*, March, 15–16.

Smith, T. (1995). Vision of changes in textile markets. *Indian Textile Journal*, **105** (4), 166–7.

Solomon, M. R. and Englis, B. G. (1998). Consumer preferences for apparel and textile products as a function of lifestyle imagery. *National Textile Center Briefs*, March, 28.

Tandem Corporation (1997). Decision support in retail: unlocking the power of retail data. *Retail Solution Brief* <http://www.tandem.com/INFOCIR/HTML/BRFS_WPS/DSSRETSB.html>.

Turner, J. D. (1991). Activating the creative process. *Textile Chemist and Colorist*, **23** (2), 21–2.

van Praag, L. (1987). Managing design. In *World Textiles: Investment Innovation Invention*, pp. 303–8. The Textile Institute. Papers presented at the Annual World Conference, 4–7 May 1987, Como, Italy.

Watkins, S. (1988). Using the design process to teach functional apparel design. *Clothing and Textiles Research Journal*, **7**, 10–15.

Wickett, J. L., Gaskill, L. R. and Damhorst, M. L. (1999). Apparel retail product development: model testing and expansion. *Clothing and Textile Research Journal*, **17** (1), 21–35.

Young, J. G. (1998). What is creativity? *Adventures in Creativity, A Multimedia Magazine* <http://www.volusia.com/creative/2mag1.htm>.

9

The mechanics of fashion

Pammi Sinha

Introduction

Speed of response and capital investment are two of the driving forces of competitiveness to any business, but to the fashion industry design and marketing are crucial. The discussion that follows aims to understand the fashion design process and, more specifically, to examine the role of design and the designer in the fashion design process.

- The first section (of four) describes the environment that UK fashion designers work within and the role of design in the business of fashion.
- The second presents the designer's perspective of the process and their experiences of the design process.
- The third describes the different types of fashion design processes and the role of the fashion designer in the organization.
- The fourth, concluding section discusses the general implications in relation to issues about designers and design management.

The environment that the fashion designer works within

The clothing industry is a vast network of raw material suppliers, designers, manufacturers, agents, wholesalers, retailers and businesses that promote and publicize the products (Carr and Pomeroy, 1992; Bohdanowicz and Clamp, 1994). The UK clothing manufacturing sector has been in long-term decline, with productivity levels of woven clothing, knitted and crocheted fabric, underwear, workwear and clothing accessories falling progressively since 1995. In 1995, it was the sixth largest manufacturing sector in the UK; it is now ranked as the ninth of 11 manufacturing sectors classified in the SIC (92) industry classifications, with a turnover of £17.7 billion for 1998 and exports of over £5.1 billion in 1999 (Key Note, 2000). This gloomy picture of the UK clothing industry clearly shows an industry challenged by price pressures, especially from low-priced imports from Europe and Asia, as well as the success of the discount retailers (Key Note, 2000). A recent report from the Textile and Clothing Strategy Group, however, while acknowledging that large-scale manufacturing may not be competitive against the low-cost importers, has highlighted four areas in which UK manufacturers can compete, other than through price (DTI, 2000). These are:

- Design and product innovation: of great importance in differentiating products and adding value.
- Marketing and branding: increasingly important for the designer and manufacturer to understand and implement.
- Speed of response: recognized as being the one vital strength in manufacturing and delivery of products to buyers as the number of seasons increase to sometimes four-week cycles.
- Capital investment: required for long production runs benefiting from automization to some degree.

The role of design in the organization

Design has an important place in the business of fashion. Diffusion ranges from the big brand designers such as Pearce Fionda and Jasper Conran have proved successful for Debenhams, as have Marks & Spencer's new Autograph collections (just-style.com, 2000). As the clothing market becomes increasingly polarized, an understanding of the core values of a brand and design skills has become a necessity to not only survive, but to compete. The high-end British brands such as Daks, Aquascutum, Austin Reed, Scotch House and Burberry have concentrated on understanding their consumers' perceptions of their brands to redesign their classic offerings and advertising campaigns. Burberry was reported to have a 110% increase in their profits following the revamp of their image and design (Arlidge, 2000). The success of Marks & Spencer's announced restructuring of the 'selection departments' and the creation of new job roles of 'category managers' along 'lifestyle areas' rather than their current 'product areas' to allow for greater responsiveness to consumer demands remains to be seen, but has been long overdue (Carruthers, 2000). Focus groups and feedback from selling managers in each unit are to be used to gauge opinion on products in store from Spring 2001. As far back as 1996, the Marks & Spencer Design Department had speculated that it was necessary to incorporate lifestyle considerations in product offerings (Godbald, 1996).

Design management has been noted to be a powerful source of differentiation in mature industries, contributing to price and non-price competitiveness of enterprises and to economic growth environmentalism, as well as expressing identity, culture and lifestyle (Kotler, 1991; Cooper and Press, 1995; Turner et al., 1998). Building on Porter's (1985) value chain concept, it has been noted that design management creates value at three different levels: management of design activities, integration of the design function into all the business processes and integration of the design methods and decisions to the design vision within the company mission and strategy (Cooper and Press, 1995; Borja de Mazota in Bruce and Jevnaker, 1998). The upturn in the Finnish fashion firm Marimekko Oy's fortunes when the designer was given a more strategic role (Ainamo, 1998) illustrates that strategic design management requires 'a thorough knowledge of the activity of design . . . an understanding of design thinking in terms of its cognitive structure' (Borja de Mazota in Bruce and Jevnaker, 1998, p. 248). This understanding might create opportunities for incorporating 'designerly thinking' and design decisions into organizational strategy. The case studies conducted demonstrate this to be not purely a function of company size or market constraints, but more about organizational culture and management.

The fashion designers' perspectives of their design processes

So just what *exactly* does the fashion designer *do* in the UK fashion industry? Are there differences between what designers do across differing market levels? What is it like being a designer in today's climate? What are the stresses and the pressures of being a fashion designer? What do fashion designers need to be able to do? This section and the next discuss the interviews that looked at the fashion designer's experiences of the process. These interviews were conducted with designers in womenswear manufacturing companies, as market segmentation in the UK womenswear sector is particularly well defined in comparison with other clothing sectors (Sinha, 2000). Significant issues/phases and their sequence were identified, and models of individual processes constructed, compared, variables in the fashion design process identified and differences in the process across market levels considered. The case study companies are presented in Table 9.1. Although Company A

Table 9.1 The case study companies

Market segmentation factors	Company				
	A	B	C	D	E
Company age (years)	87	61	52	6	5
Type of business organization	Part of conglomerate	Part of enterprise/ conglomerate	Holding company	Small business	Small business
Total employees	70 000	40 000 (1467)	210	25–30	3
Group interviewed	Ladies' shirts, trousers and separates (casuals)	Coats	Special occasion/ eveningwear	Stretch separates	Ladies' wear
Distribution by retailer type	Variety	Specialist multiple	Specialist independents and department store	Specialist multiples and others	Specialist independents
Distributors	Marks & Spencer	Own retail and concessions in House of Fraser	Agents and own concessions in House of Fraser	Concessions in Top Shop and wholesalers/retailers	Independent retailers, e.g. Koh Samui, Pellicano

No. of UK retail outlets	280 (M&S)	238	About 80	4–20	1–3
Retail price range	15–50	65–199	45–500	14–40	60–800
Market share (approx., %)	4	1	Up to 1.4	0.02	Up to 0.022
Consumer age	30+	30–40	30+	15–29	25+
Consumer spending power	Medium	Medium/high	Medium/high	Low/medium	Very high
Consumer needs	Fit, comfort, durability, appropriateness	New fashions appropriately toned down	The right 'look', reliance on certain brands	Fashion details, latest trends, fashionability	Individuality

recently withdrew from contract supply, they have been included as an example of just how precarious a position manufacturing of large-scale production is in the UK, because the design process was almost a textbook example of design management and relationship building. This is discussed further later in this chapter.

What does a fashion designer do?

Perhaps the first question that comes to mind when thinking about what a fashion designer does is to try and define the term fashion designer. Without delving into the debate about the terms 'fashion' and 'clothing' (if it is possible to do so), any definition of the term 'fashion designer' seems to depend on how one defines 'fashion' and 'clothing'. The UK Fashion Report described the fashion designer as being '... involved in creative and individual collections ... characterised by high value, low volume sales and mainly small-scale enterprise', where 'the names had attained a certain cachet' and were regarded as 'inspiring trends and refreshing the look on the high street' (EMAP, 1997, p. 435). In contrast, Pamela Stecker reasoned that any definition of the modern fashion designer is dependent on the designer's experience, the company, the type of garments produced and the constraints upon the design (Stecker, 1996). In this section, the skills that fashion designers interviewed felt were needed are discussed, as are their experiences and how and why they came to be designers in the organizations for which they were working.

Skills required

Skills required of the fashion designer range have been documented as being a market researcher of visual and qualitative data, an analyst of the collected data, an interpreter of meanings, anticipating trends and moods to acting as a conduit for expressing current moods (Atkinson, 1995; Potter, 1989). The fashion designers interviewed gave a wide array of answers, but they all emphatically stated that their role was to make money for their organization. Other skills that the fashion designers require are:

- **Communication**
  All the designers felt that communication was vital. Drawing and conversation were important. All the designers worked with a team of pattern cutters, sample machinists and, in some cases, buyers. The drawings were useful tools to communicate design ideas but were also used to understand a design better; for instance, Designer B felt that she was able to think about and get to know her customer better as she drew. Drawing became increasingly important with company size. Designer A's team at Company A used drawing to work out their new ranges for the season with the selectors in the sketch and swatch meetings. A 'process of elimination' decided

possible fabrics for mainly the basic shapes, which were previously successful garments which had been constructed using clients' pattern blocks that suppliers were required to use.

Designer E used his drawing skills to promote his collections at the beginning of a season through the magazines. Draping was more evident at Company D and Company E. The designers worked closely with the sample-making teams and their production machinists, and were available to explain matters arising. Designer E stated that he used a combination of draping on the stand and sketching to design. The larger companies with larger market share ordered their fabrics at a very early stage of the process, most of which were 'repeat' orders from the previous season. The designers were aware of the fabric's behaviour and so did not need to drape the fabric to assess its behaviour on the body. Company E was a very small company, whose consumers preferred something 'individual', used fewer repeat fabrics and so needed to assess the draping quality of fabrics.

Communication as a means of forming relationships was an extremely important element to Designer E and Designer A's team. Designer E's only form of feedback about his collection (other than re-orders or no orders) was from talking to his buyers; sales figures were not released from the boutiques. Designer A's team working within Company A endeavoured to forge close relationships with their selectors in order to discuss ideas for next season. In addition, Company A strove to maintain links with fabric manufacturers to enable production of new fabrics (an important element in updating their classic styles). Designer E did not have the financial resources to make links with fabric manufacturers, but did have a network of freelance textile designers who worked with him on his collections.

- **Belief in oneself**
  This was crucial as designers often had the confidence in their work to convince buyers, finance and production functions within companies that their samples were appropriate for the market. This need to have self-belief was also commented on by Angela McRobbie (1998) in her enlightening study of the fate of new UK trained fashion graduates and the many problems facing them in finding creatively rewarding work in the UK industry.

- **Commitment**
  All the designers felt that their student days had been excellent training for a life as a designer. They had had to build up stamina and energy to maintain the peaks and troughs of working in a studio. The designer's work is not nine to five and during preparation of a collection, they may stay well into the late hours of the evening, returning in the small hours of the morning to get the collection ready. The perpetual round of visiting exhibitions, sourcing fabrics and trims and time keeping for the company was an aspect that was stressful to at least two of the five designers interviewed.

Experiences and approach to design

Common interests that the case study designers had prior to becoming fashion designers were a love of clothes and fantasy, a period of study in fashion (either at B.A. or M.A. level) and the construction of garments. All the designers were capable of cutting their own patterns, even though they were not required to produce patterns as part of their work. The differences occurred in their approach to designing.

Designer A had enjoyed the drawing element of designing and, after graduating from Newcastle Polytechnic in 1991, she had worked for a year for a prediction agency in New York. While she enjoyed the work, she was frustrated by the lack of construction requirements in the work. She wanted to 'design totally in reality' and return to the challenges of garment construction.

Designer B had been a student at a time when couture was no longer the aspiration of all and youth fashion was making its presence felt. After winning a competition to design the uniforms for the BEA air stewardesses' uniforms while studying at the RCA during the late 1950s and early 1960s, Designer B became inspired to dress many women, rather than her original, singular, 'vision from Vogue'. Her personal design agenda is to express the new moods and trends in clothes that suit her customer's age, income, needs and desires, and finds it personally rewarding when many different types of women choose to wear any one particular style that she has designed.

Designer C was inspired by clean, dramatic lines and endeavoured to create drama and glamour in her designs. She had an interest in the complete look (she had trained to be a hairdresser prior to studying fashion). Designer C was also keenly interested in the construction of her garments and worked closely with her pattern cutter. This was her first design job after graduating from the RCA, and, possibly because the garments were intended for special occasions, Designer C appeared to need to understand her customer's lifestyle more than their age and income.

Designer D had always enjoyed fashion and stated during one interview that, while a student, she preferred to wear something that was unusual and trendy, even if it was slightly uncomfortable or impractical, than to wear something that was ordinary. Her overriding concerns for this company were to express the current trends and fashion at appropriate prices for her customers. With the price point and ease of manufacture being immediate issues that she deals with, she finds it particularly rewarding to produce a sample that embodies all her design intentions and still meets the business criteria.

Designer E enjoyed colour, texture, display and exhibition. He had originally trained as a chef for 2 years prior to trying to enrol on a fine art course. Designer E was also interested in self-expression and used to modify clothing to express his moods. At the interview for enrolling for foundation courses, he took his clothes and the interviewers suggested to him that as the fine art courses were booked up, perhaps he should enrol to do a fashion course. Designer E specialized in printed textiles with his fashion and graduated from Middlesex Polytechnic in 1991. Designer E produced his first collection to appear under the 'New Generations' banner at the London Fashion Show in 1993 alongside Alexander McQueen, Copperwheat Blundell, Sonnentag Mulligan, Lisa Johnson and Paul Frith. He won the 'New Generation Designer Award'. Designer E has gained a reputation for producing delicate, ethereal collections that make use of hand embroidery and hand-finished elements, such as pleating, petals caught onto fine fabrics, etc. His personal reward from his work is in making garments that are sensual and pleasurable to wear. He particularly enjoys the idea that his clothes are not definable into any particular period in time or category, such as special occasion or eveningwear. He enjoyed the fact that one of his clients reported that she had bought one of his thick silk garments and felt comfortable wearing it with boots when she went camping.

The designers interviewed all had very common constraints and pressures that they had to face in their work pattern.

- **Time**

  All designers had to produce their collections within a certain time frame and all felt the pressures of producing samples worthy of selection for manufacture. Designer D produced a new range of samples every 4 weeks for wholesale and for TopShop concessions. Designer A's team produced a large range (upwards from 60 pieces) every 5–7 months. They also produced smaller, more fashion-orientated ranges within the season and also liaised with the factories and selectors at Marks & Spencer to ensure that the garments manufactured were as agreed. Designer B has spent a lot of her time 'between seasons' with fashion colleges lecturing, being involved in many college projects, and is external assessor for many fashion degree and technical courses. For the last 14 years, Designer B has been a jury member for the RSA Design Bursaries Competition (Fashion) and a Fellow of the RSA for the last 10 years. The MBE was conferred upon her in 1990. She also physically visits the shops and gets to know her customer by observing not only what and how they buy, but also how they are dressed when they come into the shops. Designer C began her next season's collection as soon as the samples were selected for manufacture. Designer E, being the company director, as well as designer, had to ensure that all business and manufacturing concerns were cared for. For example, in chasing orders and payments, overseeing production and quality, liaising with his buyers and clients for their 'special orders'.

- **Price point**

  All the designers were conscious of the need to meet the pricing constraints in their designs. Designers expressing particular concerns about the pricing issues were those at Companies A, B and D. Designer E's garments were sold in boutiques around London, Paris, etc. and price point was not as great an issue, if the design justified the expense. Designer C found that, through her success at the company, she could argue for a style not to be modified for pricing if the changes opposed her design integrity.

- **Budgets**
  All designers' budgets for the forthcoming season depended on the success
  of the previous season. An added pressure was if the budget was increased
  due to a particularly good season, as the expectations were that this season
  needed to be at least as good (if not better).

The fashion design process

There is a wide diversity of scales of operations and organization of the
fashion industry, including wholesaling and retailing as well as manufacturing
(Baynes et al., 1990). Typically, the fashion design process has been regarded
as being phased, with the first stage as 'research', followed by 'design
development' and 'manufacture' (Frings, 1991; Drew, 1992; Carr and
Pomeroy, 1992; Stecker, 1996). As individual models were compared, a
'generic' design process model was constructed and is illustrated in Figure
9.1. Each of the five generic phases of the process provided opportunities for
the uptake of market information. The development of the styles was
iterative, i.e. amendments continued until the style was deemed to be of
appropriate fit, quality, size, etc. for manufacture. Once in this phase, it was
too expensive to accommodate changes to design and manufacturing specifications. The phases that differed between the companies were synthesis,
selection and manufacturing. These differences were related to company size,
type of consumer, number of retail distribution outlets (potential market
size), finance available, how information was taken on about the market, its
analysis and the ultimate use of this information. The comparisons are
discussed below and simplified individual flowcharts are presented as a
comparison in Figure 9.2.

Phase A1: research and analysis

All the designers were responsible for collecting and analysing information
about design trends (design audit). Market research was described as
information about market trends, as well as retail sales figures for the past
season. This information was in the form of visuals through magazines and
sketches of new styles and details, fabric swatches and colour trends. It was
interesting to note that none of the designers mentioned making use of the
commercial market reports and/or quantitative market information about
consumer trends. The business functions of the company (e.g. marketing, sales,
accounts) were responsible for analysing sales figures and assessing organizational resources (business audit). The results of the design audit (inspirational
strategy: initial conclusions about design directions that the designers would
like to take) were combined with the business audit (styles that had proved to
be successful commercially). This combination provided the company with a
strategy (confirmational strategy) for the rest of the season. The differences are
tabulated in Table 9.2.

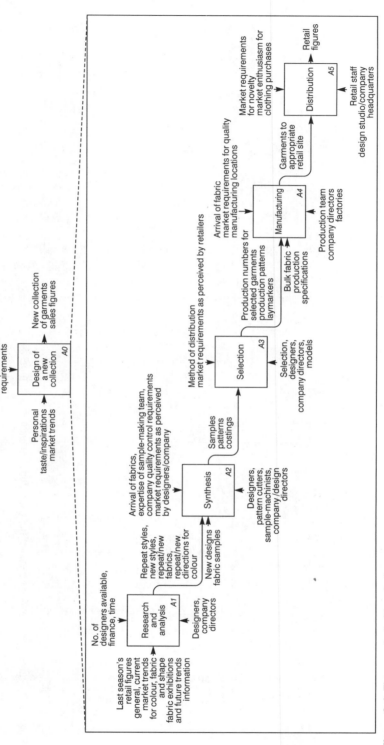

Figure 9.1 The generic fashion design process.

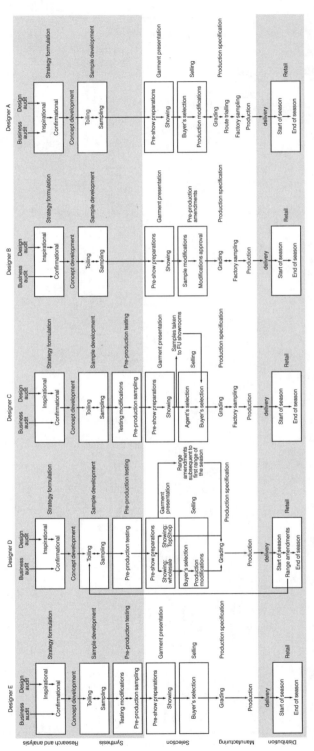

Figure 9.2 Summary comparison between the case study company design processes.

Table 9.2 Differences between the case study companies in the research and analysis phase

A	B	C	D	E
Shortest percentage of time spent in this phase than the other companies; has the most number of designers working for the client's account (94)				Largest percentage of time spent in this phase than the other companies, also the smallest company
Designers worked as a team and shared the information amongst the company		Designers worked as a team but did not share the information amongst the company	Designer worked with sales director	Designer was the company director, therefore responsible for conducting all business and design audits
Designers mainly concerned with gathering design trends information				Perceived his customer as requiring individuality and stated that he avoided much of the styling research, preferring to source fabrics, gardening and interiors magazines for colour and texture inspirations
Produced the most in terms of tangible results of research and analysis: reports of the trends, gaps in their buyers' market, as well as conducting focus groups to understand their (and their major buyers') core customers				
Results from business audit combined with the inspirational strategy and Marks & Spencer's analysis of the design directions; considerable interaction between Company A and Marks & Spencer in formulating the confirmational strategy				

Phase A2: synthesis

All designers developed concepts and produced samples of the designs that were to be considered for manufacture. Styles were only manufactured or bought after viewing as samples. The process of sample making was a vital part of the process because it enabled the following:

1 Visual appearance of the design could be assessed for suitability of the fabric, colour and style.
2 The look of the design was viewed as it would look like when bought.
3 The appropriate amount of fabric for the appropriate price point could be assessed.
4 Quality control tests for the fabric and manufacture were possible on the sample.
5 Further sizes could be graded from the sample.

Major differences between the companies are tabulated in Table 9.3.

Phase A3: selection

All the companies prepared their garments for showing to a group of selectors, resulting in the specification of style numbers, their colours, sizes and numbers to be manufactured. Differences between the companies are tabulated in Table 9.4.

Phase A4: manufacture

This phase was concerned with the production of selected samples according to the order specifications. This was the second longest phase, varying between 20% and 45% of the design process. Differences between the companies are tabulated in Table 9.5.

Phase A5: distribution

Manufactured samples were delivered to the appropriate retail outlets for selling to the public. This was the longest phase of the design process, varying between 25% and 50%. All companies collected their wholesale figures over the season. Availability of retail figures, which provided the most direct information about consumer buying and success of the design, varied. The differences between the companies are tabulated in Table 9.6.

The comparison between the case studies identified the following variables that changed according to market segment, company size and market share, i.e. links between the design process and its market segmentation:

● Market research efforts
● Understanding the consumer
● Analysis of trends data

Table 9.3 Differences between the case study companies in the synthesis phase

A	B	C	D	E
Phase distinguishable from previous phase	Phase increasingly indistinguishable			Indistinct from previous phase
Buyer involved in sample making decisions; largest percentage of process for this phase than other companies	Shortest phase than other companies	Longer time than other companies; samples modified at this stage to make ready for manufacture. Samples shown to buyers as examples of their quality as well as styles		
Greatest proportion of 'repeats'			Least proportion of 'repeats'	
Least use of draping; shapes constrained by buyer's templates				Greatest use of draping

Table 9.4 Differences between the case study companies in the selection phase

A	B	C	D	E
Modifications made in this phase for manufacturing		No further modifications from buyers undertaken	Further modifications from wholesalers undertaken if very small changes	Very few modifications undertaken from buyers
Buyer selected manufacturing range and specified modifications	Shortest percentage time in this phase in comparison with other companies; retail as well as manufacture, no third party involved in selection		Longest percentage of time in this phase in comparison with others. Separation of samples from Top Shop and wholesale. Also produced new range every four weeks to update their offerings	

Table 9.5 Differences between the case study companies in the manufacturing phase

A	B	C	D	E
	Factory samples necessary because factories located at some distance			Production took place on site, no factory sampling
Own factories enable 'route trialling' to ensure smooth production and delivery of garments	Sourcing of factories necessary		Longest in comparison between companies because new range produced every four weeks	
		Some own factories		

Table 9.6 Differences between the case study companies in the distribution phase

A	B	C	D	E
Strong supplier relations with Marks & Spencer; retail figures available	Own retail sites; all retail figures available	Retail figures from own concessions		
		Boutiques or wholesalers did not release retail figures; usually rely on relationship with them to get feedback		usually rely on
				Private orders from customers gave some indication of consumer wants and needs from face-to-face discussion

- Building relationships within the industry
- Efforts in quality checking
- Sizing variations and proximity to manufacture
- Use of computer technology
- Level of standardization
- Importance of fabric to the new range
- Design process organization and the role of the designer
- Time variance in preparing all samples for selection.

The relationships between the variables are summarized in Figure 9.3, which is a causal network diagram arranged so that each variable is numbered from top to bottom of the page, allowing for 'streams' to be viewed. For example, factors involved in classic styling:

1 A factor in classic styling (variable **28**) involved a high reliance on fabric (**20**).
2 High reliance on fabrics was the result of either a high level of product standardization (**21**) or reduced effort in researching the fashion trends (**15**).
3 Reduced efforts in market research were the result of a lower market share (**4, 3**), which indicated a lower age group of customers with requirements for either the latest trends or something different from the rest.
4 A high standardization level (**21**) coupled with a high sizing variation (**22**) was the result of a large effort in understanding the consumer needs (**17**), strongly linked to consumers of 30+ years of age.
5 The number of consumers in the 30+ age group is high (**4**), indicating a large market share leading to increased finance availability (**5**).
6 Increased finance lessened the proximity of manufacturing locations (**24**) and allowed a greater use of computer technology (**14**).

Because the manufacturing locations are distant (**24**), there is increased sizing variations and greater number of quality checks (**25**) for fit and durability, indicating classic styling.

The role of the fashion designer within the fashion organization

Table 9.7 illustrates that all case study company designers were responsible for their designs until the stages of manufacture, i.e. grading and styling checks. Designer E was involved throughout the design process, as he was the company director. While the case studies had primarily been concerned with the operational nature of the fashion design process, the designers indicated during the interviews how design decisions were made and were ranked according to how influential to the company they felt their design recommendations to be.

As expected and illustrated in Table 9.8, Designer E ranked the highest, as he was the company director as well as designer. Designer E described how his interest in colour and texture led him to experiment with and focus on the

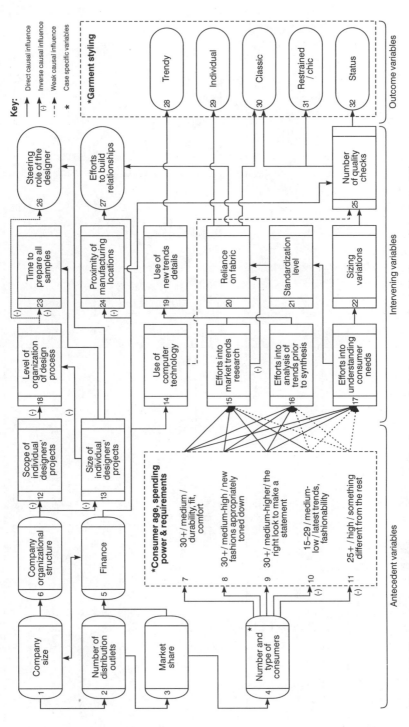

Figure 9.3 Change in fashion design process variables for manufacturing companies with the market segmentation.

Table 9.7 Differences between the case study companies for involvement of the designer

Stage no.	Sub-stage no.	Sub-stage description	A	B	C	D	E	Number of sub-stages within phase
Phase A1: research and analysis								
A11		Business audit	*	*	*	*	*	A=4, B=4, C=4, D=4, E=4
A12		Design audit	*	*	*	*	*	
A13	A131	Strategy formulation (inspirational)	*	*	*	*	*	
	A132	Strategy formulation (confirmational)	*	*	*	*	*	
Phase A2: synthesis								
A21		Concept development	*	*	*	*	*	A=3, B=3, C=5, D=4, E=4
A22	A221	Sample development (toiling)	*	*	*	*	*	
	A222	Sample development (sampling)	*	*	*	*	*	
A23	A231	Pre-production testing (modifications)			*	*	*	
	A232	Pre-production testing (sampling)			*			
Phase A3: selection								
A31		Garment presentation (pre-show preparations)	*	*	*	*	*	A=4, B=4, C=4, D=4, E=3
	A312	Garment presentation (showing)	*	*	*	*	*	
	A313	Garment presentation (agents' showing)			*			

Code	Sub-stage	A	B	C	D	E	
	A314	Pre-production amendments (sample modifications)	*	*	*	*		
	A315	Pre-production amendments (modifications approval)	*	*	*	*	*	
A32	A321	Selling (buyers' selection)	*	*	*	*	*	A=4, B=4, C=4, D=4, E=3
	A322	Selling (production modifications)	*	*	*	*	*	
Phase A4: manufacture								
A41	A411	Production specification (grading)	*	*	*	*	*	
	A412	Production specification (route trialling)	*					
	A413	Production specification (factory sampling)	*	*	*			A=4, B=3, C=3, D=2, E=2
A42		Production	*	*	*	*	*	
Phase A5: distribution								
A51		Delivery	*	*	*	*		
A52	A521	Retail (start of season)	*	*	*	*	*	
	A522	Retail (range amendments)				*	*	A=3, B=3, C=3, D=4, E=3
	A523	Retail (end of season)	*	*	*	*	*	
		Total number of substages =	18	17	19	18	16	

*The sub-stage is present in the company, shaded areas indicate involvement of designer.

Table 9.8 Design decisions taken by the designer

Score of designer influence	Designer alone decides on colour	Designer alone decides on fabric	Designer alone decides on style	Designer alone decides on conceptual range	Designer alone decides on manufacturing range	Score (maximum score = 25)
5	E	E	E	E		E = 21
4			B, D			B = 16
3	B	A, B, D		B	B	D = 12
2	C, D	C	A, C	A, C, D		C = 9
1	A				A, C, D, E	A = 9
	Decision specified	Decision specified	Decision specified	Decision specified	Decision specified	

fabric to guide him for new shapes. His efforts were directed at interpreting his personal inspirations. Designer E's success through peer review is evidenced through being awarded the New Generation Designer Award 1993 and profiled in magazines with wide circulation numbers, such as *Vogue* and *Marie Claire* (Armstrong, 1995; *Marie Claire*, 1993). That he is still trading with no financial backers after 5 years is also testament to his skills in business as well as design. Company E is due to produce a range of lingerie and nightwear for the designer area at Debenhams (Whitehead, 2000).

Designers A and C (where the company employee numbers were about 70 000 and 210, respectively) ranked lowest among the case studies for their influence in the decision-making process, indicating that the steering role of the designer is not merely a factor of the company size. Companies A, B, C and D had gained commercial success. Company A, in particular, had been successful for a number of years through their very strong relationship with Marks & Spencer. The design management at Company A was reorganized during 1996–1997 and was a textbook example of team structure and good practice in that it allowed for improved relationships with the clients and between team members (Hill and Jones, 1998). This did not, however, prevent a reduction in sales to Marks & Spencer in 1999 and, finally, withdrawal from contract supply (Company A Annual Reports and Accounts, 1999; Reuters, 2000). Moreover, the large production numbers, distance of factory locations and all the ensuing problems of maintaining design and quality integrity, and time taken for new styles to enter into retail make for an apparently inflexible process. As has been noted, the large organization is disadvantaged because it is risk aversive and has slow movement of information due to its hierarchical structure, while the small companies benefit from remaining flexible and agile (Champion and Carr, 2000). Company A's withdrawal from contract clothing makes a compelling argument for, among others, the role of the designer and designerly thinking to be more strategically involved in the company.

Conclusion

The designer in the smaller companies has a more strategic role than in the larger companies and it may be time to reassess how much autonomy the designers ought to have in the design process. From the case studies it was clear that the designers' understanding of the consumer needs and wants, interpretation of this into desirable designs and their ability to communicate this to the relevant people efficiently in the sample-making process were crucial to the success of the design. A comparison of the designers' activities confirmed the literature review about the definition and role of the fashion designer as market and trends researcher, analyst and team leader in the sample-making process. These skills look set to become an even more critical factor for a labour-intensive industry beset by cost-cutting strategies that large retailers and their suppliers appear unable to avoid, however dire the consequences.

Considerations may be given to vocational training in strategic thinking, business development and creating support mechanisms to increase the feeling of being a stakeholder in the business. Integrating design thinking into corporate strategy may be possible through strategic change and innovation, termed organizational learning by MacLean and MacIntosh (1997). Indeed, it would appear to be necessary to encourage 'risk taking' in the manner in which designers such as Designer E are able to exercise for companies to remain innovative and able to function in the current business climate (Champion and Carr, 2000).

References

Ainamo, A. (1998). Design and competitive advantage: the case of Marimekko Oy, a Finnish fashion firm. In *Management of Design Alliances* (M. Bruce and B. Jevnaker, eds). Wiley.

Arlidge, J. (2000). Future of Britain's luxury brands is in the past, 3 October <http://www.just-style.com>.

Armstrong, L. (1995). Made in England. *Vogue*, February, 92.

Atkinson, S. (1995). Designing and marketing fashion products. In *Fashion Marketing* (M. Easey, ed.), pp. 107–34. Oxford: Blackwell Science.

Baynes, K., Brochocka, K. and Saunders, B. (1990). *Fashion and Design* (a Penguin self-starter). Harmondsworth: Penguin.

Bohdanowicz, J. and Clamp, J. (1994). *Fashion Marketing*. London: Routledge.

Bruce, M. and Jevnaker, B. (eds) (1998). *Management of Design Alliances: Sustaining Competitive Advantage*. Wiley.

Carr, H. and Pomeroy, J. (1992). *Fashion Design and Product Development*. Oxford: Blackwell Scientific.

Carruthers, R. (2000). More jobs to go as staff restructuring bites at M&S: focus is on lifestyle buying. *Drapers Record*, 20 May, 3.

Champion, D. and Carr, N. G. (2000). Starting up in High Gear: an interview with Vinod Khosla. *Harvard Business Review*, July/August.

Company A (1999). Annual Reports and Accounts.

Cooper, R. and Press, M. (1995). *The Design Agenda; A Guide to Successful Design Management*. Wiley.

Drew, L. (1992). *The Business of Fashion*. Cambridge: Cambridge University Press.

DTI (2000). *A National Strategy for the UK Textile and Clothing Industry*, June. London: DTI.

EMAP (1997). *The UK Fashion Report*, Market Tracking International Ltd. London: EMAP Fashion.

Frings, G. S. (1991). *Fashion: From Concept to Consumer*, 3rd Edn. Englewood Cliffs, NJ: Prentice-Hall.

Godbald, B. (1996). A personal interpretation of consumers and marketing in the future. Seminar presentation for the Textile Institute, 24 October, Manchester.

Hill, C. W. L. and Jones, G. R. (1998). *Strategic Management, An Integrated Approach*. Boston: Houghton Mifflin.

just-style.com (2000). Marks and Sparks fly, 27 January <http://www.just-style.com>.

Key Note (2000). *UK Clothing and Footwear Market Sector Report*. London: Key Note Publications.

Kotler, P. (1991). *Marketing Management: Analysis, Planning, Implementation and Control*, 7th Edn. Englewood Cliffs, NJ: Prentice-Hall.

MacLean, D. and MacIntosh, R. (1997). Conditioned emergence: an approach to transformation using business process re-engineering and organisational learning. *British Academy of Management Conference*, London Business School, Queen Elizabeth II Conference Centre, London, 8–10 September <http://bprc.warwick.ac.uk/bam4.htm>

Marie Claire (1993). New designers, supplement to main magazine. *Marie Claire*, October.

McRobbie, A. (1998). *British Fashion Design: Rag Trade or Image Industry?* London: Routledge.

Porter, M. E. (1985). *Competitive Advantage: Creating and Sustaining Superior Performance*. New York: Free Press (Macmillan).

Potter, N. (1989). *What is Designer: Things, Places, Messages*, 3rd Edn. London: Hyphen Press.

Reuters (2000). Company A to sell off contract unit, 6 September.

Sinha, P. (2000). A comparative study of fashion design processes in the UK women's wear industry. Ph.D. thesis, Institute of Social Research, University of Salford.

Stecker, P. (1996). *The Fashion Design Manual*. Australia: Macmillan Education.

Turner, R., Kelley, T. A., Fricke, P. et al. (1998). Eighteen views on the definition of design management. *Design Management Journal*, Summer, 14–19.

Whitehead, D. (2000). Debenhams chases M&S share of lingerie market. *Drapers Record*, 3 June.

10

Consumers and their negative selves, and the implications for fashion marketing

Emma Banister and Margaret K. Hogg

Introduction

The primary focus of this chapter is the interaction between consumers' views of themselves and their use of fashion products and brands as symbols to enhance these views, and more specifically the 'non-choice' or avoidance of other products, and the relationship of these products (or brands) with the self. In its discussion of the self-congruency theory, this chapter primarily concentrates on the purchase of clothing brands, the choice of fashion retailers and the selection of images in accordance with views of the self. However, the theory and ideas put forward are of high relevance to any product or product category which can be considered to be high in symbolic meaning. Initially, existing literature concerning symbolic consumption, the self-concept and congruency theory will be outlined and useful references will be provided for those of you who would like to read more fully around the areas. This will be followed by a discussion of the negative aspects of symbolic consumption and a consideration of the influence of *negative selves* on consumption decisions.

Symbolic consumption

Product and brand symbolism recognizes the inability of the economic value of an object to fully capture the actual value of products or brands for many consumers (Levy, 1959; Richins, 1994; Hirschman and Holbrook, 1980; Solomon, 1983), and represents value above the functional value of the product (or brand). In fact, branding is often used by manufacturers as a means of adding symbolic value to an item.

In order to convey symbolic meaning, a minimum of two conditions must be present – a symbol should be identified with a group, and within this group it should communicate similar meanings (Hirschman and Holbrook, 1980; Ligas and Cotte, 1998). The product and brand symbolism literature reflects the idea that aspects of the consumption process allow others to make certain inferences about consumers (Grubb and Grathwohl, 1967, p. 24; Solomon, 1983, p. 320; Freitas et al., 1997; Belk, 1988) and that psychological needs can be achieved through consumption choices (Escalas, 1997). Clothing is a highly symbolic product category and its high visibility means that individuals will often make assumptions about others purely on the basis of their clothing. The symbolic nature of clothing can incorporate clothing styles, brands, retailer outlets, uniforms, membership of particular sub-cultures and so forth.

> For example, Calvin Klein. When someone buys an item of Calvin Klein branded clothing, they are unlikely to buy items by the label solely as a means of ensuring warmth and cover. Wearing the Calvin Klein label hints at the sophistication and design consciousness of the consumer. The label might be worn by people who want to communicate an element of wealth in addition to an uncluttered lifestyle (the simplicity of the designs) and an appreciation for quality and the finer things in life is likely to be assumed by others.

Symbolic consumption is not limited to the purchase and wearing of fashion items, but includes all social practices. The purchase of products, newspapers and magazines, visiting museums, watching films, even the food that we eat, all these practices are saturated with meanings and values. The meanings and values combine to contribute to consumers' sense of who they are (and who they are not) and what they represent (or do not represent).

Self-concept

Any discussions about identity and the relationship between consumers and their possessions should feature the notion of the *self-concept*. A fairly early definition by Rosenberg (1979, p. 7) is perhaps the most widely used, and considers the self-concept to denote the 'totality of the individual's thoughts and feelings having reference to himself as an object'.

A number of different dimensions of the self-concept have been identified. The most widely explored components are the actual or current self (how a person perceives him or herself), the ideal self (the qualities that an individual would like to possess but falls short of) and the social self (how a person believes that others will perceive him or her). The self-concept is essentially a dynamic structure that changes according to the nature of the social surroundings or situation. Possible selves (which include both hoped for and feared possibilities) can function as incentives for future behaviour (Cross and Markus, 1991; Markus and Nurius, 1986). The central idea, and the importance of possible selves to consumption decisions, is based on the premise that what an individual is striving for is as important as what they currently are. Consumers will make use of negative possible selves as incentives to change their current self or as a motivation to act and consume in a certain way.

The audience

In addition to the self-concept, the notion of an audience plays a significant role in the communication of products' and brands' symbolic properties. The idea of an audience of 'significant others' draws upon Bearden and Etzel's (1982) research concerning reference[1] groups. Consumers will form associations with certain groups that will then influence their behaviour. Consumers will also form stereotypes of the generalized user of the product and form product images, which will then serve to influence the consumer decision-making process (Erickson, 1996). Positive reference groups will encourage consumers to consume in a certain way, while negative groups will discourage the consumption of certain items, with consumers making negative associations on the basis of the negative reference group.

> For example, in schools, cliques of children often exist who tend to dress in similar ways to each other. The style of dress is often informed by other consumption decisions common to the group – for example, the type of music favoured by group members. Often other pupils (outside of the group) will form general assumptions about the personality of the group rather than relying on the cues of individual group members. The influence of the group therefore functions in two directions. On the one hand, individual group members will be influenced by others within the group, and so their clothing and appearance may be similar. In addition, others (outside of the group) will make certain assumptions about group members on the basis of the generalized group image.

[1] Reference groups are defined as 'a person or a group of people that significantly influences an individual's behaviour' (Bearden and Etzel, 1982, p. 184). For a more detailed explanation of group influence on consumers' behaviour, see Solomon et al. (1999, pp. 268–98).

Product and brand imagery

When consumers interpret the imagery associated with a product or a brand, it is often highly linked to the stereotype of the generalized user of the product – Sirgy et al. (1997) refer to this as the product-user image. It is this image (often informed by the views of the audience) that is considered by Sirgy et al. (1997) to be the most significant in the generation of self-congruency theory. Consumers therefore make judgements and consumption decisions regarding fashion products and brands based on their stereotypical opinions about products and the 'typical consumers' of those products.

> For example, at an airport the observation of others' choice of luggage alone might lead us to make certain assumptions about consumers' lifestyle and even their holiday destination. A Louis Vuitton luggage set would communicate wealth and style, and observers might assume that the owner is jetting off to an exclusive resort. An old rucksack may be used by someone with a considerably smaller budget, and could indicate a sense of adventure – perhaps someone intending to backpack around the world. The symbolism that consumers attach to these brands would become confused if contradictory messages were communicated – for example, if the old rucksack was carried by someone wearing an Armani suit.

Self-image/product image congruency

The theory of self-image/product image congruency proposes that connections exist between an *individual's self-image* and their *consumption decisions* (Erickson and Sirgy, 1992; Kleine et al., 1993; Grubb and Grathwohl, 1967). The *image congruency hypothesis* (Grubb and Grathwohl, 1967, pp. 25–6) links the evaluation and interpretation of product and brand imagery with the self-image and the views of an audience (Figure 10.1). In effect, products and brands are used as instruments to improve individuals' self-image, and the socially attributed meanings of the product are then transferred to individuals through consumption.

An important assumption of the image congruency hypothesis is that the self-concept is valuable to consumers and that individuals therefore will seek to protect and enhance it (Sirgy, 1982, p. 289). This means that if, for example, you are purchasing an item of clothing, you are likely to select a brand name or retailer that conjures up a positive image for you. Often, this positive imagery will be formed on the basis of the *typical user stereotypes* that you associate with that brand. So, for example, you may have a certain set of brands – termed the evoked set – that you would consider acceptable. You would hope (consciously or subconsciously) that by purchasing and wearing an item of clothing identifiable to others as being one of these brands, that the qualities associated with the brand will then be identified with you and effectively communicated to the potential audience.

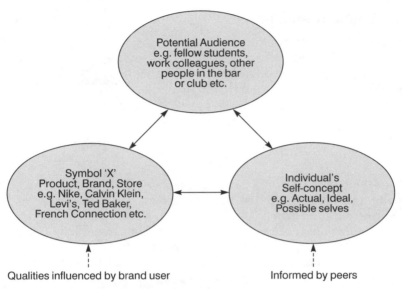

Figure 10.1 The image congruency hypothesis. *Source:* adapted from Grubb and Grathwohl (1967).

In essence, the relationship between products and brands (including fashion items) and consumers' identities functions in two directions. On the one hand, the products purchased help consumers to define who they are. On the other, individuals will seek to *maintain* their self-concepts by purchasing items perceived to be congruent with their identity. Therefore, we can see that both the actual self and the ideal self are important players in this relationship.

Self-congruency theory supports the existence of a system of *appearance management*, whereby individuals use clothing as a flexible means to negotiate their identity (Kaiser et al., 1991). We can see from Figure 10.1 that the 'chosen' identity could vary depending on the potential audience (and the situation). Therefore, different sets of brands or fashion retailers would be deemed appropriate in different situations.

Negative symbolic consumption

So far, we have considered how individuals use their identities and the positive images of products and brands to influence their consumption decisions. However, it is also important for fashion marketers and manufacturers and those studying consumer trends to form an understanding of those items, brands and trends which are not attractive to consumers, and more importantly to appreciate *why* items acquire the images that they do. It is suggested that *what we choose not to consume* is an important aspect of both individual and group identity (or identities). Consumers' rejection of fashion items and brands often says as much about them personally and socially as those which they opt to consume. A framework has been developed that incorporates the negative aspects of symbolic consumption, along with congruency theory, in an attempt to understand consumers' rejection of fashion items for symbolic reasons.

Possible selves were presented in the self-concept section as *a set of* imagined roles or states of being that can be either positive or negative (Markus and Nurius, 1986). Negative selves work in a conflicting manner operating as (dis)incentives for future behaviour – representing selves to be rejected or avoided (Markus and Nurius, 1986).

Much is made of the concept of taste – e.g. tastes in clothing, furniture, and art – yet it is significant that tastes are often asserted in negative terms. Consumers usually have less difficulty talking about products that they dislike and would not consume than they do in expressing their desires and preferences (Wilk, 1997). Consumers also tend to have little difficulty identifying and articulating the negative product user stereotypes and the negative inferences that can be associated with product cues.

Similarly to the positive self-concept, a number of negative selves exist. These negative selves operate within the context of possible selves. Two categories of negative selves have been identified, the *undesired* self (Ogilvie, 1987; Banister and Hogg, 2001) and the *avoidance* self (Banister and Hogg, 2001). The characteristics of these and their influences on individual consumption activities will be discussed.

Framework

A framework (Figure 10.2) is depicted which seeks to identify the means by which consumers attach undesirable qualities to items and the likely negative influence of these on their purchase decisions (i.e. rejection or avoidance). This complements the work of Grubb and Grathwohl (1967), who looked at the

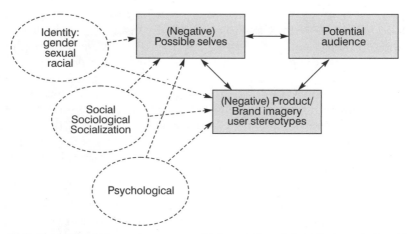

Figure 10.2 Conceptual framework: consumers' interpretation of (negative) product and brand meanings.

purchase of products and brands as a means of *self-enhancement*. The framework seeks to understand how *individual* consumers use the consumption process (i.e. in terms of those products they decide to avoid consuming) as a vehicle for creating meaning.

The framework (Figure 10.2) depicts the means by which product and brand meanings are interpreted by consumers in the context of (negative) possible selves, and the product and brand user imagery that these negative selves activate. The spheres on the left and the broken arrows depict the probable influences on individual consumer's (negative) possible selves and the stereotypes that are important to them. These influences reflect the fact that different consumers interpret products and brands in different ways, and that much of this variety will depend on their particular identity, as well as social forces and their psychological make up.

Two main facets of negative possible selves will now be outlined; these are the undesired self and the avoidance self. One of these selves, the undesired self, was identified by Ogilvie (1987) and the other was identified by Banister and Hogg (2001). The main difference between the two facets is the more extreme and permanent nature of the undesired self, as opposed to the sometimes temporary or transient nature of the avoidance self.

The central idea of these negative selves is that they function as important reference points for consumers, and therefore are significant aspects of identity creation. They will be used by individuals to assess how close or distant they are from being like their most negative (or worst) images of themselves (Ogilvie, 1987; Eisenstadt and Leippe, 1994). Ogilvie (1987) made comparisons between the undesired self and the ideal self, and found the push (of the undesired self) to be more effective than the pull (of the ideal self) in terms functioning as a standard for measuring one's present place in life.

The undesired self: 'so not me!'

The *undesired self* represents those images that consumers consider to be the most alien to their identity, that is 'so not me!'. The *undesired self* is the most extreme view of the negative self, compared with the *avoidance self*. It is less abstract than the ideal self and consumers often have clear views of the type of people (i.e. the negative user stereotypes) that they would associate with this image – i.e. those consumers who would wear the outfits, brands or retailers that they are rejecting. Some of the characteristics associated with the *undesired self* will now be discussed.

Stereotypes

Consumers make use of negative product stereotypes as a means of understanding the product and brand imagery that accompanies fashion items. These negative stereotypes used by consumers are often labelled, with ideas and assumptions about consumers' lifestyles and their consumption activities accompanying the stereotypes. In this way, negative stereotypes form an integral aspect of the undesired self, and a means by which to express why particular brands, images and retailers are 'so not me!'.

Behavioural and personality assumptions

The main difference that exists between the *undesired self* and the *avoidance self* is the notion that specific 'undesirable' qualities accompany the undesired self. These behavioural and personality assumptions are informed by the negative stereotypes that are identified with the undesired self, and in certain cases adversely affect individuals' behaviour towards others (Feinberg et al., 1992). It should be remembered that what represents a negative image for one person may well be interpreted positively by a different individual (with a different set of influences on their consumption decisions).

It is not always complete images, but even small details of a person's dress that can communicate fairly specific messages about consumers. For example, an individual with their shirt untucked from their trousers could be assumed to be disorganized on the basis of the lack of organization of their clothing. Where these negative comments concern personality traits, they often serve to ensure that the observer would not consider dressing in a similar way, illustrating the 'push factor' of Ogilvie's (1987) argument concerning the undesired self.

Experience related

It was argued by Ogilvie (1987) that the undesired self is more experience based and less conceptual than the ideal self. Negative images that are connected with clothing are often formed on the basis of previous experience. This previous experience can relate to (usually disliked) others, or it might be defined by an image that individuals used to have in the past – for younger consumers the 'past image' will often have been influenced by their parents. Sometimes, undesired selves that are informed by 'past experience' translate into not making previous 'fashion mistakes' again.

The avoidance self: 'just not me!'

The *avoidance self* can be contrasted with the *undesired self*. The undesired self is *always* viewed negatively – whether in relation to the individual or in relation to someone else. The avoidance self is viewed negatively in relation to the individual, but might well be viewed positively on someone else who has a different lifestyle, is at a different life stage, a different appearance, personality and so forth.

A different set of criteria is significant when looking at the avoidance self – specifically age, body image, character/personality, situation – and many of these are less permanent characteristics than those that are associated with the undesired self.

Age related

The age dimension is one of the most important characteristics of the *avoidance self*. Clothing is often used by others to indicate the age of the wearer, and consumers tend to have established ideas about what form of dress is appropriate for particular age groups. When clothing is worn that is considered to be inappropriate to an individual's age, it is often interpreted to be 'bad taste' and forms an aspect of the avoidance self. The age dimension functions in two directions. On the one hand, individuals are ridiculed for wearing clothing that could be considered as too 'young' for them – 'mutton dressed as lamb'. In addition, much is made of children (especially girls) wearing clothing that is considered to be too old, and therefore inappropriate. In some ways, the 'choice' associated with fashion items is reduced as consumers become older and more concerned about their body image, and this is perhaps again particularly true for women.

The avoidance self recognizes that, throughout an individual's life, different patterns of consumption will be deemed appropriate (and this is particularly the case with clothing), and consumers will adjust their image accordingly, sometimes with items that a few years before represented an avoidance self for them.

Body image

Consumers' body images are relevant to their avoidance self and the associated avoidance of clothing items, brands and images. In many cases, consumers' body image is related to their age. It is usually important to individuals that they wear clothing that is flattering to their body shape, as well as appropriate. Rules about appropriateness will differ between cultures and will also depend on individual lifestyles.

Character/personality

It is important for consumers that the clothing that they wear is considered to be congruent with their character or personality (an aspect of the self-congruency theory). Wearing clothing which does not 'suit' the individual, in terms of their character or personality, is perhaps the major way in which clothing could be considered negatively (activating the avoidance self), in spite of its recognition as a positive image on someone else.

Therefore, individuals need to be aware of what their image is and the type of dress that they can 'get away with' and, linked to this, the particular 'limitations' that exist for them.

> For example, outrageous designs might be considered acceptable for someone with a vibrant and outrageous personality, although on someone a little more reserved they might be viewed as inappropriate or ill-suited.

In this way, it is likely that some items/images may be rejected for symbolic reasons (i.e. because of the messages they communicate), but without negative connotations becoming attached to the clothing.

Situational

The clothing that consumers purchase is likely to reflect their individual life situation and the contextual nature of consumption. Davis (1985) saw the relevance of wearer, occasion, place and company to the meanings that clothing communicates.

Consumers' life situations will be partly dictated by occupation, life-stage, age or simply their priorities at a particular point in time (Martineau, 1957). Often, situational influences will be a reflection of an individual's very specific ideas about what represents 'me' and therefore by contrast 'what is not me'. At times, what can be termed 'situational not mes' will become relevant. Situations which deviate from the 'norm' for individuals, such as job interviews, functions (e.g. weddings and other formal dress occasions) will represent occasions when participants may 'play' a role that is different from their usual (and often preferred) one. In these situations, it becomes necessary for consumers to embrace an image which might normally be associated with their avoidance self.

> For example, a successful job interview could result in a student most happy in jeans and a T-shirt becoming accustomed to wearing a suit on a daily basis. What might have initially represented an 'avoidance self' for the student essentially becomes a part of their positive image or at the very least a 'situational self', that is part of their image in specific situations.

The work environment is a particularly relevant factor in decisions about what to wear in many countries, and it is often felt to be imperative that the correct signals (e.g. formal, professional, non-sexual) are communicated at work.

The negative self: a summary

Different aspects of the negative self can be identified and classified under two headings. The undesired self ('so not me') embodies the most extreme notions of what is 'not me' and can be linked to the rejection of products/ brands and product/brand user stereotypes. The avoidance self ('just not me'), in comparison, embodies less strong views about 'not me' and can be linked to feelings of aversion and the avoidance of products/brands and product/brand user stereotypes. What clearly differentiates the undesired from the avoidance self is that the latter incorporates images that are negative when the images are applied to ourselves, but these images could be viewed positively on someone else.

Implications for fashion marketing

A greater understanding of negative symbolic consumption and knowledge about the different facets or criteria identified with negative selves is important for fashion marketers attempting to understand consumers. Rather than concentrating solely on the positive aspects of product or brand selection, it would be beneficial for those involved in fashion to understand the negative stereotypes and symbolism that is (or becomes) associated with brands, retailers and images. This information can be used in decision making right the way through the supply chain: from design, buying and merchandising, through to the formulation of effective promotional strategies.

It is important that designers, buyers and manufacturers do not produce or attempt to sell clothing and fashions which conjure up negative associations to their intended customer base. The implications for promotional strategies are twofold. On the one hand, it is important for advertisers to ensure that negative stereotypes and associations do not become attached to products, brands or retailers by consumers within their target market. It should also be possible for advertisers to use a knowledge of negative symbolism or negative selves in advertising campaigns that *encourage* consumers to attach negative stereotypes to the competition. This aim can be achieved without alluding directly to competitors but through the use of slogans[2] and images that play on their target consumers' undesired and avoidance selves.

In order to fully appreciate the 'make-up' of their customer base and potential customers, it is important for companies, particularly those involved with the fickle world of fashion, to begin to form an understanding of this area. It is essential for them to be aware of not just who their customers are, but who they are not, enabling a greater insight into fashion and clothing consumption.

References

Banister, E. N. and Hogg, M. K. (2001). Mapping the negative self: from 'so not me'. . . to 'just not me'. In *Advances in Consumer Research* (M. C. Gilly and J. Meyers-Levy, eds), Vol. XXVIII. Utah: Association for Consumer Research Conference (in press).

Bearden, W. O. and Etzel, M. J. (1982). Reference group influence on product and brand purchase decisions. *Journal of Consumer Research*, **9** (September), 183–94.

Belk, R. W. (1988). Possessions and the extended self. *Journal of Consumer Research*, **15** (September), 139–68.

Cross, S. and Markus, H. (1991). Possible selves across the life span. *Human Development*, **34**, 230–55.

---

[2]   To some extent, this is already being done, through the usage of such slogans as 'beware of cheap imitations' or 'stand out from the crowd'.

Davis, F. (1985). Clothing and fashion as communication. In *The Psychology of Fashion* (M. R. Solomon, ed.), pp. 15–27. Lexington Books.

Eisenstadt, D. and Leippe, M. R. (1994). The self-comparison and self-discrepant feedback: consequences of learning you are what you thought you were not. *Journal of Personality and Social Psychology*, **67** (4), 611–26.

Erickson, M. K. (1996). Using self-congruity and ideal congruity to predict purchase intention: a European perspective. *Journal of Euromarketing*, **6** (1), 41–56.

Erickson, M. K. and Sirgy, M. J. (1992). Employed females' clothing preference, self-image congruence, and career anchorage. *Journal of Applied Social Psychology*, **22** (5), 408–22.

Escalas, J. E. (1997). Meaningful self-brand connections: the incorporation of brands into consumers' self concepts. Unpublished paper.

Feinberg, R. A., Mataro, L. and Burroughs, W. J. (1992). Clothing and social identity. *Clothing and Textiles Research Journal*, **11** (1), 18–23.

Freitas, A., Davis, C. H. and Kim, J. W. (1997). Appearance management as border construction: least favorite clothing, group distancing and identity . . . not! *Sociological Inquiry*, **67** (3), 323–35.

Grubb, E. L. and Grathwohl, H. L. (1967). Consumer self-concept, symbolism and market behaviour: a theoretical approach. *Journal of Marketing*, **31**, 22–7.

Hirschman, E. C. and Holbrook, M. B. (1980). Symbolic consumer behaviour. *Proceedings of the Conference on Consumer Esthetics and Symbolic Consumption*, May. New York: Association for Consumer Research.

Kaiser, S. B., Nagasawa, R. H. and Hutton, S. S. (1991). Fashion, postmodernity and personal appearance: a symbolic interactionist formulation. *Symbolic Interaction*, **14** (2), 165–85.

Kleine, R. E., Kleine, S. S. and Kernan, J. B. (1993). Mundane consumption and the self: a social-identity perspective. *Journal of Consumer Psychology*, **2** (3), 209–35.

Levy, S. J. (1959). Symbols for sale. *Harvard Business Review*, **37** (4), 117–24.

Ligas, M. and Cotte, J. (1998). The process of negotiating brand meaning: a symbolic interactionist perspective. *ACR Competitive Paper* (1999), *Proceedings*.

Markus, H. and Nurius, P. (1986). Possible selves. *American Psychologist*, **41** (9), 954–69.

Martineau, P. (1957). *Motivation in Advertising: Motives that Make People Buy*. New York: McGraw-Hill.

Ogilvie, D. M. (1987). The undesired self: a neglected variable in personality research. *Journal of Personality and Social Psychology*, **52** (2), 379–85.

Richins, M. L. (1994). Valuing things: the public and private meanings of possessions. *Journal of Consumer Research*, **21** (December), 504–21.

Rosenberg, M. (1979). *Conceiving the Self*. New York: Basic Books.

Sirgy, M. J. (1982). Self-concept in consumer behaviour: a critical review. *Journal of Consumer Research*, **9** (December), 287–300.

Sirgy, M. J., Grewal, D., Mangkeburg, T. F., Park, J., Chon, K., Claiborne, C. B., Johar, J. S. and Berkman, H. (1997). Assessing the predictive validity of two methods of measuring self-image congruence. *Journal of the Academy of Marketing Science*, **25** (3), 229–41.

Solomon, M. R. (1983). The role of products as social stimuli: a symbolic interactionist perspective. *Journal of Consumer Research*, **10** (December), 319–29.

Solomon, M., Bamossy, G. and Askegaard, S. (1999). *Consumer Behaviour: A European Perspective*. London: Prentice Hall Europe.

Wilk, R. R. (1997). A critique of desire: distaste and dislike in consumer behaviour. *Consumption, Markets and Culture*, **1** (2), 175–96.

11

B2C online strategies for fashion retailers

Ruth Murphy and Margaret Bruce

Introduction

This chapter examines the factors to be considered in developing online strategies for clothing retailers. In doing so, it offers a brief overview of the clothing retail marketplace, together with identification of drivers of e-commerce technologies. It then analyses strategic positioning in online environments and how a website's strategic potential may be enhanced via online marketing communications. Adopting a business to consumer (B2C) perspective, the chapter strives to identify what websites are doing in terms of creating value for the consumer and in turn how this too may enhance the strategic potential of a website. Finally, the chapter presents an account of the development together with an analysis of strategies adopted by two clothing retailers, the start-up company Boo.com, which has now been taken over by Fashionmall.com, and Marks & Spencer.

Drivers of online fashion retailing

Until recently, the traditional UK bricks and mortar clothing retailers have been reluctant to embrace Internet technologies. Rather, it has been the new entrants or start-ups that have engaged in such with the encouragement from enthusiastic investors. Whilst not all have been successful, for example Boo.com, they have helped to stimulate an awareness of the Internet's potential for selling clothing in an online environment. To date, a number of UK clothing retailers such as Marks & Spencer, Arcadia and BhS have undergone cost cutting, rationalization and management changes in an attempt to revive their businesses. The middle market is being attacked on several fronts. Firstly, competition is evident from the lower end of the market from companies such as Matalan, New Look and Peacocks. Secondly, the medium-sized fashion-led chains, such as Oasis, French Connection and the recent UK entrants Morgan, Kookai, Mango and Zara, are all performing well competing via their own label brands. In all, the market is in a state of unrest and whilst the low cost competitors strive to offer high fashion at bargain prices, both the successful medium-sized fashion chains and the struggling middle players are adopting a multi-channel strategy selling clothing via their high street stores, home catalogues, the Internet and some into digital TV. However, it is uncertain how they will exploit these channels in order to obtain a sustainable competitive advantage. A survey undertaken by Mintel (2000) found that some clothing retailers considered it was imperative to have a web presence, the reason being that it is important to be seen to be doing something. This perhaps indicates that, for some retailers, no clear strategy has been thought through and therefore raises an element of doubt amongst these retailers as to whether the value of retail trading over the Internet is truly going to pay off. However, perhaps it is too early to make any judgements, for whilst the Internet has become a familiar household name, it is a minority of UK households who have access to it from their homes, and whilst this continues to be the case, consumer spending via this medium will remain low (Keynote, 2000). Nevertheless, despite this, drivers of such technology are clearly sufficiently strong enough to encourage retailers to engage in some level of online activity.

Sources driving retailers to build websites are various. Within Britain, the UK government is committed to a goal of universal access to the Internet by 2005 (DTI, 2000), thereby enlarging the potential market for online purchasers. Further to this, the European Union aims to 'establish a clear environment for all actors in the information society in the EU from providers to consumers' (Likanen, 2000), thus further helping to stimulate the growth of consumers using the Internet. In terms of a website's attractiveness over 'bricks and mortar' stores, Key Note (2000) suggests that, as the Internet is global, retail operations are able to penetrate a wider marketplace. Further to this, the low cost entry model of the Internet means that either start-ups or existing high street retailers, regardless of size, are able to enter the home shopping market.

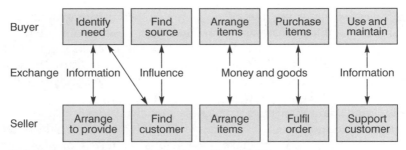

Figure 11.1 Electronic commerce model. *Source:* Nissen (1995).

Together with the above drivers, e-commerce provides retailers with the capabilities to buy, sell and provide support for any kind of business to business (B2B) or business to consumer (B2C) transactions via computer networks: in effect, all the activities which are common to the combined efforts of each of the three channels conventionally used in the buying and selling process, these being communications, transaction and distribution channels. Consequently, in an online environment, a website is able to advertise products, allow consumers to pay for them, and in the case of digital software distribute the product via a download (Li et al., 1999). With regards to non-digital products such as clothing, communications and transaction functions are achieved on a website, but not distribution. Nissen (1995) illustrates this in his model of electronic commerce that passes through the traditional stages of adoption of a product from unawareness to awareness, evaluation of alternatives, purchase and use (Figure 11.1).

Strategic positioning and online fashion retail strategies

Throughout its recent history, the retail industry has been prominent in the quest for productivity and operational effectiveness, employing such technologies as EDI, EPOS, intelligent packing and smart tagging to achieve this (Rawlinson, 1997). Whilst these technologies may have resulted in improved productivities, Porter (1996) suggests that many companies may be criticized for not being able to translate this into gaining strategic advantages. This he maintains can only be achieved through performing different activities from rivals or performing the same activities, but in a different way. He maintains that it is through the adoption of a generic strategy, whether it is differentiated or low cost, or in the case of Matalan a combination of both, offering high fashion at low prices (Jones et al., 2000), each organization determines the means by which it intends to successfully meet strategic challenges. Further to this, according to Prahalad and Hamel (1990), strategies must be built upon the organization's core competencies and have cognizance with changes in the external environment. Walters and Hanrahan (2000) identify significant changing events affecting the retail sector as being: the growth of global companies; changing customer characteristics; new formats such as the Internet and customer loyalty. In all, what gives retailers significant competitive advantages is by deploying their core capabilities to deal with environmental changes and, in so doing, position themselves within the marketplace which is unique to their competitors.

Walters and Hanrahan offer a business model in which customer service, market and product decisions form the choice of areas in which retailers, regardless of their format, make judgements in terms of their strategic positioning within the marketplace (Figure 11.2).

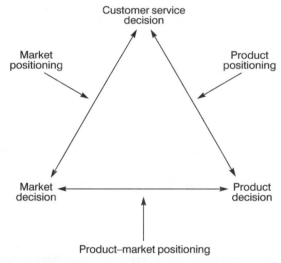

Figure 11.2 Developing strategic positioning in retail strategy. *Source:* Walters and Hanrahan (2000).

Applying this model to online clothing retailing, a number of online business models may be identified. Whilst they are not the only models to be found, in terms of identification of strategic positions online clothing retailers are carving out, they help to illustrate Walters and Hanrahan's model and offer a snapshot of competitive activities (Table 11.1).

Strategic potential via marketing communications

Simeon (1999) considers that the prime objective of a website is to attract visitors, whilst its ultimate objective is to increase the chances that a commercial transaction will take place. He therefore suggests that the site's ability to attract, inform, position and deliver is crucial in terms of assessing the strategic potential of a website. In doing so, he identifies two strategic

Table 11.1 Strategic positions related to online retail business models

Strategic position	Definition	Online business model
Market position	The result of a combination of market decisions and customer service factors.	METAMEDIARIES: a third party that provides a single point of contact between the customer and a community of suppliers. They function to assemble all products and services into an integrated bundle (Sawhney, 1999). An example of such a website is www.theknot.com. Offers online wedding planning service: dress, accessories, scheduling, invitations, registry booking, honeymoon and related travel services.
Product position	Customer service decisions with regards to product attributes.	CLOSE RELATIONSHIPS: develop close relationships with customers though facilities such as e-mail (Maes, 1998). Examples include websites which offer price comparison services, e.g. Ybag, which enables users to request specific goods via the Internet and then invites retailers to respond with their best offers.
Product–market position	Specific product attributes in terms of where product is positioned within the marketplace.	ONLINE BRANDED RETAILER: Market research suggests that consumers value brand names in an online environment as they act as 'familiar simplifiers of choice' (Reynolds, 2000). For example www.boo.com offered a lifestyle site competing on premium brand selection.

outcomes, these being profitability and virtual branding. He defines virtual branding as the 'ability of the website to gain recognition and establish its presence in the minds of customers and the public at large'.

Drawing upon marketing communications activities undertaken by current online clothing retailers, virtual branding may be achieved in a variety of ways. This is illustrated in Table 11.2.

In Simeon's (1999) view, profitability may be achieved by reducing the communication and distribution costs behind the numerous types of commercial transactions, or by generating revenues from either selling goods online or from advertisers advertising on other firms' web pages. A number of clothing portal sites adopt this strategy, such as Fashionmall.com.

Table 11.2 Online marketing communications activities leading to virtual branding

Marketing communication	Comment
Production of information	Annual Reports, locations of dealers and outlets in the user's area. Company history/news. Aim to increase user awareness
Open communications	E-mail facility for users to offer comments, suggestions and complaints. Opportunity to build relations and get closer to the customer, e.g. snowandrock.com
Club membership	Provide facility to join online clubs pertaining to company's products. Opportunity to build customer loyalty, e.g. boo.com
Give aways	Provide users with accessories that support their computer environment e.g. screensavers. Presents an advertising opportunity, e.g. agentprovocateur.com
Entertainment	Provide users with incentive to visit the website, e.g. games and competitions. Has the potential to keep visitors interested, e.g. gap.com
Virtual tour/experience	Offers users the opportunity to 'tour'company facilities, e.g. Liberty.co.uk's scarf hall. Attract visitors to the site
Capture digital pictures	Attracts visitors to the site by providing them with the opportunity to take digital pictures whilst they are online, e.g. capture images of fashion show videos
Instructional support	Provide users with information on how best to use a product/service, e.g. how to wear accessories
Complementary services	Offer hot links to sites containing information pertinent to the firm's products or services, e.g. boxfresh.co.uk

Strategic potential via identification of consumer value

So far, this chapter has established that the strategic direction of the retail firm comprises a selected strategic position sought out by the retailer based upon decisions around customer service, the product and the market. Successful online strategic outcomes, identified as profitability and virtual branding, may be achieved through effective marketing communications and are the result of effectively deploying the firm's core capabilities. However, ultimately, as Walters and Hanrahan (2000) point out, the overall performance or success of the organization will be determined by customer satisfaction.

Customer satisfaction is largely dependent upon consumer value. Therefore, whilst a retailer may be able to attract a visitor to a website, through such marketing communications as outlined above, in turn the consumer must be able to derive some kind of value from visiting the site. Here, the retailer has an opportunity. If they can appropriately identify desired consumer values in an online environment, and position themselves accordingly, in so doing they will be able to differentiate themselves in the marketplace. Overall, in order to think of online retail strategies which create value for the consumer, it is important to consider the various concepts surrounding the term consumer value.

Perceived value may be defined as 'benefits customers receive in relation to total costs', or what Zeithmal (1988) refers to as the overall assessment of what is received relative to what is given. Alternatively, Holbrook's (1999) definition focuses on the interactivity between the consumer and the offering, as he defines value as 'an interactive relativistic preference experience'. Taking this perspective, he has identified various types of consumer value, a brief explanation of which is offered in Table 11.3.

Using these, Holbrook developed a matrix, as shown in Table 11.4, where each cell of the typology presented represents a distinct type of consumer value.

Holbrook (1999) proposes that the model is flexible enough to be able to apply it to a variety of consumer experiences. To test this, we have applied it to online retail sites' offerings, the prime purpose being to assess how online clothing retailers are currently creating value for consumers via their websites.

Table 11.3 Types of value identified by Holbrook (1999)

Type of Value	Description
Extrinsic:	The offering is not valued in itself but rather for its ability or function to achieve something, e.g. the extrinsic value of money or value of a hammer which exists to function to drive in nails.
Intrinsic:	Relates to the essential nature of the offering, which is valued as an end in itself, e.g. a music concert.
Self-oriented:	The source of value derived from an offering is its capacity to contribute to an individual for his or her own sake, e.g. reading a book for pleasure.
Other oriented:	Value derived from an offering is in terms of what or how the offering may affect or influence others, e.g. family and friends or the community, society, the country.
Active:	Value is active when it involves a physical or mental manipulation of a tangible or intangible offering, e.g. value derived from using time saving devices such as ATM machines instead of queuing in a bank to access money.
Reactive:	Value is reactive when something is undertaken by the offering or with a consumer being part of the consumption experience, e.g. the experience of receiving a quality service.

Source: Holbrook (1999).

Table 11.4 Holbrook's typology of consumer value

		Extrinsic	Intrinsic
Self oriented	Active	**Efficiency** Convenience	**Play** Enjoyment
	Reactive	**Excellence** Quality of product or service	**Aesthetics** Beauty of offering
Other oriented	Active	**Status** Success communicated to others via offering	**Ethics** Virtue communicated to others via offering
	Reactive	**Esteem** Reputation communicated to other via offering	**Spirituality** Faith embedded in offering

Source: Holbrook (1999).

Efficiency

The extrinsic value of a website may be gained in the form of saving time, e.g. not having to physically go to a high street store to buy goods, rather ordering them from the comfort of your own home plus having them delivered there. All online clothing retailers who are transactional offer this efficiency. Efficiencies may also be accrued by way of the convenience of accessing information online, e.g. written details of product attributes together with illustrations of product offerings. Landsend (www.landsend.com), for example, illustrate their clothing products in the form of 3-D product presentations. By way of further convenience, they also offer a personal model whereby the user may select their clothes based on their own shape and lifestyle. Another example of convenience is offered by the website Pres.net, a single website of department stores throughout the world that offers a reminder service and address book so that users will be e-mailed to remind them of birthdays or special occasions.

Play

Enjoyment may derive from individuals accessing websites which offer puzzles to be solved. Pleasure for its own sake can also be derived from undertaking information searches, e.g. hobbyists seeking to build up their knowledge in their areas of interest. A number of clothing websites provide value to various enthusiasts in this way, e.g. forming online clubs or communities such as Nike's London initiative website (www.nikelondon-.co.uk), which acts as a site to help Londoners arrange football games after work and at weekends, for instance featuring a 'where to play' section, including details of venues in the London area. In seeking to provide entertainment for its users, Top Shop (www.topshop.co.uk) sells personalized CDs from its website, whereby a visitor is able to select a 10-track CD from a choice of 80 music tracks after listening to 30-second samples.

Excellence

Excellence may be acquired through quality, for example the standard of service offered via home deliveries, e.g. delivering goods when they state they will be delivered, or information regarding product attributes, e.g. sizing information with regards to clothing such as that offered by lingerie retailer Rigby & Peller (www.rigbyandpeller.com), whose site provides a fitting advice centre. Value in excellence may be derived from the functionality of the website in terms of adequately satisfying consumers' needs, e.g. department store group Alders, who offer an online wedding gift service that enables customers to register a wedding, access wedding lists and buy gifts (www.alders.com). Further to this, other examples of value in excellence include ease of accessing information or ease of making transactions, payment security and returns policies, plus visual representations offering clarity of detail of products.

Aesthetics

Consumers may react positively and value the look and feel of the website in terms of its attractiveness. The visual representation of products may also be valued by way of attractiveness of the nature of the offering, e.g. Liberty of London's website (www.liberty-of-london.com) offers a facility for the user to view the Regent Street store's scarf room around a 360° panorama.

Ethics

Holbrook (1999) argues that purchasing products or services which are environmentally friendly or for ethical reasons is a form of intrinsic value and therefore such behaviour is valued for its own sake, what is referred to colloquially as 'virtue is its own reward'. Here value is accrued via the virtue one communicates to others by making such a purchase. Benetton (www.benetton.com) encourages such purchases, using their website to communicate the values embedded within the company, for example a quote on one of their web pages is 'All Human Beings are Born Free and Equal in Dignity and Rights'.

Status

It is suggested that status is derived from individuals actively manipulating their behaviour as an end in itself to achieve a favourable response from others (Solomon, 1999). In terms of using a website to engage in status-seeking behaviour, chat room facilities such as that offered by the sportswear retailer

Ellis Brigham (www.ellis-brigham.com) offers a forum where snowboard enthusiasts have the opportunity to engage in discussions about their sport.

Esteem

Esteem is defined as an outcome as a result of an individual reacting to a response to others' appreciation of that individual (Holbrook, 1999), i.e. the high regard of others when they view what they own or have accomplished. In the context of a commercial website, this may be achieved through the publication of individual names who have achieved something specific, e.g. sportswear retailers providing an account of athletes who performed in the Sydney 2000 Olympics, as the Nike.com website has done.

Spirituality

Holbrook defines spirituality as being a sense of communion one may feel within himself or herself and with humanity. In Brown's (1999) view, purchasing activities are not typically determined by such convictions and therefore this dimension of consumer value is not considered here.

The above typology is useful as shown from the examples given; online retailers, through capturing particular consumer values, are able to build strategic outcomes. Examples of virtual branding may be evidenced through Nike in the case of its association with successful athletes holding them in high esteem or alternatively through building online communities focused on playing football. Virtual branding is also developed through providing efficient and excellent services such as the convenience of home deliveries offered by all transactional websites or the convenience of returning unwanted goods back to the high street store, such as is the online policy of Marks & Spencer. Virtual branding is further achieved through the quality of service offered by Alders' wedding lists. Also, profits may be accrued via efficient and excellent services in dealing with customers' transactions.

Whilst examples have been offered for each of the dimensions of Holbrook's typology of consumer value, with the exception of spirituality, it is interesting to note that one can see that some elements could comfortably fit into more than one box of the matrix, an example of this being information, i.e. the value of information may be aesthetic, playful, convenient or excellent. It may even be a combination of all four. Further to this, one could also argue that the elements of a website may impart different types of value to different users, and it is therefore, as reflected in Holbrook's definition, from the perspective of the individual that one can truly understand the value that has been created for their benefit. Consequently, identification of consumer value for specific lifestyle segments and/or household types would be helpful to online retailers in determining what value would be most appropriate for their target market and in turn help them to develop their positioning strategy. For example, whilst one consumer, who is time poor, may value efficiency highly, another user, who is time rich, may value play more highly.

Case studies

In further examining the factors associated with developing online strategies for clothing retailers, it is useful at this point to examine the Internet strategies actually adopted by clothing retailers. These are presented below. The first company we examine is the start-up company Boo.com and the second Marks & Spencer, the traditional 'bricks and mortar' clothing retailer.

Boo.com's Internet retail strategy

Boo.com's retail proposition was one of a branded Internet retailer selling sportswear labels to non-sports people rather than merely a broker to high profile established brands. Unlike companies such as Amazon.com, who currently follow and target the mass market, Boo.com's web strategy was to offer a lifestyle site competing on premium brand selection rather than price. The company identified a core age group of male and female 18- to 35-year-olds who they felt corresponded to their target market description. The purpose of the website was to be both a content provider and to make sales. In terms of offering information and to support the lifestyle image, the site contained a multimedia 'webzine' called Boom that aimed to offer a 'cultural and high brow lifestyle magazine good for building brand awareness' (Chandiramani, 2000). Further support to customers was offered in the form of the virtual assistant Miss Boo, who performed the role of a personal shopper. Aims of the site were ambitious, deciding not to present their goods in a static catalogue format, typical of many e-commerce companies; innovations included a zoom facility that enabled users to gain a close-up view of fabric, stitching and colour. All advertising was carried out offline through TV, cinema, the style press and national newspapers, plus fly posters and promotions in clubs.

Given that the clothing market is generally considered mature in terms of expansion opportunities, lifestyle positioning presents growth prospects and therefore differentiating themselves in this way seemed a good strategy for Boo.com to adopt. Further to this, choosing not to sell on price kept Boo.com out of the high risk category Internet retailers who are subject to price comparison shopping bots. In all, Boo.com were faced with the major challenge of building up an Internet business from scratch, unlike 'bricks and mortar' retailers such as Marks & Spencer, who have experience of selling clothing both within the high street and via their mail order catalogue, knowledge of home shopping.

Their business model was quite different to other Internet business start-ups, who typically have started small and scaled up when their audience has grown, Amazon being an example of this. Rather, Boo.com attempted to create all the instruments of an international brand from the outset (Michel, 2000). They achieved this on the launch day by launching in 18 countries simultaneously, with seven different language versions of the site tailoring Miss Boo to each country (Chandiramani, 2000).

The launch of the website was 3 November 1999, 5 months after its announced initial date of launch, May 1999. The company put the reasons for the delay of the site being, firstly, underestimating the complexity of launching in multiple countries. Throughout its 18-month life, the firm's strategy altered in a number of ways. For example, in terms of pricing, although it set out to be a premium retailer it reduced its prices after being online for only a few months. Although it invested heavily in technical resources using advanced technology, when the site did eventually go online, its zoom technology was not available to 99% of European and 98% of US homes due to lack of the high-bandwidth access needed. A further problem was that Mac users could not access the site (Torris, 2000). It seems as though the company set itself up offering a business model that it subsequently could not deliver on. As a consequence, this attracted further media attention.

The main assets of the company were clearly its brand, a functional multi-lingual site and an affluent target market. Fashionmall.com, who subsequently purchased the company, did not purchase any of their physical assets. This is largely because Boo.com's 3-D product presentation has ceased to provide differentiation, as companies such as Landsend now also have such facilities, plus this technology can now be acquired from NxView or Xippix, down-loadable programs which are multimedia viewers that can be added to a web browser.

The Boo.com experience has no doubt shown the dangers of uncontrolled growth and highlighted the difficulties of B2C propositions. However, the notion of rapid growth is not unique in Internet businesses regardless of the product or service offered. The low barrier to entry that the Internet offers encourages new Internet businesses to rapidly build their brand and market share in order to defend their position before others 'get in'. But what are the basic issues? As Weir (2000) points out, 'Boo has shown, in spectacular fashion, that cash simply isn't enough to execute a business model well', as he considers the company showed the inability to handle the basic fundamentals of business. For instance, Michel (2000) deems that the major failing of Boo.com was that the founders fell for the 'hype of a few graphic designers looking to their portfolio, rather than the needs of customers'. The fact that the company's strategy kept changing, for example in terms of it pricing policy, implies that, whilst they may have had a good proposition, it was poorly thought through (Lord, 2000). Basically, the company failed to play on an innovative idea that was to enhance clothing presentation through online innovation. With regards to a B2C business model, Fashionmall.com's interest in the company indicates that building high brand recognition is the key, together with identification of niche cash-rich target markets.

The history of Boo.com raises a number of questions. There are some who consider that the greatest business potential of the Internet is to be found in business to business (B2B) activity (Birch, 2000). Certainly, B2B offers greater economic rewards in that less brand building activities need to be undertaken, unlike with the B2C market. Those who are cynics may speculate that Boo.com is just one of the first dotcom companies which will collapse. Indeed, Price

Waterhouse Coopers has been quoted during the time of the collapse as saying that one in four British Internet companies will run out of finances within 6 months (Rushe, 2000). Without doubt, other Internet companies will be dismayed with the outcome of Boo.com, as the event has shaken the confidence of investors. Other companies cited in the media, such as Lastminute.com's falling shares also occurring during May 2000, will have contributed to this.

Marks & Spencer's Internet retail strategy

Marks & Spencer launched its presence on the Internet as an information website offering corporate information such as annual reports, recruitment information and company history. It has subsequently launched itself as a transactional site. Marks & Spencer's problems have been well documented in the media. For instance, recent announcements made declare underlying pre-tax profits fall by 7 per cent to £480.9 million (Voyle, 2001) compared to recent years when they reached profits of more than £1 billion (Lewis, 2000). Whilst the company is currently in the process of selling Brookes Brothers, the US clothing chain's website has been among the US's top ten clothing sites and therefore will have provided a valuable source of information for Marks & Spencer's own e-commerce launch, which took place in Spring 2000. Previous to its full launch, that aimed to sell 3000 products online, including food, clothing and household goods, the company undertook two trials: firstly, early in 1999 to BT employees on their Intranet and, secondly, towards the end of 1999 to all Internet users selling a selection of Christmas gifts (Sturgeon, 1999). Compared to the retail start-up Boo.com, the company has a customer database of 5.2 million card holders and, together with its financial services, had a strong platform to start a transactional website from (Lewis, 2000). With the company's mail order catalogue, Marks & Spencer have integrated their site into their existing customer service, involving an online shopping tool available for customers in-store to order out-of-stock goods from and then check on the progress of their order via the company's website (Sturgeon, 1999). Alternatively, they may view product offerings at home before making a visit to the store to make their purchase, thus suggesting that by merging their fulfilment operations, the company is not concerned by which channel the consumer chooses to shop. In terms of logistics, as an established retailer with a developed warehouse, delivery system and call centre for its catalogue, Lewis (2000) considers that the company was in a good position to avoid the fulfilment problems that some start-up companies have experienced.

According to Lewis (2000), their core proposition is designed around four central principles: product availability, ease of use, reliability and speed. For instance, information regarding the availability of stock is given to customers at the time of ordering, e.g. if a product is out of stock, it will not appear on the site; if the product line is running low, users will be alerted to this (Sturgeon, 1999). Customers are also able to obtain refunds for their online purchases from the high street store, together with the facility to exchange items. In terms of pricing policy, the company considers that offering goods at a cheaper price online than elsewhere is problematic in terms of returning goods to the high street store. Therefore, the company has kept their pricing the same whatever channel is used, not wishing to damage their price integrity (Sturgeon, 1999).

One may have considered that launching a website may have provided Marks & Spencer with the opportunity to reposition their brand within the marketplace and change public perceptions, especially given the negative publicity the chain has attracted recently (Sturgeon, 1999). However, they have chosen to draw upon the brand's long-established image of quality and trust, the rationale for this being that the public know who Marks & Spencer are. As Lewis (2000) points out, the company considers that their offering is well suited to the Internet, as their products are so familiar with customers; one will know exactly what they are getting. The strength of their brand in terms of communicating trust may help to dispel any users' concerns over credit card security (Williamson, 1999).

Like Boo.com, Marks & Spencer have faced difficulties. In February 2000, they planned to launch their new Spring season collection online. However, they had also taken the decision not to accept credit cards until May 2000, therefore limiting Internet shoppers to pay by Switch, Delta or Marks & Spencer Chargecard (Chandiramani, 1999). The rationale for this decision was that without the facility for high street stores to accept credit, problems would be encountered by Internet users who had purchased products via credit cards and then wished to return them to a high street store.

Future plans are that the company's website will not be confined to the UK, rather it will give Marks & Spencer access to global markets without the expense of developing new stores (Williamson, 1999). This is an important consideration for the company given their experience of closure of their stores in Canada and the more recent announcement of its plans to shut 18 stores in France as part of its move to close all 38 continental European stores (Voyle, 2001). It is reported that prime countries for targeting in order to offer their website facilities are those in Europe, the US, Australia and large expatriate communities (Chandiramani, 1999).

Not only has the company made investments in launching its own website, Marks & Spencer Ventures, the company's investment division funded the development of a lingerie website (Splendor.com). Whilst now no longer in existence, like the Brook's Brothers site, it will have provided the company with information regarding such things as consumer behaviour in an online environment. Further to this, along with Boots the Chemist, the company also sells their gift vouchers online through the VoucherExpress website (www.voucherexpress.com) (Scott, 1999).

As part of the company's marketing communications, it intends to put its website address on all of its storefront façades and shopping bags. In terms of getting close to the customer, Marks & Spencer intend to implement systems that will enable each store to manage the content of their own details on the national site, locally. Users will be encouraged to e-mail their local store branch manager (Williamson, 2000b).

Marks & Spencer have received some criticism in the press as a result of the launch of their e-commerce site, suggesting that the rationale for this undertaking is part of a bigger programme of the company changing its image for the future (Lewis, 2000). One may argue against this if the company is claiming to retain their central proposition of offering consumers quality and trust. In turn, this will help to draw their core customer to their website. However, they have also been criticized for having lost touch with their customers (Plender, 1999) and therefore it is difficult at this point in time to assess the viability of their website. What is unique is the integration of the company's various selling channels, mail order, the high street and the Internet. This is a similar strategy to other bricks and mortar fashion retailers such as the Arcadia Group, who also pursued an information-to-transaction strategy.

Summary

This chapter has sought to examine the factors to be considered in developing online strategies for clothing retailers. In so doing, it has presented the drivers that have stimulated clothing retailers to engage in e-commerce. It has suggested that effective strategic positioning in the retail sector is based upon decisions surrounding customer service, the product and the market. Various online marketing communications activities have been outlined, together with identification of possible strategic outcomes. The chapter has also investigated ways of enhancing the strategic potential of a website via identification of consumer values that may be derived from online environments. Finally, the chapter offers two cases studies, Boo.com and Marks & Spencer, in order to examine the online strategies of clothing retailers.

Conclusion

Both established clothing retailers and start-up companies are developing online strategies to sell and market goods on the Internet. Each is having various degrees of success. However, what is clear is that there is no one distinct business model that is appropriate to this format. Rather, various business models are being pursued and therefore suggestions for further research include the production of a clear classification of these models based upon various strategic positions, various marketing communications activities adopted and various attempts at deriving consumer value within an online environment.

Mintel (2000) point out that Internet retailing for clothing currently constitutes a very tiny part of the market. They consider that this trading format will not replace the traditional high street due to the fact that women like to see, feel and touch clothing items. However, they do think that sales via websites will grow. In particular, they believe it will be more likely to be successful for basics than for special purchases. Whatever their predictions or indeed anybody else's, what is clear is that the Internet has the potential to increase consumer choice dramatically and those companies who can position themselves appropriately, differentiate their offerings in such a way as to add meaningful consumer value and in turn deliver that value are going to succeed.

References

Birch, A. (2000). Reality hits virtual shopping. *New Media Age*, 2 March, 26–9.

Brown, S. (1999). Devaluing value: the apophatic ethic and the spirit of postmodern consumption. In *Consumer Value* (M. B. Holbrook, ed.), Ch. 8. Routledge.

Chandiramani, R. (1999). M&S range to go online without credit card facility. *Revolution*, 10 November, 3.

Chandiramani, R. (2000). Ridicule is nothing to be scared of. *Revolution*, 16 February, 30–4.

DTI (2000). *Knowledge 2000, DTI Conference on the Knowledge Driven Economy*. Tony Blair's speech.

Holbrook, M. B. (1999). *Consumer Value: A Framework for Analysis and Research*. Routledge.

Jones, P., Clarke-Hill, C. and Hillier, D. (2000). The growth of Matalan stores management. *Research News*, **23** (5/6), 82–8.

Key Note (2000). *Home Shopping*, January.

Lewis E. (2000). St Michael prays for on-line success. *New Media Age*, 9 March, 26–8.

Li, H., Kuo, C. and Russell, M. G. (1999). The impact of perceived channel utilities, shopping orientations, and on the consumer's online buying behaviour. *Journal of Computer-Mediated Communication*, **5** (2) <http:www.ascusc.org/jcmc/vol5/issue2/hairong.html>.

Likanen, E. (2000). A strong e-economy for all in Europe. Paper presented at *E-Agenda for Business* seminar, Dibb Lupton, Alsop, 23 February.

Lord, R. (2000). Boo, Boo black sheep, have we a lesson to learn? *Business Revolution*, 24 May, 7.

Maes, P. (1998). Software Agents and the Future of Electronic Commerce. <http:pattie.www.media.mit.edu/people/pattie/ECOM>.

Michel, S. (2000). The post Boo fall out. *New Media Age*, 25 May, 20.

Mintel (2000). *Womenswear Retailing*. August 2000.

Nissen, M. E. (1995). *Commerce Model and the Intelligent Hub*. CommerceNet CALS Working Group Presentation, November.

Plender, J. (1999). A prime case of complacency. *Financial Times*, 22 May.

Porter, M. E. (1996). What is strategy? *Harvard Business Review*, Nov/Dec.

Prahalad, C. K. and Hamel, G. (1990). The core competences of the corporation. *Harvard Business Review*, May/June.

Rawlinson, R. (1997). The future of fashion. *Drapers Record Focus*, February, vii–viii.

Reynolds, J. (2000). eCommerce: a critical review. *International Journal of Retail and Distribution Management*, **28** (10), 417–44.

Rushe, D. (2000). From Boo to bust. *The Sunday Times*, 21 May, Business Focus, 5.

Sawhney, M. (1999). Meet the Metamediary. <http:www.sawhney.kellog.nwu.edu/metamed/metamediation.htm>.

Scott, J. (1999). M&S and Boots sell gift vouchers online. *Revolution*, 20 October, 12.

Simeon, R. (1999). Evaluating domestic and international web site strategies. *Internet Research: Electronic Networking Applications and Policy*, **9** (4).

Solomon, M. R. (1999). The value of status and the status of value. In *Consumer Value* (M. B. Holbrook, ed.), Ch. 3. Routledge.

Sturgeon, E. (1999). How M&S is targeting the Christmas market. *Revolution*, 8 December, 32–4.

Torris, T. (2000). Analyst speak. *New Media Age*, 25 May, 51.

Voyle, S. (2001) Marks & Spencer's profits fall 7%: Vandevelde scales back promises of speedy recovery. *Financial Times*, 23 May.

Walters, D. and Hanrahan, J. (2000). *Retail Strategy, Planning and Control*. Macmillan Business.

Weir, J. (2000). Beating the growing pains. *New Media Age*, 25 May, 13.

Williamson, D. (1999). M&S tries its luck on the web. *Revolution*, 17 November, 20.

Williamson, D. (2000a). M&S backed lingerie site suffers launch delay. *Revolution*, 7 June, 3.

Williamson, D. (2000b). M&S rebrands stores with web address. *Revolution*, 1 June, 5.

Zeithmal, V. A. (1988). Consumer perceptions of price, quality and value: a means-end model of synthesis of evidence. *Journal of Marketing*, **52** (July), 2–22.

12

The making and marketing of a trend

Martin Raymond

The fashion business has come a long way from the days when trend predictions were all about attending the industry's key trade fairs and catwalk shows and coming away with a set of sketches or complimentary kit of trend boards with appropriate fabric swatches attached. Certainly this still happens, at events like Premiere Vision, Pitti Filati or indeed the twice yearly catwalk extravaganzas in London, Paris, New York and Milan, but more and more, the industry is moving away from this rather inaccurate and intuitive model of trend prediction, and onto more ethno- and socio-graphic versions. Ones where a whole battery of marketing tools, observation methods and techniques are being used to underpin the looks and lifestyle gambits promoted by an ever increasing number of brands and labels.

Yes, middle market retailers and department stores still use mood boards and fabric swatches to brief their studios, the Urban Nomad Look, the Techno-Warrior look, the City Sophisticate or, if they have less imagination and a dull fashion sense, comparative shoppers who travel the globe and bring back key items to deconstruct and copy. But these techniques are happily on the wane. At the branded end of the market at least, designers more and more realize that fashion is no longer a matter of clothing, but one of lifestyle – a multi-faceted, multi-purpose entity where fashion is just one part of a heady, highly complex way of living. One that requires the true designer to look to the houses we live in, the furniture we sit on, the clubs we go to, the bars we socialize in, or indeed the office environments we spend our days or nights in before he or she can be confident that the collections they are working on have any value or real meaning.

More and more we require these things from our clothes if we are to part with the ever-increasing amounts of money designers and retailers demand from us. Meaning, justification, a sense that the jacket we desire, or the dress we cherish, is not just going to clothe us, but send out the required social and sexual messages as well – here is a man or woman who is a player, a doer, a party animal; someone who knows not just what the latest fashion is, but *why* it is.

To do this properly, trend prediction agencies (really trend research agencies) braille[1] the culture, as in reaching out to touch, feel and sense its emerging sub-currents – which, for the moment, and the immediate future (a core or extreme trend can boil for a year before the mainstream even gets wind of it) is about glamour, irony, optimism, retro power dressing or the idea that we are living a 24-hour day.

We know from futurologists like James Gleick (1999) and Leon Kreitzman (1999) (author of *The 24 Hour Society*) that the current zeitgeist is also about speed, compression culture, urbanity, being plugged in and part of that great Western rush towards a notion called the New Economy – hence clothes, clubs, labels and lifestyle choices that are all about the super-casual, the super sexy, but also the super-utilitarian: garments and accessories made from neoprenes, plastics, rip-stop nylons, fabrics that are streamlined (sharkskin bodysuits from Speedo) fast forward, with pockets, closures, linings and shell outer layers that tell others you are part of a new mood, a new world order that works a 24-hour clock, that lives a portable, ever on the move lifestyle.

All this explains why we are beginning to see clothes with pockets and smart fabrics that can accommodate wrapround communications (Levis and Philips ICD+ range of jackets with wireless mobiles and MP3 connections), diagnostic interfaces (shoes from Fuseproject that can tell manufacturers and retailers just how comfortable or otherwise they are when you wear them), wearable computers (Charmed Technology's embroidered mainframes with keypads), magic skin macs (Sofinals self-healing fabrics that can be repaired with a brush of the fingers), aromafabrics (Elizabeth de Senneville's Cosmetic Concept collection that allows you to deliver moisturizers to the body), medi-fabrics (Soldier Systems Center, a research unit with the US army, are currently testing smart fabrics which detect gun wounds on the body and alert medics to the depth and dangers of the wound via remote wireless access), sonic fashions (fabrics that carry positive and negative charges in filaments that work together when crushed to play music or to whisper soothing sounds) or indeed

---

[1] Brailling, term coined by futurologist Faith Popcorn.

the more familiar multi-purpose ones that have been given a new lease of compression culture life by labels like Vexed Generation, CP company or artists like Lucy Orta, whose garments can become tents, sleeping bags or indeed pods to accommodate up to five people.

In many cases, the above began as socio-artistic experiments, as blue skies research, or as ideas that started on the counter-cultural periphery and worked their way in to become part of the accepted mainstream. Think combats, sushi, Pokemon toys, Hello Kitty memorabilia, G-shock watches, or labels like Abercrombie and Fitch and you get the idea, now quite commonplace, 10 years ago were the first stop choice of the informed few.

How we find out about these things, and how they are subsequently catapulted into the greater culture, is what trending is really about – not seeing into the future, but searching the present for potentially viral items that are set to infect and pollute tomorrow's fashionscapes. So not a matter of crystal ball gazing then, but a careful mix of judicious research and knowing where and how to look. And this is what the best trend analysts do; look, listen, search and ask the right questions about what they are seeing. Go back to the clothing types we listed above and ask yourself this: As a trend where did they come from? Were they inspired by music? Increased casualization of the work ethic? Shifts in the way we view work (from a career-based activity to a project-specific one), or the ways we are altering how we break up and negotiate our day – from the old economy nine to five model, to the new 24-Seven option inventions like the Internet have thrown up?

The answer of course is all of the above. I know this from searching and surveying this particular part of the culture. Likewise, if I am to look at the job categories of the people who adopt this look, or catapult it on (in trending argot this is also known as sneezing), I get a fuller and more in-depth picture of their lives and lifestyle activities. Club promoters, DJs, start-up tsars, designers, illustrators, drum and bass musicians, bar owners, club owners, models, fashion photographers, fashion designers, and zine publishers and editors – job categories that have quite a lot in common, wouldn't you say? Media, music, modelling and fashion; in other words plugged-in, in the know, ahead of the posse. Now, when I look closer at these categories, I notice something else, where their businesses are located, in the Hoxton, Shoreditch, Commercial Road triangle.

Again, I ask myself why, and again the answer only becomes clear when I actually visit the area. Victorian and Edwardian warehouses, open plan walk ups, a rundown terrain of dingy streets, dilapidated shops and now desolate factories once upon a time inhabited by immigrant sweatshops, artisan workshops and a succession of ethnic minority groups from Lithuanian Jews, to Chinese coolies, to Irish, Somalian and Bangladeshi refugees, all of whom have left a unique and highly charged stamp on the area.

They also left the kind of infrastructure the people we are brailling like – a place of low rents, high ceilings, easy to convert buildings and a 24-hour access policy that is denied in most other parts of a city that follows fairly traditional and increasingly outmoded work practices. Creatives are inevitably lured to this kind of place – in Paris it is the sentier, in New York the lower east side, in Dublin Temple bar – and here studios are opened, bars, late night clubs, galleries, design ateliers, Internet companies, recording studios, magazine publishers and all slotting into a routine and a way of life that develops its own social codes, work practices, and way of eating and chilling out.

And out of this, of course, comes the *look*, the Hoxton look, if that's what you want to call it, or as Richard Benson, a one-time editor of *Arena* magazine and now head of lifestyle consultancy, Bug, named it, the flexecutive look, or to give this tribe its now accepted name, Generation Flex.

The look is now all too familiar, but 5 years ago it was still on the fringes, still boiling. As Benson explains it, it consisted and still consists of combat trousers, fleeces and all-terrain trainers – but the labels are consciously flash. Sure, there was Nike, Adidas, New Balance Caterpillar, the North Face, Berghaus, Clarks, Spiewak, ironic Kappa and genuine army surplus, but there was also US only Carharrt, Prada, Sport, Napapijri, Helmut Lang, Left Hand, DKNY, 6876, a little Merrill footwear and some Jacqueline Rabun jewellery, etc. (Benson, 1998).

As this look solidified, many who did not live in the area, or indeed worked in those industries we have mentioned, began to copy it, replicate the sense of the look without living the life of it, even down to the goatee, the one shoulder rucksack and now ubiquitous micro-scooter. This is what fashion is really about, and why trend analysis and trend prediction is no longer done with mood board and fabric swatches but on the street, in the club, around and about fashion flash points, or lifestyle hotspots (Pillot de Chenecey, 2000).

For lifestyle as a concept and as a badge of social office has completely reversed the flow of design and trend prediction and how these things are done. Once, in the 1950s, it came from Paris, and the twice yearly couture shows there, and trickled down, via a slow process of copying and adjusting to the average man or woman's wardrobe, She of Slough and He of Hanley finally getting to wear a version of the original look long after designers, retailers, manufacturers, or the local tailor or seamstress diluted it down to whatever was deemed acceptable for the class or social category they were selling into. Now the look, key ones at least, start on the street and work their way up and are copied, adjusted or cleansed of any subversive element by the designer or manufacturer, who makes them more palatable for their target market group.

More to the point, the look, as we have seen with the flexecutive, springs out of a lifestyle choice (flexecutive fashions are all about function, portability, the idea that the person wearing them would not be seen dead in the City, in a suit or a dead-end nine to five job), or from shifts and subtle movements in that part of our social or leisure lives that may not be initially visible to the retailer, designer or manufacturer caught up in the endless cycle of production, distribution and retailing.

This is why we now have cool hunters – connected, plugged-in researchers who scan the culture or travel the globe for early signs of activities that are set to become key and major trends brand leaders and designers need to know about and incorporate into their design philosophy – futurologists, ethnologists, cultural analysts or lifestyle consultancies such as The Future Laboratory, Promostyl, The Intelligence Factory, BrainReserve, Trend Union, Bug, The Henley Centre, Captain Crikey or Media Street Network, all of whom eschew the instinct-only approach to trend analysis in favour of a more scientific, and less problematic, methodology of making lifestyle predictions.

These can vary from the more traditional tools used by market research companies – telephone polling, focus groups, data mining, face to face interviews, Q&A surveys – to ones that borrow heavily on the procedures and techniques used in the not unrelated fields of ethnology and anthropology – the use of urban hides, field researchers, culture scouts, hidden cameras or cultural brailling, a reading of the culture via its magazines, TV programmes, Internet sites and chatrooms, that requires the analyst to have a thorough and in-depth knowledge of current and emerging trends, and how these are likely to impact on the cultural mainstream, or indeed fragment, and mutate into something new. Dress Down Friday, and the subsequent fall-off in suit sales in the UK and US, is a good illustration of this.

In the 1980s and early 1990s, suits were symbolic of power, position and taste (if you wore designer ones), but also of a sense of purpose, privilege and status. Silicon Valley, the rise of dotcom culture and the sartorial attributes associated with it – jeans, casual shirt, no tie, cross trainers – changed all this. Here were people who were creative, cool, engaged in some wacky and wonderful social and societal adventure, and look, no suits! Better still, they were *wealthy* with no suits. More pointedly, they looked like they were enjoying the jobs they did, in Seattle, in Silicon Valley, in Hoxton, and yes, they seemed to work at them longer (where our current 24-Seven culture came from), make few distinctions between when they played at the office, or indeed when their offices became a place for playing and partying in, and certainly when you saw them out in bars, at Starbucks (the original dress down coffee shop), or at a Nirvana gig, the one thing they had in common (apart from platinum Amex cards) was the fact that they did not wear suits.

Imagine that, no suits and yet they were still earning, still respectable members of society, still being wined and dined by old world players. But, and this was a big but, they actually seemed to be having a good time. So much so, many opted out and joined them – lawyers, PRs, advertising agencies, financial houses, venture capitalists and so on. Which made the business behemoths of the old economy sit up and take notice. How to stop the drain? How to keep their embattled, embittered employees happy? By making their offices fun places to work in? By making them more egalitarian? By making them more casual and less corporate? All of this – hence offices that now have communal work stations, chill out areas, sleep seats, or companies that have stakeholders instead of shareholders, many of the stakeholders being valued employees they want to keep. But, on top of this, they also allowed people to dress casual, to feel creative by looking creative. In other words, imitating the dress sense of the Silicon Valley set.

In trend reporting and analysis, this kind of behaviour is called mirroring, or the placebo effect – where one socio-economic group hopes that wearing the clothes or looks of another will somehow endow them with the other's lifestyle choices. In other words, if you want to look the part, dress it. Fashion then has less and less to do with the sometimes bizarre dictates of designers, and it has to be said even less to do with manufacturers copying the look for half the price, or indeed retailers offering discounts or blue cross sale days. If anything, it has to do with shifts in the greater culture that impact on something as ordinary and everyday as the suit in a way that not only affects how we view it sartorially, but also how we view it sociologically – from being an object of desire, respect and stability to one that suggests a lack of imagination, a personality that is dull, colourless, truculent and all that was stodgy and backward looking about the old economy.

Indeed, this general revolt towards casualization on one hand and individuality on the other by the consumer has left much of the middle market retailers and brands in turmoil – Marks & Spencer, Arcadia, Moss Bros. Ironically, these are the very groups that continue to cling to the mood board method of trend prediction, continue to use the comparative shopper, the in-house studio that visits all the right fabric fairs and catwalk shows, that continues too to use outmoded class and social categories to sell clothing, continues to their peril to ignore the science of trend and societal analysis and prediction – that which replaces what the customer wants with what the customer desires, that which allows for individual input, which turns shopping into a relationship-based activity, and one that is highly interactive and immersive, rather than one based around the idea of exchange, money being handed over for a product handed back.

However, good trend analysis is also about knowing the realities of how the population is broken up, not only by new social categories (Flexecutives, Soft Lad, Ladettes, Grit Girls, SINDIES, The New Tasteocracy, Hedonists, The Limelight Generation, etc.) (*Viewpoint*, 2000), but by group trend consultants know as Antenna groups, Early Adopter groups, Late Adopters and Laggards.

Antenna people are those who see new ideas, or indeed invent them or place them into a particular social context. Adopters are a larger, more sociable group of people who take the ideas introduced by Antenna people and make them more widely visible and less threatening in appearance. They are also known as sneezers, people who literally spread ideas, like germs, at an incredible and highly volatile rate. Then comes the Early Adopters, those of us who see ourselves as fashion-orientated, and change and tweak things to suit ourselves, and then, we have Late Adopters, the high street mainstream who need to be reassured that what they are wearing is not too outlandish, or likely to go out of date so quickly they will not get enough wear out of it. Finally come the Laggards, who talk about clothes rather than fashion, and who mysteriously believe that clothes are about looking tidy, presentable or/and never worn to stand out.

It is by surveying these groups that the new generation of trend consultancies or viral marketeers get a feel for how a specific trend, i.e. a clothing trend, or a more lifestyle-orientated one (a growing demand for organic foods, foods that are GM free, for ethically sourced clothes or products, for adventure holidays, easy Internet access), is set to move and trickle through the culture.

But they also look at context, at how the trend or life change is most likely to be transmitted or passed on, by word of mouth (also known as viral marketing), word of mouse (on the Internet, in chatrooms and on bulletin boards) via music, clubs, in fashion magazines, in the office, through advertising, by one ethnic or socio-economic group mimicking or aping the look, characteristics or coolness factor of another. Think here how clothes associated with ragga, gansta rap, skateboarding, the Spice Girls, punks, Neo Romantics, Grunge or bands like Oasis filtrate across or down and become part of the visual, fashion or cultural aura of groups who are far removed from the originators of the look.

In his book, *The Tipping Point*, Malcolm Gladwell (2000a) breaks these categories down into specific types of people: mavens, connectors and salesmen; in short, those who know (mavens), those who pass ideas on (connectors) and, most importantly perhaps for the mainstream, those who sell ideas in ways that are more culturally and socially acceptable – body modification, tattooing and piercing are good examples of this. Once they were badges of the fetishistic fringe, extreme activities associated with sexual branding, gang membership or a criminal past. Now, thanks to the way we have mitigated piercing and tattoos through music (the Spice Girls), fashion (Naomi Campbell and Kate Moss), or by selling it as something celebrities do (Madonna, David Beckham, Brad Pitt), it becomes more widely acceptable, if not a desirable passport to a world that we want to be part of, the *beau monde*, the celebrity party. These processes and procedures of such trend progressions are all part and parcel of the new way of measuring, brokering and ultimately predicting them.

But to understand how trends spread (from the cultural extremes inwards to the suburban mainstream), we also need to understand why. And nowhere is this more compellingly explained than in Gladwell's *The Tipping Point* (2000a), a book, along with Naomi Klein's *No Logo* (2000), Paco Underhill's *Why We Buy* (1999) and Seth Godin's *Unleashing the Ideavirus* (2000a), that has become core to understanding how trends work, and how these new generation forecasting groups function as a consequence.

Gladwell (2000a) explains it thus. Occasionally a book, a building or a fashion look impinges on our culture and we have no idea where it came from or why. One day nothing, then the next, you are on the underground and there's that book everybody seems to be reading (*Divine Secrets of the Ya Ya Sisterhood*, *Harry Potter and the Goblet of Fire*, *The Tipping Point*). Or maybe it's a pair of shoes, Hush Puppies say, or a one shoulder rucksack; an odd kind of way to design a bag, but look about you and from Hoxton, to TriBeCa, Barbés, to Berne, there they are. Everywhere. And yet there has been no advertising for them.

And what of Palm Pilots and the WAP phone, the i-Mac or Dyson cleaners, sushi bars or stainless steel kitchens, wood floors or the New Tasteocracy's obsession with wallpaper, soft-form furniture, Pilates, micro-scooters or fashion labels like Abercrombie and Fitch? Invisible then rampant like a disease, a virus. Because they are new? Perhaps, but not all the time. Gladwell (2000a) and Godin (2000a) have a much different theory, and one that has given rise to trendland's latest buzz phrase, viral marketing, and the launch of a whole new generation of trends and guerrilla marketing agencies: The Future Laboratory, Media Street Network, Captain Crikey, Cake, Mother, Headlight Vision.

And in many ways the job of the viral marketeer and the trend analyst is interchangeable; each, after all, is chasing after the same thing, the Big Idea – for if Gladwell's book is about locating the trend and explaining its spread, Godin's is about locating it and then telling you how to spread it. And if you look at trends closely you will see that a trend can only become a trend if somebody somewhere wants to adopt or adapt it.

Take the Hush Puppies thing (Gladwell, 2000a, pp. 5, 7, 8). Comfortable, the kind of shoes dad wore at weekends to look casual in. Not exactly a hip and happening fashion statement, but there you go. And there they went. By 1995, sales were down to 30 000 a year and falling. Even the backwoods outlets in America's mid-west could not get rid of them. Then one fine day, a miracle. At a fashion shoot two Hush Puppies executives, Owen Baxter and Geoffrey Lewis, ran into a stylist from New York who told them that the classic Hush Puppies had suddenly become hip (*Viewpoint*, 2000), that there were re-sale shops in the Village, in Soho, where the shoes were being sold. People were going to the Ma and Pa stores, the little stores that still carried them, and were buying them up.

As Gladwell (2000a) tells it, these two hard-bitten sales reps were puzzled. Then came calls from designers like Issac Mizrahi (I think it's fair to say that at the time we had no idea who Issac Mizrahi was), John Bartlett, Anna Sui and LA designer Joel Fitzgerald, all asking for Hush Puppies for their forthcoming shows. Joel was even opening a Hush Puppies store he told them, gutting a place next door to his Hollywood boutique he said, and putting a 20-foot inflatable Basset hound on the roof (the Hush Puppies symbol) because the demand for Hush Puppies in that area had gone nuclear and he wanted people to know his was the shop that could satisfy all their cravings.

Naturally, the Hush Puppies people were thrilled, but they still did not get it. Had no idea why sales had rocketed from 30 000 pairs per year in the Autumn of 1995, to four times that amount the following year, and the year after that still more, until Hush Puppies were once again a fashion staple in the wardrobe of with-it kids from Seattle to St Louis. The publishers of *The Divine Secrets of The Ya Ya Sisterhood* were to see similar patterns in how the book shot from obscurity to become a runaway international best seller overnight. Ditto Bloomsbury, who publish the Harry Potter tales, and Fendi, whose Baguette has revived the fortunes of that company almost single-handedly. Nothing. Then bang. Like a plague, a virus, a hyper-infectious contagion.

And that, according to Gladwell (2000a) and Godin (2000a), is exactly what it is; not a trend, not a fad, not a mood board idea being slavishly replicated down the line, but a sartorial or intellectual virus. And Gladwell should know;

for years he did the science and medicine beat for *The Washington Post* and encountered viruses and infectious diseases aplenty. What he was not banking on, however, was how areas of interest such as epidemiology or virology would impact so profoundly on his other interests: why trends as in social or fashion trends happen the way they happen, how movements or ideas run through the culture the way they do.

We think, for instance, that they happen slowly, he says, and over a long period of time, moving carefully and measurably through those categories cool hunters or trend forecasters are so fond of using – from innovators, to Early Adopters, to Early Majority, to Late Majority and finally onto the Laggards – as each one of us takes it on when we are ready, familiar with the shape of that shoe for instance, or comfortable with the textures and surfaces of that chair or that house (Gladwell, 2000b).

But no, Gladwell, with his knowledge of virology, noted that the opposite was the case. That ideas and products and messages and behaviours spread just like viruses do. More bizarrely, he noticed that the spread corresponded to characteristics found in all infections, that they were not slow to infect, but did so rapidly and in strict geometric progression. More peculiarly, he observed that it only took one or two people or carriers to spread the disease, and that once this infection process began, it showed up as a dramatic and upward curve. The point at which this curve hits critical mass has been named the Tipping Point, the title of his book.

For Godin (2000a), it is a similar procedure. For him, in future all ideas and fashion statements will be spread this way. His book is a perfect example of this. Launched with no advertising budget, it is a paradigm of that process; you can download it from the Internet (at www.ideasvirus.com) and, when you do, it tells you how the book can be spread like a virus via chatrooms, e-mails to friends, by firestorming bulletin boards or by word of mouth (Godin, 2000b). This of course is how fashion and lifestyle trends can be spread most effectively. All of which throws into doubt much of what we have always believed about how trends spread, why they spread, and the part or otherwise advertising, the media and big budget marketing play in spreading them.

The latter not a lot, if you are to believe the central plank of Gladwell or Godin's thesis. Indeed, for both, word of mouth (viral marketing) is by far the best way for trends or ideas to spread, and this happens best and most effectively – not by TV, by advertising (interruption marketing) or niche advertising as one would suspect – but via a network of people Gladwell calls mavens, connectors and salesman, yes, by word of mouth.

These are a small but influential (his Law of the Few) group of men and women who, because of their positions (connectors), the way they garner and store information (mavens), or indeed disseminate such information in a way that is more palatable to the slow to catch on majority (salesmen), are core to the whole process of how tastes, trends and ideas are brokered or spread to the rest of the population. Media Street Network, a successful US trends consultancy and media marketing agency run by 23-year-old Reggie Styles, does this by recruiting teams of teenagers from the street who will either tell him what's hot and what's not, or if his company already has a hot trend, product or music idea to promote, it will use these teenagers to connect with Early Adopters and transmit or pass on the required idea. This is known as firestorming, or trend salting (Godin, 2000b).

There are other factors to be considered, however: the Stickiness Factor, for example, and the Power of Context. The former is of course that elusive Holy Grail all trend analysts, marketing and advertising agencies are obsessed with identifying and isolating, the thing or tick that makes us recall a product, place or fashion moment instantly and with the corresponding need to purchase it. The latter is the context in which we surround things so that they become sticky or appealing in the first place.

Again, look to Hush Puppies; they were always there, dormant, or in decline, like quite a few of our current social illnesses, then something happens, a stylist (maven) maybe at a particular downtown club (context) sees one or two people wearing them and thinks, that's a tip, that's a thing I can take and promote, so they do, telling their friends, or one particular friend who is a heavy socializer, gets to all the other downtown hotspots (a connector) and tells everybody he/she meets about the Hush Puppies thing, and since they are unaffiliated, not seen to be a representative of the company or advertising agency, everybody says, hey, that's cool (the stickiness factor) and starts telling others, and so on, until the rest of us are saying very much the same thing as well.

What's fascinating about this is that it is true for all areas, not just fashion, but design, technology, art, politics, media and modes of behaviour; why, for example, hedonism has become such a Big Thing at the moment, or endurance holidays, or vigilante consumerism, or Intellectual capital, or such notions as social and ethical responsibility. They are not new, merely finding their moment, their way in from the counter-cultural fringes.

In fashion terms then, it is easy to not just predict the next big trend, but to get it right; we know that chatrooms, bulletin boards and target youth groups are live with the re-emergence of the brand as king. We know too that it is a lifestyle issue rather than a fashion one. Furthermore, we know that words and phrases like ethical responsibility are in the air, ditto sustainability, accountability, the hollow corporation, relationship selling, so the next big trend must surely be towards the citizen brand concept or trend, products, looks or ideas that reassure us, and do not disappoint us across all categories.

Nike and Adidas, for instance, may be gods in fashion, but there is a query about their third world working practices and labour rights issues. This of course taints how we view the brand, and offers us one less reason for buying the brand. Tommy Hilfiger has suffered a similar fate, ditto Gap and Starbucks. This does not tell us, however, what specific trends will appear – we need to survey the culture closely for this – but it can tell us what categories they will or should fall into. We know too from research that health and leisure are among the largest growing sectors of profit, that the over fifties – Silver Surfers – are among the wealthiest and the most leisure orientated. We know too that thirtysomething women, Grit Girls as they are called, are now one of the most powerful economic forces to be reckoned with – women own 9 million companies in the US alone, and within a decade will employ half the US workforce – so we can look to these sectors to throw up the next big trends (Popcorn and Marigold, 2000).

We also know that biogenetics, biotechnology, our concerns about global warming and our planet's increased lack of water are increasingly occupying our thought processes – which can only have a knock-on effect in what we wear or how we wear it. Take the colour blue for instance, in, out, in, out, but over the next 5 years, as water becomes an issue between the have and the have nots, the depletion of the ozone layer a more strident reality, blue is certainly the colour most likely to dominate not just the sense and sensibilities of fashion designers, but designers and architects everywhere.

Blue is also about spirituality, poetry (other words being picked up in chatrooms), the sky and the sea, but also in its darker shades, about science (electricity), mystery and some would say evil – biotechnology, genetic modification. So blue then would be a safe colour to choose as the most dominant colour of the next decade – just like beige was the colour of the 1990s (minimalism, softness) and black the key colour of the power-suited 1980s. How do we know? The greater indicators are there, but also smaller, quieter ones on the cultural periphery. It is only a matter of seeking them out – not guessing them out – a case of applying science to the requirements of futurology, along with instinct, intuition and a broader appreciation of things from other aspects of our cultural roots besides fashion. Fashion, after all, is a reflective medium not a proactive one.

References

Benson, R. (1998). Flexi living. *Viewpoint*, issue 6, 77.

Gladwell, M. (2000a). *The Tipping Point*. London: Little Brown.

Gladwell, M. (2000b). Interview by Martin Raymond. *Viewpoint*, issue 8, 36, 37.

Gleick, J. (1999). *Faster; The Acceleration of Just About Everything*. London: Little Brown.

Godin, S. (2000a). *Unleashing the Ideavirus*. Published from www.ideavirus.com

Godin, S. (2000b). Interviewed by Tim Adams. Culture section, *The Observer*, 6 November, 4.

Klein, N. (2000) *No Logo*. London: Flamingo/HarperCollins.

Kreitzman, L. (1999) *The 24 Hour Society*. London: Profile.

Pillot de Chenecey (2000). Captain Crikey, interview by Martin Raymond. *Viewpoint*, issue 8, 61.

Popcorn, F. and Marigold, L. (2000). *EVEolution: The Eight Truths of Marketing to Women*. London: HarperCollins Business.

Underhill, P. (1999). *Why We Buy, The Science of Shopping*. London: Orion Business Books.

Viewpoint (1999). New social categories for measuring lifestyles against. Issue 8.

Viewpoint (2000). The limelight generation, October 2000.

The final word

The various chapters in this book have hopefully given readers a good insight into the variety of issues facing people and organizations in the contemporary global fashion industry when identifying, analysing and taking decisions related to marketing. It is essential that the research agenda considers a rich variety of issues that face fashion marketing decision makers and that different researchers with their different perspectives are able to make their contributions to the field. Research should follow four major canons in this respect: it should be rigorous, it should be useful, it should be timely and it should provide practitioners with 'food for thought'. It is with this in mind that I would like to leave you with a final thought which is not to lose sight of reality in your search for new concepts and new applications. There are very seldom general solutions to specific problems and one size does not fit all. Capturing the zeitgeist, searching for new customers, new markets, applying new business models or simply trying to understand existing customers, consumer behaviour and the impact or opportunities that globalization or e-business presents is not easy. It is always useful to take a 'reality check' after considering the various pieces of advice that practitioners, academics and consultants have given before taking action.

S-Commerce – A new B2C retail craze?

They're calling it shops or 'S-Commerce' and it's being rolled out in towns and cities nationwide. It's a real revelation, according to Malcolm Fosbury, a middleware engineer from Hillingdon. 'You just walk into one of these shops and they have all sorts of things for sale.' Fosbury was particularly impressed by a clothes shop he discovered while browsing in central London. 'Shops seem to be the ideal medium for transactions of this type. I can actually try out a jacket and see if it fits me. Then I can visualize the way I would look if I was wearing the clothing.' This is possible using a high definition 2D viewing system, or 'mirror' as it has become known.

Shops which are frequently aggregated into shopping portals or 'high streets' are becoming increasingly popular with the cash rich time poor generation of new consumers. Often located in densely populated areas people can find them extremely convenient. And Malcolm is not alone in being impressed by shops. 'Some days I just don't have time to download huge Flash animations of rotating trainers and then wait five days for them to be delivered in the hope they will actually fit', says Sandra Bailey, a systems analyst from Chelsea. 'This way I can actually complete the transaction in real time and walk away with the goods.' Being able to see whether or not shoes and clothing fit has been a real bonus for Bailey, 'I used to spend my evenings boxing up gear to return. Sometimes the clothes didn't fit, sometimes they just sent the wrong stuff.'

Shops have a compelling commercial story to tell too, according to Gartner Group Retail Analyst, Carl Baker. 'There are massive efficiencies in the supply chain. By concentrating distribution to a series of high volume outlets in urban centres – typically close to where people live and work – businesses can make dramatic savings in fulfilment costs. Just compare this with the wasteful practise of delivering items piecemeal to people's homes.'

Furthermore, allowing consumers to receive goods when they actually want them could mean an end to the frustration of returning home to find a despatch notice telling you that your goods are waiting in a delivery depot the other side of town.

But it's not just convenience and time-saving that appeals to Fosbury, 'Visiting a shop is a real relief for me. I mean, as it is I spend all day in front of a bloody computer.'

Source: Anonymous (June 2000)

The views expressed in this short piece demonstrate some of the myths and realities surrounding e-business applied to fashion retailing and support the need for critical thinking when conducting research or in applying new business ideas.

Index